THIS PLACE OF PROMISE

This Place of Promise

—— ❧ ——

A Historian's Perspective on 200 Years of
Missouri History

GARY R. KREMER

UNIVERSITY OF MISSOURI PRESS

Columbia

This book was made possible with the generous support of
The State Historical Society of Missouri

For Lisa A. Kremer and our children,

Randy, Sharon, and Becky,

and for our grandchildren,

Dustin, Brooke, and Bladen Kremer,

Logan, Kaden, Halston, and Saylor Bax,

and Brennan Dazey.

And for our sons-in-law, Travis Bax and Jeffrey Dazey.

With love and gratitude.

"If, in moving through your life, you find yourself lost, go back to the last place where you knew who you were, and what you were doing, and start again from there."

Bernice Johnson Reagon, quoted in Carol Stack, *Call to Home: African Americans Reclaim the Rural South*

"History will always find you, and wrap you in its thousand arms."

Joy Harjo, Poet Laureate of the United States, "Break my Heart," in *An American Sunrise: Poems*

Contents

Illustrations

Acknowledgments

THIS BOOK HAD its origins in Missouri House Concurrent Resolution 7 (HCR7) passed by the 97th General Assembly, tasking the State Historical Society of Missouri (SHSMO) to develop "plans, ideas, and proposals to commemorate and celebrate" the Missouri Bicentennial of statehood, and to provide "guidance and direction to a statewide effort to promote and celebrate the State of Missouri's rich and complex history." The SHSMO Board of Trustees quickly envisioned a book about Missouri's first two hundred years of statehood as part of that commemoration and celebration.

As I began to think about the shape and direction this book would take, I pondered the many ways this state and its history have shaped my life. I also thought about the many ways I have benefited from the scholarship of other Missouri historians over the course of more than half a century. Many of those historians are no longer with us, but I learned much from them through their writings and through countless conversations with them over the years. I wish to acknowledge publicly the time they spent with me and the lessons they imparted to me. I owe a great deal to these scholars: Lawrence O. Christensen, John C. Crighton, Robert L. Dyer, Thomas G. Dyer, Robert H. Ferrell, Thomas E. Gage, Lynn Wolf Gentzler, Robert K. Gilmore, James W. Goodrich, Lorenzo J. Greene, Alan R. Havig, Lawrence H. Larsen, David D. March, Duane G. Meyer, Paul C. Nagel, James C. Olson, James Neel Primm, Adolf E. Schroeder, and Arvarh E. Strickland. Perry McCandless and Robert B. Flanders, who are no longer active in the field of history, also helped and inspired me. Paul C. Nagel's 1976 book, *Missouri: A Bicentennial History*, served as something of a model for this volume.

I have also learned from my association with long-time Missouri historians who continue to work in the field, including Brooks Blevins, John F. Bradbury, Dominic J. Capeci, Jr., James M. Denny, Keona K. Ervin,

Michael Fellman, John C. Fisher, William E. Foley, Louis S. Gerteis, Colin Gordon, Debra F. Greene, Antonio F. Holland, John Herron, Patrick J. Huber, Walter Johnson, Richard Kirkendall, Virginia Laas, Howard Marshall, Diane Mutti Burke, Lynn Morrow, Jeremy Neely, William E. Parrish, Christopher Phillips, William Piston, Joel P. Rhodes, Brett Rogers, Jarod Roll, Walter Schroeder, Bonnie Stepenoff, Dick Steward, T. J. Stiles, Jon Taylor, LeeAnn Whites, and Kenneth H. Winn.

I wish to thank, also, members of the SHSMO Board of Trustees for their support of this project and for allowing me time to work on this book. I am especially grateful to the following trustees who contributed financially to subvent the publication in an effort to lower the cost of the book: Roy D. Blunt, James Leon Combs, Virginia A. Laas, Stephen N. Limbaugh Jr., and Beatrice Litherland Smith.

Likewise, I wish to express my appreciation to my co-workers at SHSMO who picked up the slack when my work on the book took me away from administrative responsibilities. Gerald Hirsch was especially helpful, but so were Melissa Wilkinson, Jennifer King, and Maggie Mayhan. Christina George was always ready and able to help me with computer problems.

Librarians and archivists are the essential workers without whom historians could not do their work, and SHSMO has some of the best in the business. Librarians Tatyana Shinn, Amy Waters, Kevin George, and Clinton Lawson were especially helpful, as were archivists Laura Jolley, Elizabeth Engel, and Heather Richmond. Fellow historians and co-workers Danielle Griego and Sean Rost were also helpful.

Laura Jolley led the effort to illustrate the book. She was ably assisted by SHSMO staffers Elizabeth Engel, Beth Pike, Aubrey Rowden, A.J. Medlock, Kathleen Seale, Carole Groggin, Lucinda Adams, Whitney Heinzmann, and Joan Stack. I also appreciate the assistance of Missouri State Archives Visual Materials Archivist Erika Woehlk and local historian Betty Chillington.

A number of individuals read the manuscript in whole or in part and made helpful suggestions for improvement. They include John Brenner, Lawrence Celani, Andrew Davidson, Kimberly Harper, Laura Jolley, Lisa Kremer, and Virginia Laas. I also benefitted greatly from the suggestions of two anonymous readers for the University of Missouri Press; I wish to thank them for their judicious and timely readings and helpful suggestions for improvement. I am also grateful to the editors of the *Missouri Historical Review* for publishing a chapter from this book in the July issue of that journal.

Speaking of the Press, this is the ninth book I've produced through the Press, and the most enjoyable process I have experienced to date. This positive experience I attribute largely to the professionalism, kindness, commitment, and editorial skill of Editor-in-Chief Andrew Davidson. I am thankful for the opportunity to work with Andrew. I feel fortunate, also, to have been able to work with staff members Mary Conley, Robin Rennison, Deanna Davis, Drew Griffith, and Megan Casey-Sparrius. Susan Curtis copyedited the manuscript. I am especially grateful for her deep knowledge of Missouri and U.S. history, and her skill as a writer and editor. Her attention to detail greatly improved the finished product.

You would think that with all the good help I have received, I would have produced an error-free book. Such a prospect seems unlikely, primarily because of my stubborn reluctance to accept advice, even when it is both well-intentioned and correct. Errors that remain in this book are mine and mine alone.

Finally, I wish to thank the members of my family for their individual and collective patience and indulgence through the years, as I pursued my passion for Missouri history: my wife, Lisa, son Randy, daughters Sharon and Becky, and their spouses, Travis Bax and Jeffrey Dazey. I also want to thank our eight grandchildren: Dustin, Brooke and Bladen Kremer, Logan, Kaden, Saylor, and Halston Bax, and Brennan Dazey. All the grandchildren have come to know my fondness for talking about and visiting Missouri landmarks, such as Clark's Hill, Painted Rock State Park, Stieferman's Bluff, and scores of other places around the state. The words "history lesson," shouted by a grandchild, have come to be a warning signal that "Papa" is about to launch into a well-meaning, if not always fully welcomed, lecture on a historical topic of his choice. My family inspires me and enriches my life on a daily basis, which is why this book is dedicated to them.

Gary R. Kremer
Jefferson City, Missouri
March 31, 2021

THIS PLACE OF PROMISE

Prologue

My Missouri

"All that goes to make the me in me began in a Missouri village. . . ."

Mark Twain, *Following the Equator* (1897)

AS I BEGAN to think about writing this book commemorating the two hundredth anniversary of Missouri statehood, I began, also, to think about my own Missouri history, and the countless ways in which this state has shaped me. I am who I am because of where I was born, and when and where I grew up. The way I experienced the world over the past seven decades and more was largely determined by the timing of my birth, my gender, my race, my religion, and my parents' ethnicity and socioeconomic standing. My personal story is a Missouri story, tied intrinsically to this state's history. Without it, I would not be me. The same is true for all Missourians.

Missouri is a place that I have always called home, as have four generations of Kremers who preceded me, and two (and counting) generations who succeed me. Like so many Missourians past and present, I am descended from immigrants. My great-great grandfather, P. Gustav Kremer, came to Osage County, Missouri, from Krefeld, Germany, during the early 1840s, shortly after the county was established in 1841. As a young man in his early twenties, he came to Missouri in search of greater opportunities, a chance for a better life. He settled on a 103-acre farm, purchased from the federal government, near the village of Loose Creek, about 15 miles east of Missouri's capital, Jefferson City. Soon thereafter (1844) he married a fellow German immigrant by the name of Agnes Dahler. The couple started a family the next year, with the birth of my great-grandfather, Joseph, in 1845.

Like too many men on my father's side of the family, Gustav died young, not yet fifty years of age, in May 1865, soon after the end of the American

3

Civil War. Four years later, his eldest child and only son, Joseph, married Anna Koenigsfeld, who lived several miles north of her husband's birthplace, a farm along Cedar Creek, a Loose Creek tributary only a few miles from the Missouri River. Within a year of the marriage, Joseph and Anna purchased that farm and began their own family.

Between 1870 and 1885, Anna Koenigsfeld Kremer bore six children and was pregnant with a seventh when forty-year-old Joseph died of double pneumonia. Fifteen-year-old Henry, my grandfather, became the man of the house upon his father's death, and with the help of his younger siblings continued to try to make a living on his parents' farm. Over time, as he reached adulthood, he was able to purchase a farm adjacent to the one owned by his widowed mother.

Like so many Missourians during the mid-to-late nineteenth century, these three generations of Kremer men were farmers whose crops and livestock were largely consumed by their families. The 1880 federal agricultural census indicates that Joseph owned twenty acres of tilled land, two acres of

Fig. 1: Built in 1892, this served as Our Lady Help of Christians Church and School until a new church was built in 1922. Heinrich (Henry) Kremer is second from left. The author attended school in this building from 1954 to 1961. The building was razed in 1963. Photograph taken ca. 1894. Credit: Our Lady Help of Christians Parish.

"Permanent Meadows," and eighty acres of "Unimproved" land—woodland and forest. The value of his farm, including land, fences, and buildings to-taled $1,500. His farming implements and machinery were worth $80 and his livestock was valued at $250. The livestock consisted of two horses and two mules, four "Milch" cows, whose milk allowed the family to produce twenty-five pounds of butter. He also had four "other" cows. Three calves were "dropped" during the preceding year. Joseph sold five head of cattle during the previous year and slaughtered one for his family's food. He also had sixteen head of swine, and his poultry flock numbered 100. The latter produced 100 dozen eggs over the course of the year. Presumably, the few cattle that were sold provided cash that allowed the family to acquire basic commodities that they could not or chose not to produce: salt, sugar, coffee, tobacco, and some limited clothing, including shoes. It is likely that butter and eggs were bartered for some of these commodities as well.

Joseph raised one ton of hay on one acre of land, no doubt the hay going to feed his livestock. Similarly, he produced 200 bushels of "Indian corn" on sixteen acres of land and 475 bushels of wheat on twenty-three acres. One quarter acre was devoted to the production of sugar cane, which yielded fifteen gallons of molasses. Another quarter acre of land produced twenty-five bushels of potatoes. A half-acre was devoted to the production of apples, although there appears to have been no harvest of apples during the year preceding the taking of the census.

Such was the limited produce of a hardscrabble farmer with a wife and four children, ages one month to nine years. Joseph's twenty-one-year-old sister, Mary, lived with the family and is listed on the federal census return as "househelp."

Their lives were burdened in many ways by the early deaths of men in the family, who did not live long enough to accumulate significant capital to pass on to the next generation. Thus, each of these three men had to start over, without the benefit of his father's accumulated wealth, save for the land he tilled.

Another burden of multi-generational early death was a keen awareness of the fragility of life and the recognition of one's own mortality. Perhaps this encouraged a deep commitment to religiosity and the Catholic faith that they shared with the overwhelming majority of their neighbors and friends.

None of the three men had much in the way of formal education. Henry, the youngest of the three, attended school for only six years. It is likely that his father and grandfather had even less schooling. Formal education had little value in the Missouri they knew, and there were no schools beyond the elementary grades anywhere nearby.

My own father was born on the farm of his father in 1914, the youngest of three surviving children from my grandfather's second marriage (the first ended when his young wife died). My grandmother, a widow when she married my grandfather, brought two children to her second marriage. The eldest, Martin Kaver, was her biological son. The second, Joseph, was an "orphan train" boy from New York City. Orphan trains originated with New York minister and philanthropist, Charles Loring Brace. Troubled by poverty-stricken, homeless children in New York City, Brace and his successors transported orphan children by train to midwestern states, including Missouri, in the hope that rural and small-town life in the Midwest would improve the lives and lot of these children. Between 1854 and 1929, as many as 200,000 children left New York City by means of orphan trains.

Tragedy struck my father's family in 1915, when his mother died of cancer. My father was only eighteen months old at the time. He never knew his mother, and he suffered her loss throughout his too-short life: he died in 1979 of the same cancer that claimed his mother. He was only sixty-five years old.

So, my father was raised in a large, extended, blended family by his grandmother, an unmarried aunt, and an older sister. Like my grandmother, my great-grandmother had taken in an orphan-train child, a young girl from New York named Helen.

Like his father before him, my father had a limited education: eight years of elementary school. According to the 1880 census, my grandmother could neither read nor write. As a teenager during the Great Depression, my dad hired out to local farmers as a laborer, sometimes cutting railroad ties for fifty cents per day and cordwood for whatever price it would fetch during the winter months. During the late 1930s, he was fortunate enough to get a job with the Works Progress Administration (WPA), one of President Franklin Delano Roosevelt's anti-Depression agencies. In 1939 he worked as a "common laborer" in addition to working fifteen weeks on a WPA project for annual wages totaling $125.

Bernard Kremer, my father, enlisted in the U.S. Army on June 16, 1941, nearly six months prior to the Japanese bombing of Pearl Harbor. He spent the bulk of the war with Company E of the Sixty-Third Infantry Regiment of the Army's Sixth Division, a unit often referred to as "Red Star." This unit spent more than 300 days in combat in the jungles of New Guinea and on the island of Luzon in the Philippines between 1943 and 1945.

Bernard, or "Ben" as he was commonly called, was discharged from the Army on November 1, 1945. His years of military service and the brutal war experiences weighed heavily on him for the remainder of his life. He became active in a local VFW chapter and tried to attend as many veterans' funerals as possible. He also attended annual reunions of his old army unit. He knew the sacrifices his fellow veterans had made. During the era of the Vietnam War, he often chafed at references to the conflict as being American soldiers' first exposure to guerilla warfare. He knew better.

Following his discharge from the Army, Ben returned to the community where he had grown up. His elderly father had sold the farm, so he went looking for work elsewhere. He found employment with the Missouri Pacific Railroad.

Like so many men of his generation, Ben remained unmarried into his early thirties; it was difficult enough for him to provide the basics of life for himself, much less for a wife and family.

His marital status changed on November 6, 1947, when he married Gertrude Hausmann Broker, a widowed mother of a three-year-old whose husband had died in the war.

Initially, the newlyweds and Gertrude's daughter moved to a farm in the fertile Missouri River Bottom in northern Osage County. Ben left his job with the railroad because it required him to be away from his new family during the week. For roughly the next eighteen months, he worked on the farm in exchange for a salary of $100 per month, plus an old farm house to live in, a cow for milking, two butchering hogs, and access to a garden plot and a potato patch. The effort at farming was short-lived: a Missouri River flood in the spring of 1949 sent the family packing to higher ground. Eventually, they settled in a house in the village of Frankenstein that had once belonged to Ben's grandmother. By the late 1940s, the house was owned by Ben's Aunt Kate, the youngest of his father's siblings.

Aunt Kate was a spinster who "kept house" for the local Catholic priest and lived in the rectory of Our Lady Help of Christians parish. Her duties included cooking and cleaning for the pastor. She rented the house she had inherited from her mother to my parents for $6.00 a month. As part of the bargain, my parents took over the responsibility of caring for Aunt Kate's elderly brother, who happened to be my father's dad and my grandfather.

Aunt Kate's house became my home for the better part of the next two decades. It was a ramshackle one-and-a-half-story frame structure with a tin, cat-slide roof and absolutely no sign of paint on its weather-boarded walls. It had no running water, meaning no indoor plumbing and no bathroom. Instead it featured a two-seat outhouse and a cistern near the house from which water could be pumped by hand.

My father's lack of formal education led him to work at a series of manual labor/unskilled jobs: first as an assistant in an auto body repair shop, then as a store clerk, and, for much of my childhood, as a "grease monkey," one who greased cars, changed their oil, and cleaned them. For the last twenty years of his working life, my father toiled as a boiler fireman for the Missouri Department of Corrections. None of the jobs he held over the course of his life paid very well, our family living paycheck to paycheck. Money was neither "saved" nor "invested."

In truth, my father, like so many rural Missourians of his generation, was unprepared for the world he entered as a mature, young adult during the mid-1930s. His most obvious deficiency was his lack of formal education. He did not benefit from the GI Bill that helped so many other WWII veterans. He may not have even known about it, and even if he had, his isolation in a small homogeneous community left him unprepared to access and benefit from it or, for that matter, most of the other innovations of the modernizing world.

As for my mother, she had no aspirations beyond those of being a wife and mother, roles in which she excelled. She had escaped the isolation and homogeneity of rural Missouri farm life for a few years during the late 1930s, when she was sent to a St. Louis suburb by her widowed father to work as a domestic servant in the private home of a multi-generational family. The 1940 federal census reveals that she, as an 18-year-old "maid," worked fifty-two weeks in 1939. She worked sixty hours during the week of March 24–30, 1940. Her salary for the entire year of 1939 was $198, or $3.81 per week. If the sixty-hour week was a normal one for her, that means that she earned 6 cents per hour, plus, of course, the all-important "room and board."

I grew up in the farming community where my parents had grown up, in a house with no running water, no bathroom, no central heat or air-conditioning, and no television or telephone, at least not in the early years of my memory. My life centered around my mom and my dad, a sister, Sharon, who was four years my senior, another sister, Janet, who was three years my junior—and, of course, Our Lady Help of Christians Catholic Church and School.

Fig. 2: Our Lady Help of Christians Catholic Church, Frankenstein, as it appeared during the author's youth. The church was built in 1922 and has always been the spiritual and social center of the community. Credit: Raymond Laughlin.

I started school in the first grade (there was no kindergarten) in September of 1954. That was the year of the *Brown* v. *Board of Education* U.S. Supreme Court decision, which outlawed racial segregation in public education. I knew nothing of *Brown*. There were no African Americans in my community, although the nuns at Our Lady Help of Christians Parochial School taught us that racial bigotry was wrong. Archbishop Joseph Ritter, head of the St. Louis Archdiocese, which included my community, had threatened Catholics who stood in the way of racially integrated schools under his jurisdiction with excommunication, the ultimate punishment for a Catholic.

I don't recall ever questioning a Catholic teaching or teacher as an elementary school student. Priests and nuns (we called them "sisters") were absolute authority figures in my community. Because I lived only a few hundred yards from the school and church, I was often called upon to assist the priest and nuns. My sisters and I picked wildflowers (mostly daisies and black-eyed Susans) from nearby pastures to decorate altars in the church. I and my best friend, Tim Samson, who also lived nearby, served Mass when no other altar boys were available, which was much of the time, and we fired up the large wood-burning furnace in the school basement because our parish priest's frugality prevented him from hiring a school janitor.

Fig. 3: Priests and others gathered in celebration of the centennial of the founding of Our Lady Help of Christians Catholic Parish, 1963, Frankenstein, Missouri. Author is fourth from the left. To his immediate right is best friend Tim Samson. Credit: Our Lady Help of Christians Parish.

There was little that was memorable or profound about my elementary school education. Like most American students of the 1950s, I learned to fear godless communists. In 1957, in the wake of the shock of the Soviets' launch of the first satellite, Sputnik, I and several of my classmates who were deemed to be of above-average intelligence were moved from the third to the fifth grade, having skipped the fourth grade, presumably, out of the new national commitment to "catching up" with the Soviets.

One of the most memorable events of my years of elementary school came on January 20, 1961, the day that John F. Kennedy was inaugurated as the thirty-fifth president of the United States, the first Catholic to hold that office. It was the only time in my memory that a television was brought into Our Lady Help of Christians School. I was moved then, even as I continue to be today, some sixty years later, by Kennedy's call to service and idealism: "Ask not what your country can do for you," the new president suggested, "but what you can do for your country."

My idealism knew no bounds. Like many other children of the 1960s, I wanted to change the world. At first I thought I could do this by becoming a priest. While we were in the eighth grade, Tim Samson, still my best friend, and I made plans to enroll in the fall of 1961 at St. Thomas Aquinas Preparatory Seminary in Hannibal, Missouri. I turned thirteen during my first week of classes at the seminary. I had never been away from home for more than a day or two at a time, usually an overnight stay with a cousin, and was homesick beyond belief.

I spent two years at the seminary in a highly structured social environment that was punctuated by academic rigor. The most memorable event of those two years happened on the night of October 22, 1962. It was a Monday evening, and all of my fellow students and I were in our mandatory evening study hall. A television was brought into the room so that we could all watch President Kennedy deliver his Cuban Missile Crisis Speech. Nearly six decades later, I still remember the absolute terror I felt in hearing the president of the United States deliver an ultimatum to USSR Premier Nikita Khrushchev and the Soviet Union. I and most of the others in the room felt certain that nuclear war and annihilation were imminent. Some of the other students were crying. Others actually asked permission to use a phone so they might reach their parents in order to tell them goodbye.

A fear of the Soviets pervaded my childhood and adolescence. I had continuing nightmares about an invasion of Frankenstein, population all of 38, and how I was forced to fight off Soviet soldiers, armed only with my antique Winchester pump .22 rifle.

Of course, a nuclear war in which all of us died never came, but my fear of communists did not diminish. A couple of years later, after I abandoned my goal of becoming a priest and began attending a central Missouri public high school with a Catholic name (Fatima), I was selected by school officials to participate, along with three of my classmates, in a live television program titled "Communism Looks at Youth." The program was mistitled.

It should have been called "Youths Look at Communism," or, even more accurately, "Youths Give Communists Hell!"

The program was hosted by Missouri Supreme Court Commissioner Alden A. Stockard. Panel participants were asked to read *Masters of Deceit*, a book written by the virulently anti-communist director of the Federal Bureau of Investigation, J. Edgar Hoover, and then discuss the nefarious deeds of communists described therein, by means of leading questions and comments posed by Commissioner Stockard. I remember little of what transpired during the half hour program, although I do remember the feeling of fear I had upon leaving the television station when the program was over. More precisely, I feared that communists might have been watching the program and, having heard what I had to say about them, might be planning to retaliate against me in some violent way, perhaps by affixing a bomb to my car. Indeed, once inside the vehicle, I hesitated to start the engine, then actually heaved a sigh of relief when it started without exploding.

Concerns about communism aside, I was largely politically unaware during most of my high school years, although I remember vividly the assassination of President Kennedy and the accompanying feeling that the entire nation was in trouble as a consequence. As anyone of my generation can tell you, I remember exactly where I was and what I was doing when I heard the news of the assassination. I was sitting alone in a classroom at Fatima High School in the Osage County village of Westphalia, taking a makeup test for a biology class that I had missed because of travel with the school's basketball team. Suddenly, I heard the unmistakable voice of the school superintendent over the school intercom. The voice said that the president had been shot and everyone should go to the gymnasium. Once in the gym, the superintendent told us that our beloved president was dead.

I could not believe it. I had never experienced anything like this. President Kennedy had seemed so alive and energetic, so invulnerable. Like millions of my fellow Americans, I was glued to the television set for the next several days, watching Walter Cronkite and his colleagues at CBS News cover all the activities resulting from the assassination. I was still watching two days later, when Jack Ruby stepped in front of Lee Harvey Oswald and mortally wounded him during a live national broadcast. At that moment, I began to wonder if instead of being America the blessed, we might not be America the cursed.

Another thing that deeply troubled me during my high school years were the events associated with the Civil Rights Movement, and especially the violence perpetrated against African Americans in the South in the early to mid-1960s. I feel certain this was the case because of television and the presentation of countless cases of injustice inflicted upon Black Americans by racist whites. I remember being so troubled by racial injustice in the United States that I made the topic the subject of a speech I delivered in a speech class during my senior year in high school.

I graduated from high school on a Friday in May 1965. Three days later, I started a job as a clerk-typist for the Missouri Division of Employment Security in Jefferson City. It was a full-time, 40-hour per week job, for which I earned $206 per month. My take home pay was $183 per month. It was the most money I had ever seen in my life.

Nonetheless, I knew that I did not want to transcribe field auditors' reports for the rest of my life. In the fall of 1965, I enrolled as a freshman at Central Missouri State University in Warrensburg. My intended major was sociology. I wanted to do something meaningful to improve the world. I wanted to be a social worker.

CMSU was not, however, a good fit for me. I was not yet ready for college, still too young and immature. After less than three months at college, and soon after my 17th birthday, I dropped out and returned home to hang out with high school friends and look for a job.

I returned to work for the state of Missouri as a clerk-typist on December 27, 1965, the new stint on the job reconnecting me with a high school classmate, Paul Hasenbeck. Over the next few months, Paul and I became close friends. The war in Vietnam was heating up, but because I was still only 17, I was not yet eligible for the draft, not so my friend Paul. Before we knew it, he was drafted into the U.S. Army, reporting for basic training in the fall of 1966. Within a few months, he was in Vietnam. Within a few more months, in April 1967, I heard that Paul was Missing in Action, something that drove the war home to me in a very real and personal way. Paul is still MIA as I write this, more than half a century later. I still miss him.

By the time Paul disappeared in a faraway land, I had begun to develop a very negative attitude toward the Vietnam War. I had enrolled as a student at Lincoln University the same fall that Paul reported for basic and had begun to think ever more deeply about which Americans were doing most of the fighting in Vietnam and about the long-simmering, now seemingly exploding, civil unrest in America, with violence against Blacks and riots erupting in places such as Detroit and the Watts neighborhood in Los Angeles.

In the fall of 1967, I enrolled in a U.S. History course taught by Dr. Wayne E. Johnson, a professor who had a profound impact on my intellectual development. He was a brilliant and entertaining lecturer who made history seem fun and useful. He was also an unapologetic liberal who was opposed to the Vietnam War and President Lyndon Johnson's handling of it. The next year, I enrolled in a Black history course, taught by Lorenzo Johnston Greene, one of the preeminent scholars of African American history in the country. Over time, Dr. Greene became both my mentor and my friend.

All in all, 1968 may have been one of the most traumatic years I have ever experienced. Early that year I had become very politically and socially conscious. First came the Tet Offensive in Vietnam, an event that confirmed to me and millions like me that our government had been lying to us about how the war was going, that the United States was not in fact winning it. That sentiment gave rise to the surprising success of antiwar presidential candidate Eugene McCarthy. His strong finish in the Democratic New Hampshire presidential primary in March 1968 led directly to Lyndon Johnson's announcement that "if nominated I will not run, if elected I will not serve another term as your president."

Nothing, however, could have prepared me for the shock of Martin Luther King Jr.'s assassination in Memphis on April 4, 1968. I was doubly shocked to learn, subsequently, that the alleged assassin, James Earl Ray, was an escaped convict on the lam from the Missouri State Penitentiary in Jefferson City. I was deeply troubled by King's assassination and the violence that followed it. King was murdered on a Thursday. The next day I was so upset that I left my job and went to Lincoln University, just to walk around campus, even though classes had been cancelled. I felt the need, I think, to be around African Americans, to say or do something to show solidarity with them, perhaps even to apologize to them on behalf of the entire white race.

Friday evening, April 5, 1968, my girlfriend and I were driving around Jefferson City when suddenly the voice of city mayor John G. Christy came on a local AM radio station. Christy was responding to a protest march by Lincoln University students held earlier that day. The students had demanded the retraction by the Jefferson City *News Tribune* of an anti-King editorial published the previous day. In truth, the protest was minor in comparison to what was happening on college campuses and in cities around the nation, especially Washington, D.C., Newark, and Chicago. Christy was tearfully pleading with protesters not to burn down his city. I thought at the time, and I still do today, that his appeal was a melodramatic one.

In addition to being the most troubling, 1968 was also one of the most stimulating, exciting, challenging, traumatic, and interesting years of my life. It was the year I entered the world of the mind and decided I wanted to live in that world. I began to read voraciously, and I became socially and politically engaged. I also got married, four days before my twentieth birthday, to a young woman six weeks beyond her eighteenth birthday. To state the obvious, we were both too young and worldly unwise.

We were married in a Catholic church, with a Catholic ceremony, and by a Catholic priest whom I had come to know and appreciate and value. I had sought him out on many occasions to discuss my growing ambivalence and frustrations with the church. (Decades later, I discovered he was one of the priestly predators who brought shame to himself and the church). I was deeply and completely Catholic, having attended Catholic schools where for nine years the only teachers I knew were priests and nuns.

But there were many things that bothered me about the Catholic Church. One was what I perceived as my own parish priest's lack of spirituality and a social conscience. I wanted him to be more like the then-famous Berrigan brothers, and talk about the immorality and injustice of the Vietnam War, or the "sin" of racism. Instead, his sermons focused on the parish buildings and the operational needs of the parish, along with a never-ending clamoring for more money in the collection basket. I wanted my church to take on the social issues of the 1960s. I wanted it to be open to the ordination of women priests, and I wanted it to abandon its repressive rules about "artificial" birth control. The Catholic priests and nuns I had known had always been fiercely hostile to the notion of any kind of sexual pleasure outside of marriage that excluded the possibility of procreation.

Unprepared for our union, my new wife and I added to the complexity of our challenges by bringing a child, Randall, into the world during the first year of our marriage. Thus, we began trying to raise an infant child while still little more than children ourselves.

My alienation from Catholicism grew and peaked with the sudden death of my older sister in October 1969. She died within a few weeks of the sudden onset of an aggressive malignant brain tumor. She left behind a grieving husband, a five-year-old daughter, and a mother, step-father, sister, and brother (me) whose lives and hopes and faith were shattered. My surviving sister, Janet, asked me the night our sister died, how could there be a God who could allow our good sister to die? I could not answer her question.

In the wake of my sister's death, and my angry, painful response to it, I flirted with agnosticism and even atheism. I sought out people whose lives and leanings I admired. That is how in the fall of 1970 I came to meet a sociology professor, in whose course I was enrolled, and ask him about his views on religion. Sporting a crew cut in an age of long hair, my (at the time) 37-year-old professor was perpetually underdressed and rode an old BMW motorcycle. In addition, he was iconoclastic, smart, supremely confident, well-spoken, and friendly. The day I went into his office to ask his views about religion, he surprised me with his response. He simply handed me some pamphlets, and asked me to read them and to come back to talk with him in a few days. I did as he asked.

The pamphlets were about the Baha'i Faith, a religion that I had never heard of, but to which I was immediately attracted because of its basic teachings: a belief in the unity of all the world's religions, the oneness of mankind, the equality of men and women, the need for a world government, and more. Over the course of several months of conversation, and a great deal more reading, I decided I wanted to become a Baha'i. Thus began a twelve-year odyssey that transformed my life in ways both good and bad. Like so many young people of my generation, I abandoned the religion of my birth and youth in favor of what was thought at the time by many to be an Eastern, mystical faith.

My decision was very hard on many people I loved, including my wife and parents, especially my dad, who blamed himself for my apostasy. Undeterred, I dove wholeheartedly into the Baha'i Faith, studied its tenets, and practiced its principles, including its mandate to abstain from all alcoholic beverages. The latter was not an easy thing to do for someone who came from a beer-drinking, wine-making culture in which alcohol was consumed almost as frequently as water. In time, my wife and children became Baha'is as well.

We stopped going to the Catholic Church, except for requisite funerals and weddings. This was a big deal for someone who had attended Mass every Sunday for the first twenty-two years of his life. There was no professional clergy among Baha'is, and no churches in local communities. "Services" consisted largely of "feasts" held in members' homes every nineteen days. The feast consisted of three parts, the first of which was a spiritual segment, made up of readings from the writings of key figures in what members referred to simply as "the Faith": the Bab, Baha'u'llah, Shoghi Effendi. The second portion was administrative, with each Baha'i community governed by a nine-member Local Spiritual Assembly or LSA. The LSA had authority over the actions and activities of all community members, including the enforcement of rules such as the aforementioned prohibition against the consumption of alcoholic beverages and the implementation of other Baha'i rules and regulations. During the administrative portion of the feast, the LSA might report on its activities or a member might request that the LSA take up a particular issue. The LSA's were regarded as nascent "Houses of Justice" that would one day be called upon to participate in a new world order's governance.

The third portion of the feast was purely social, with members visiting, their children playing, and everyone present snacking—what members of other religious groups might term "fellowshipping." My life, and that of my wife and our children, were to be governed by the teachings of the Baha'i Faith over the course of the next dozen years.

Meanwhile, I completed the requirements for a B.A. in U.S. history in December 1970. Now what? I began looking for jobs, but there wasn't much demand for a person with my background and training. For a few weeks in January and February 1971, I worked as a carpenter's assistant for my father-in-law in his construction business. Although I was a willing worker, I wasn't a very good carpenter (my father-in-law once told me that as a carpenter, I was a damned good teacher, a not-so-subtle statement about my lack of carpentry skills).

When it became apparent to both of us that I was costing my father-in-law more money than I was helping him earn, we agreed that I would move on to something else. I took a job for a few months as an orderly at

Still Osteopathic Hospital in Jefferson City. I worked on what was called "Three South," a geriatric ward. It was much like working in a nursing home. The patients were long-term residents, most of whom were destined to die there. I remember distinctly dealing with the first patient who passed away on my shift. I kept trying to find a heartbeat with a stethoscope, not quite convinced that he was really dead. I remember, also, an elderly patient named Napoleon Stockton, a ninety-one-year-old man from Bland, Missouri. I remember when he arrived in the hospital, probably in late February or early March 1971. I soon realized that the reason he was there was because he had no one to take care of him. He did not want to be there, and he was lonely and despondent; he cried a lot. I tried to comfort him, to spend time with him, to talk with him. Despite my efforts, he quickly went from dressing and feeding himself and being mobile to being bedfast and totally incapable of doing anything on his own. One morning I came into work at my normally early hour. Napoleon's bed was freshly made and empty. "Where's Napoleon?" I asked. "Oh, he died last night," came the answer. I was crushed. Napoleon had simply lost the will to live. Nearly half a century later, the thought of Napoleon and his demise still makes me sad. I wish I had been with him when he passed.

In the early spring of 1972, two new job possibilities presented themselves to me, both at Lincoln University. One was to serve as deputy director to my mentor, Dr. Lorenzo J. Greene, in a federally funded program he had designed and initiated to try to reduce the number of minority student dropouts in inner-city Missouri high schools. The other was a teaching position in an experimental program for Lincoln University freshmen, one that sought to make courses more "relevant" and interesting to minority-group students. As the chair of the history department at Lincoln, Dr. Greene was in charge of hiring for both positions.

Dr. Greene wanted me to take the former position as his deputy director; I wanted to teach. The problem with me taking the teaching position, however, was that it required a graduate degree, and I had not yet earned my MA. Despite the fact that Dr. Greene wanted me to serve as his deputy, and despite the fact that I had not yet finished my master's thesis, he agreed to hire me for the teaching position, contingent upon my completing the master's thesis over the summer. I assured him I could do that, notwithstanding the fact that one of the position's requirements was that I attend a six-week training session at Pine Manor Junior College in Chestnut Hills, Massachusetts (a Boston suburb).

Once I completed my thesis (a less than stellar piece of prose and scholarship), I was off to Boston. I had never flown on a commercial plane (I was 23 years old); I had never seen an ocean; I had to leave behind a three-year-old son and a wife, both of whom I missed immensely. The training consisted of myself and a couple of dozen other teachers, mostly from Southern Black schools, being exposed to the writings of a number of scholars of post-WWII African American history and literature. In addition to spending a lot of time in a classroom setting, and reading voraciously, I also set out to explore and understand Boston. It was a great experience. I was back home in time to teach four sections of a freshmen course at Lincoln that was essentially one on late-twentieth-century African American history and culture. A problem soon emerged in the history department over the fact that the students enrolled in my courses were not getting credit for taking a course in African American History but instead for having taken World Civilization, a traditional two-semester world history course that was part of the university's general education requirement. My colleagues in the history department, a majority of whom had been my teachers, objected to my students getting credit for world history classes when they were not being taught world history. I sided with the history professors, against the stand taken by the newly arrived director of what was known as the Curriculum Change Program.

My vigorous and vocal challenge of my supervisor's position won me the praise of my history department colleagues, but it nearly cost me my job. On the very first day of the 1973–1974 academic year, I received a letter from my supervisor, telling me that my contract would not be renewed for the next academic year. I, who had become the father of a second child in March 1973, a daughter named Sharon, for my deceased sister, would be out of a job by the end of May 1974. I had hit a low point in my life, but not for long.

Months of intrigue, letter writing, and cajoling by my teaching colleagues, and an all-out campaign on my part, to save my job proved successful. By the spring semester 1974 the Curriculum Change director had changed her mind and recommended that my contract be renewed.

Meanwhile, I found out about a federal program aimed at helping faculty members at Historically Black Colleges and Universities (HBCUs) to return to graduate school to work on doctoral degrees. This program was available through the Educations Professions Development Act (EPDA) of 1967. Through the EPDA, fellowships that provided a generous tax-free stipend and a tuition waiver were available at the American University in Washington, D.C., and the University of Pittsburgh.

I applied for a fellowship at American University in the spring of 1974 and was awarded the same in time to enroll in the summer session during that same year. In so doing I, a white baby boomer from rural Missouri, became a beneficiary of affirmative action. That same summer saw the demise of President Richard M. Nixon, and I found myself caught up in the drama unfolding over the Watergate scandal, which filled me with an ever-increasing conviction that the president deserved impeachment. In those long-ago days before twenty-four-hour-a-day cable news and the Internet, I could not find enough information about the investigation into the president and his administration. Each day I eagerly awaited the delivery of the *Washington Post*. Even though I was no great fan of Gerald Ford, Nixon's Vice President, I was elated when Nixon resigned. I remember the days and weeks and months leading up to that resignation, in particular the so-called "Saturday Night Massacre," which occurred on the evening of October 20, 1973. I was at a small dinner party at the home of two of my Lincoln University colleagues. I remember all of us standing around a television, wondering what was going to happen next, half expecting Nixon to come on TV and announce that he was declaring martial law, effective immediately.

On August 11, 1974, my wife, five-year-old son, and seventeen-month-old daughter got into our family car (a 1974 Oldsmobile), pulling a 6' x 9' U-Haul trailer and headed east to Washington, D.C. I was naïve and unprepared. I had contacted a couple of businesses that promoted themselves as agencies that assisted people in finding affordable housing, none of which were of any help. So my family and I arrived in DC without a place to live. We stayed in a motel for several days and spent the bulk of our time (and money) looking for an apartment that we could afford.

It was a very stressful time, especially with two kids. We quickly discovered that we could not afford anything near American University. We finally found an apartment we thought we could afford in Falls Church, Virginia, ten miles from the AU campus. It was a third-floor walkup, apartment number 10, in a complex at 6030 Vista Drive.

My wife found a job in the AU computer center. Our apartment was only a few blocks from the Bailey Crossroads Elementary School, where our son started kindergarten, and we found nearby daycare for our daughter. More than four decades after this adventure, I still marvel that we undertook it! I marvel at the faith we had that everything would work out. Today, I would be paralyzed by anxiety, about the quality of the neighborhood and our neighbors, about the trustworthiness of the teachers at the school and the caregivers at the daycare center. I was far more trusting in those days than I am now, a trust, no doubt, born out of a childhood spent in the safety of a functional and loving family and a small-town, rural lifestyle that seemed quintessentially safe.

I did have one especially memorable scare at the apartment complex that, more than four decades later, still haunts me occasionally. We allowed our five-year-old son to ride his bike around the apartment complex, with the admonition that he had to "remain in sight," meaning where I could see him from a window in our third-floor apartment. One day, I looked out that window and saw my son get into the car of an absolute stranger on the apartment complex parking lot! The car quickly exited the lot and disappeared around the corner. I raced down three flights of stairs and ran outside, but the car was gone. I stood there in a panic, preparing to call the police and provide them with the few sketchy descriptive details I could recall. And then, all of a sudden, the car reappeared from the opposite direction. It pulled into the parking lot, parked, and my son emerged, safe and smiling, from the car's passenger-side door. The driver of the car, it turned out, had been working on the car in the parking lot and my ever-inquisitive son was watching him. When the guy finished what he was doing, he decided to take the car for a spin around the block. He invited my son, who had not yet learned to fear strangers, to ride along. I quickly vowed never to allow anything like that to happen again.

For the next year, I was consumed with completing the coursework for my Ph.D. In addition to taking a full load of classes each semester and two summers, I audited as many lecture classes as I could, all in an effort to complete the necessary course work for the degree and to prepare for comprehensive exams. I also began to conceptualize a dissertation and to prepare drafts of chapters as class and seminar papers. Having ready access to the Library of Congress and the National Archives was an unbelievably exhilarating experience. In fact, my time at American University was the most enjoyable and rewarding educational experience of my life.

In the summer of 1975, my family and I returned to Jefferson City and I resumed teaching at Lincoln University. Over the next three years, I continued to take comprehensive exams and to work on my dissertation. I completed all exams and defended my dissertation by the summer of 1978 and was officially awarded the degree later that year.

Meanwhile, I had become deeply interested in the Missouri State Penitentiary (MSP) and its history. That interest stemmed from two things. First, I was fascinated by a book written by David Rothman: *The Discovery of the Asylum: Social Order and Disorder in the New Republic* (1971). I wanted to study the MSP in light of Rothman's conclusions about the creation and life of early nineteenth-century penitentiaries. Second, I began to develop a personal relationship with MSP and its residents, first by working among inmates to prepare them to take the GED, and, second by teaching university history courses there each semester through an associate of arts program offered inside the facility by Lincoln University. For roughly a decade, I taught a course each semester inside the walls of MSP. Many of my students, I quickly discovered, were exceptionally intelligent and talented. They pushed and prodded me to think deeply and to question much about what I thought I knew about the American past. There is no question that one of the most challenging classes I ever taught was a survey of Afro-American History, the students being twenty-five MSP inmates, many if not most of whom were Muslim. Although that class began with some unsteadiness, it turned out to be one of the most enjoyable and self-enriching courses I ever taught. I still have the *Koran* that one of those students gave me. That same student told me many years later that a turning point in the class for him came when I made positive and flattering comments about Malcolm X.

I continued to teach at Lincoln University until 1987. Meanwhile, my marriage had ended after sixteen years, as did the marriages of so many of my contemporaries. There were more than twice as many divorces in Missouri in 1985 than there had been thirty years earlier. As a kid growing up in 1950s Catholic Frankenstein, I hardly knew anyone who was divorced. Three decades later, it seemed I hardly knew anyone whose marriage had survived.

After a dozen years, I also abandoned the Baha'i Faith, driven in large part by my growing alienation from the people who had first introduced me to that religion. It turned out that they, too, had feet of clay, just like me. After some time of wandering in the wilderness, I returned to my Catholic roots, although the connection would never again be as strong as it once was.

I also remarried, to a Lincoln University co-worker, who, like me, was a single parent. We married in 1986 and blended our families and our careers. I left Lincoln University in 1987 to become the state archivist of Missouri. I knew little of archival work, but by this time I was deeply interested in Missouri history, a reality reflected in my modest list of publications.

It was a good job, made better still by the unfailing support and encouragement I received from my boss, Missouri Secretary of State Roy D. Blunt, whose love for and interest in Missouri history equaled my own. I adjusted to being a state government bureaucrat and remained as state archivist through most of the remainder of Secretary Blunt's tenure, but I returned to academia when the opportunity presented itself and it became clear that Secretary Blunt was going to seek a higher office.

I taught at William Woods College (now William Woods University) from 1991 to 2004, focusing my research and writing primarily on issues having to do with race and gender in American and Missouri history. In 2004 I was presented with another opportunity for a career change. My friend, James W. Goodrich, executive director of the State Historical Society of Missouri, suffered a debilitating stroke during the summer of 2003. After months of uncertainty about whether or not Jim would be able to resume his duties, the Society's Board of Trustees concluded that he could not. The board then decided to seek a new director, and asked me to consider taking the position.

I was ambivalent about abandoning a secure tenured teaching position for the second time in my career, but I was encouraged to do so by a number of my colleagues, most forcefully so by my friend Professor Lawrence O. Christensen, with whom I had co-authored one book and co-edited another. In his inimitable style and with his characteristic passion, "Chris" told me it was my duty and part of my patrimony to assume the position. I accepted his arguments.

I started work as the executive director of the State Historical Society of Missouri, housed then in the Elmer Ellis Library on the campus of the

University of Missouri in Columbia, on September 7, 2004, once again having abandoned a job whose perquisites included no summer teaching and a month off at Christmas. As a state-funded institution, SHSMO regularly suffered the vicissitudes associated with all publicly funded institutions. In 2005, SHSMO was briefly zeroed out of the state budget (and out of existence), before gaining new life, albeit with a significant budget cut. More cuts came in the wake of the economic downturn associated with the Great Recession of 2007–2009. Between and beyond those periods of austerity, SHSMO managed to increase its annual state appropriation, expand its staff, and increase its number of research centers from four—Columbia, St. Louis, Kansas City, and Rolla—to six, with the addition of Springfield and Cape Girardeau. SHSMO also moved into the digital world, with a large body of artwork, newspapers, photographs, and manuscripts online by 2020.

The crowning achievement of SHSMO came in the twenty-first century with its new home, the Center for Missouri Studies. This 76,000-square-foot building, erected largely of Missouri-made materials, was made possible by the General Assembly's authorization of a $35 million bond issue in 2015. Bonds were sold in 2016, construction began in 2017, and the building was completed in 2019. The grand opening was held on August 10, 2019, the 198th anniversary of Missouri statehood. More than one thousand people attended the event.

Roughly seven months later, the Center closed indefinitely, a victim of the novel coronavirus and the COVID-19 related state budget crisis. In August 2020, the Center finally re-opened, albeit with a significantly smaller staff working reduced hours. At this writing, I am left to ponder how this latest chapter of the Missouri experience will impact my life, the lives of my co-workers, and those of all my fellow Missourians.

Only time will tell, of course, just how much our lives will change before the end of the crises caused by the global pandemic, just as time and a multitude of experiences have determined our lives to this point. History really is a collection of local experiences, made up of people adjusting and adapting to the changes in their lives. My great-grandfather Gustav could not have imagined the life I have lived. Neither, for that matter, could I have imagined it five or six decades ago, or even a year ago at the Center for Missouri Studies' ribbon-cutting ceremony.

Fig. 4: The State Historical Society of Missouri's Center for Missouri Studies opened to the public in August 2019. Credit: Notley Hawkins, State Historical Society of Missouri.

Fig. 5: View of the Grand Staircase in the Center for Missouri Studies. Credit: Notley Hawkins, State Historical Society of Missouri.

One of the great benefits of studying history is that the process provides us with an opportunity to come to grips with why we are the way we are. This, then, is the purpose of this book. In the pages that follow, one will not find a comprehensive history of Missouri. I have not tried to chronicle all of the great events or pay tribute to all of the heroes (or villains) who have gone before us. Inevitably, some readers will find their favorite Missouri story or person missing. Rather, I have simply tried to recount some of what I regard as the significant historical occurrences that belong to this place called Missouri, and to all who call Missouri home, and to reflect upon, much as I have done with my own Missouri story, how those experiences have shaped our present and positioned us for the future, even as we do our best in the face of continuous change, to live our lives and make our way.

SUGGESTED READINGS

The literature on Missouri history is vast and ever expanding. The list of readings suggested here is not meant to be either complete or exhaustive. Rather, it is meant to suggest easily accessible sources that will allow students of Missouri history, whatever their ages or levels of expertise, to pursue additional reading on a variety of topics and periods of Missouri history.

The most comprehensive one-volume history of Missouri is *Missouri: The Heart of the Nation*, now in its fourth edition. Published by Wiley-Blackwell in 2020, the fourth edition is authored by William E. Parrish, Lawrence O. Christensen, and Brad D. Lookingbill. Although somewhat dated, Paul Nagel's *Missouri: A Bicentennial History*, remains useful. Nagel's book was published in 1977 by W. W. Norton & Company, Inc., and the American Association for State and Local History as a volume in The States and the Nation Series, edited by James Morton Smith. Also extremely useful is the *Dictionary of Missouri Biography* (1999), edited by Lawrence O. Christensen, William E. Foley, Gary R. Kremer, and Kenneth H. Winn. This 832-page volume contains the biographies of 724 Missourians who made distinctive contributions to the course of state and national history. It was published by the University of Missouri Press.

Multi-volume histories include *A History of Missouri* series, six volumes, published by the University of Missouri Press to commemorate the Missouri Sesquicentennial of statehood in 1971. This series was edited by William E. Parrish. The first volume appeared in 1971, the last in 2004. Each volume contains extensive suggestions for further reading.

There have been a number of books published over the past two decades that take up a particular topic in Missouri history, covering the scope of the Missouri experience. *Missouri's Black Heritage*, second edition, was published in 1993 and is a volume authored by Gary R. Kremer and Antonio F. Holland. The second edition is a revision of a 1980 version of the book that included co-author Lorenzo J. Greene. The second edition was published by the University of Missouri Press. Kremer's *Race and Meaning: The African American Experience in Missouri* (2014) covers the period from the Civil War to the mid-twentieth century. It was published by the University of Missouri Press. *Women in Missouri History: In Search of Power and Influence* (2004), edited by LeeAnn Whites, Mary C. Neth and Gary R. Kremer, was published by the University of Missouri Press. For a collection of essays about "Regular Folk" in Missouri, see Thomas M. Spencer, *The Other Missouri History: Populists, Prostitutes, and Regular Folk* (2004), published by the University of Missouri Press. Michael D. Patrick and Evelyn Goodrich Trickel, *Orphan Trains to Missouri* (Missouri Heritage Readers), published by the University of Missouri Press (1997) tells the story of orphan trains to Missouri.

The Ozarks has attracted a significant amount of attention, especially in recent years. Lynn Morrow's edited collection, *The Ozarks in Missouri History: Discoveries in an American Region* (2013), published by the University of Missouri Press, is a good introduction to Ozarks scholarship. So, too, are several works by geographer Milton D. Rafferty, especially his *The Ozarks, Land and Life* (2001), published by the University of Arkansas Press. Rafferty's *Historical Atlas of Missouri* (1982), published by the University of Oklahoma Press, also remains useful. Similarly, two works by geographer Russel Gerlach also remain helpful. *Immigrants in the Ozarks: A Study in Ethnic Geography* (1976) and *Settlement Patterns in Missouri: A Study of Population Origins* (1986). Both works were published by the University of Missouri Press. The work on the Ozarks that is without peer is the three-volume set by Brooks Blevins titled *A History of the Ozarks*. The first volume appeared in 2018 and is titled *The Old Ozarks*. The second volume is titled *The Conflicted Ozarks* (2019). The third volume, titled *The Ozarkers*, is scheduled for release in October 2021. All three volumes have been or will be published by the University of Illinois Press.

Chapter One

Coming to Missouri
Missouri and Missourians on the Eve of Statehood

"This is probably the easiest unsettled country in the world to commence farming in."

A traveler to the Missouri Territory in 1817

I GREW UP among and around farmers, people who never ceased to amaze me with their deep sense of hope and optimism. Their lives were uncertain and hard, and they lived with the knowledge that any number of occurrences could disrupt their well-being and postpone, if not shatter, their dreams. The farmers I knew in mid-twentieth-century Missouri worried over things they knew they could not control, especially the weather: droughts, hail, windstorms, and early frosts. They worried over their crops, how to find help to harvest them, and markets where they could sell them. They worried about diseases that could claim their plants, their animals, the lives of their loved ones, or even themselves. Despite their worries, however, they seemed to approach each new growing season with a sense of adventure and hope, a feeling that the coming year would bring prosperity and improvement in their lives.

It is not difficult to imagine that Henry Vest Bingham felt these same feelings of hope and promise when he ventured from Augusta County, Virginia, his birthplace, in the fall of 1818. He joined a group of fellow travelers on a westward trek in search of new land that he could call home. The son of a New England minister who had immigrated to Virginia, and a woman who was a Pennsylvania transplant to the same state, Bingham was looking for a new beginning, after having suffered a devastating financial setback in his birth county. As the editor of his 1818 diary noted years later, "He took the road west to begin again in search, preferably, of land that would raise the crops that were familiar to him—tobacco, corn, and hay."

The group that Bingham travelled with was a scouting party in search of new land and new opportunity. He temporarily left behind his wife of a decade, Mary, and his children, including seven-year-old George Caleb, the future artist, and resolved to come back for the family when he found them a new home.

The trip west was arduous and challenging, even dangerous. The group followed a trail that by 1818 was already well-travelled, from Virginia, through Kentucky, across the southern part of Indiana, through Illinois, and into Missouri by way of St. Louis, a distance of more than seven hundred miles.

The group arrived in St. Louis on June 8, 1818. Bingham described the city as a town of "from five to Six thousand Inhabitants," in which "The Indians Carry on a Considerable Trade . . . In furr & peltry." The St. Louis economy was highly dependent upon the Indigenous people who lived in or made regular trips to the village, a reality not lost on one of the town patriarchs, Auguste Chouteau, who had a long-established reputation of trust among them. Other St. Louis residents held less benign feelings toward the Natives. In a late-life interview published in a St. Louis newspaper called *The Republic*, an elderly St. Louis-born French woman named Cecelia (Clement) Aubuchon recalled, "When I was a little girl [she was born in 1811] Indians used to come here and camp every year. . . . We were afraid of them. . . . I hated the Indians."

After spending five days in St. Louis, Bingham's party headed west to St. Charles. He described that town as being "Scatteringly Built and mostly in the old french Stile Exept some New houses Lately Erected By Americans," adding, "It is at this time mostly Inhabited By Americans who have Commenced Improving the place Rappidly." Bingham reported that St. Charles had about 1,200 Inhabitance" at the time of his visit.

By June 17, 1818, Bingham had seen enough to determine that he would most likely make Missouri his new home. He noted in his diary, "The Lands I have Seen in this Territory Being with other Advantages Sufficient Inducements to Cause me to move here In preference to any other Country I have yet Seen I am informed from Every Source that the Country farther up [in mid-Missouri] is Still more Rich and Desirable." Bingham added, "If I do not Change my mind In favor of Some place that I may yet See Betwixt this and Augusta County Va. I Shall move my fammily to this Nighborhood Next Spring and more Effectually Explore the Territory."

Bingham did not change his mind. He returned to Virginia, gathered up his family, and made plans to move. In the spring of 1819, he transported his wife, their seven children, his father-in-law and seven slaves to the newly bustling town of Franklin, Missouri, some 150 miles west of St. Louis. The Binghams set about becoming Missourians.

The Bingham emigration story, with slight modifications, played out thousands of times between 1815 and 1821, when Missouri formally joined the United States as the nation's twenty-fourth state, and it continued to play out throughout the next generation of Missouri history.

The 1820 federal census of Missouri, taken even as the U.S. Congress debated whether and under what circumstances the territory should be admitted to the Union, revealed that 66,557 people lived within the territory's borders in that year. Approximately fifteen percent (10,200) of that number were enslaved African Americans. Indeed, slaves had been present in the territory that would become the state of Missouri for at least a century prior to statehood, and the issues of slavery and race would be central to the Missouri experience for the next two hundred years and beyond.

Most of these people, Black and white, were Old Stock Americans, like the Binghams, who had come from east of the Mississippi River in the wake of the Louisiana Purchase (1803). Although migration into Missouri slowed somewhat during the War of 1812, the population increased to 25,845 by 1814. After the war, migration increased significantly, more than doubling the population of the Missouri Territory over the course of the next six years. To John Mason Peck, an itinerate missionary to frontier Missouri, "It seemed as though Kentucky and Tennessee were breaking up and moving to the 'Far West.' Caravan after caravan passed over the prairies of Illinois, crossing the 'great river' at St. Louis. . . ." The increase was aided greatly by a second series of bounty land warrants issued by the federal government for up to 320 acres each for volunteer soldiers who enlisted in the army after December 1814. This second series of warrants entitled veterans to land in either Arkansas, Illinois, or Missouri. Among the scores of veterans who acquired land in Missouri in return for their military service during the War of 1812 were Benjamin and Joseph Cooper, who obtained land in Howard County, and Joseph Moreau (or Morian), who earned land in Ste. Genevieve County.

"The bulk of the population" in 1820, according to historian Jonas Viles, "was to be found along the Mississippi [River] and in a great island along the Missouri in the central part of the state—the Booneslick country. . . ." Not surprisingly, the largest concentration of population was in the City of

St. Louis, many of whose residents were descendants of the French founders who established the city in 1764 as a trade center for furriers. The city's location on the Mississippi River, near the mouth of the Missouri River, made it an ideal location, as those two great rivers provided access to both the supplies of furs in the interior of the North American continent as well as markets for those furs and all manner of agricultural products the settlers hoped to sell at points throughout the vast river system and all the way down the Mississippi to its terminus at the international port of New Orleans.

St. Louis did indeed appear to be a city on the cusp of dramatic growth when the federal census was taken in 1820. The population stood at 4,598 that year, a gain of 228 percent over the course of the previous decade. Much of this phenomenal growth had occurred since 1815, at the conclusion of the War of 1812. In the wake of the signing of the Treaty of Ghent, which formally ended the conflict, thousands of Americans crossed the Mississippi River into Missouri Territory in search of economic opportunity in the vast river valley and beyond.

The physical boundaries of St. Louis expanded during this period, and new houses were built at an unprecedented rate. The *Missouri Gazette*, Missouri's earliest newspaper, reported that more than one hundred new houses were built in St. Louis in 1818 alone. Between 1815 and 1821, a total of 306 new houses were constructed in the city, roughly half of them substantial structures of either brick or stone.

During this same period, St. Louis's economy was transitioning from one based on barter to money-based, with common laborers regularly earning $1.50 per day. At the same time, the city's economy was becoming increasingly diversified. John Paxton's 1821 *St. Louis Directory* identified forty-six mercantile houses, "carrying on an extensive trade with the most distant parts of the republic, in merchandise, produce, furs and peltry." Artisans in the city included silversmiths, jewelers, bricklayers, stone cutters, carpenters, blacksmiths, gunsmiths, cabinetmakers, and tailors. Virtually any service or commodity that one expected to be able to purchase in an older, more established city in the eastern United States could be purchased in St. Louis on the eve of Missouri statehood. That said, St. Louis in 1820 bore little resemblance to a modern-day American city. Indeed, writing in 1971, distinguished Missouri historian Lewis E. Atherton opined that "In many ways the business structure of Missouri towns [including St. Louis] in 1821 more nearly resembled that of medieval European cities than of twentieth-century America." As Atherton has written, "As owners of their own shops and tools and supervisors of all operations, master artisans were capitalists, managers, employers and workmen all in one." Both artisans and laborers were in great demand, with virtually everyone who belonged to the latter class aspiring to become a member of the former.

A major source of commercial activity in St. Louis in 1820 remained the fur trade. The 1821 *St. Louis Directory* credited it with nearly one-third of St. Louis's annual commerce ($300,000 of $1 million trade). There were two major fur-trading companies in St. Louis at the time: the one operated by the Chouteau family, who traded primarily with the Osages, the other the Missouri Fur Company of Manuel Lisa, who died in 1820, a few weeks short of his forty-eighth birthday. Both operations counted on the abilities of trappers and traders to work closely with Native American groups living along the Upper Missouri River.

St. Louis's connection to distant markets, facilitated by its location on the Mississippi River and its access to the Missouri River, was greatly enhanced by the introduction of steamboats. The first steamboat to arrive in St. Louis was the *Zebulon M. Pike*, named for the American explorer who died in 1813, which docked on the city's waterfront for the first time on August 2, 1817. By 1820, steamboats came into St. Louis with great frequency, and steamboat traffic on the Missouri River had become commonplace. This new means of transportation of both people and trade goods, in turn, connected St. Louis and Missouri River towns to eastern markets and helped to hasten the transition of the Missouri economy.

One can glean some insight into life in St. Louis on the eve of statehood from the recollections of a contemporary resident, David Holmes Conrad, who first visited the city on a cold, subzero-degree day on December 29, 1819. Conrad, then just a few days shy of his twentieth birthday, had travelled overland by horseback with a companion, cabinetmaker Joshua Newbrough, who had purchased 160 acres of land in the Boonslick a few months earlier. The duo travelled from Winchester, Virginia. The son of a prominent Winchester attorney who died in 1806, Conrad had recently completed his private training in the law and headed west to practice his new profession in the Missouri Territory. He obtained a law license in Missouri in February 1820.

According to Conrad, when he arrived in St. Louis, the "city" boasted a population of "not quite 5000" mostly French residents, with French being the dominant spoken language. "There were some Spanish residents as well, and a number of 'Americans,'" primarily, according to Conrad, unmarried men, suggesting that these were young men who had arrived in St. Louis relatively recently and who, like Conrad, hoped for a new start in a promising new land.

The city, or "town," as Conrad referred to it, struck him as "foreign," unlike the towns he had seen in Ohio and Indiana along the way. Most of the houses in St. Louis were made of logs, arranged vertically in the French style of building, unlike the horizontal log structures with which he was more familiar. The "old proprietors and founders of the town" lived in mansions built on large lots—Conrad specifically mentioned the homes of town patriarchs Auguste and Pierre Chouteau, and also that of William Clark, governor of the Missouri Territory.

Native peoples continued to have a presence in St. Louis when Conrad arrived there. Indeed, he attended a "council with some Indian tribes," hosted by Clark at the governor's invitation. Although the French influence remained strong in St. Louis, Conrad was struck by the fact that "the most prominent officers of the territory were Virginians," including Governor Clark, Lieutenant Governor Frederick Bates, and U.S. Surveyor of Public Lands, William Rector. "The Southern influence," Conrad concluded correctly, "was largely and decidedly predominant," and it informed and influenced St. Louis and much of Missouri for decades, especially in their reliance on the institution of slavery and their commitment to the notion of white supremacy.

Conrad was an unabashed Missouri booster. "The fertility of Missouri lands," he wrote in his memoir, "can hardly be understood by persons who have not lived there." Likewise, he observed, "The mineral resources of the country . . . are magnificent," especially its iron, lead and coal supplies. Wild fruits and nuts were available in abundance and wild game "abundant to a degree almost incredible." In short, Conrad concluded, "I never saw a country where the spontaneous product of the necessaries of life did so abound."

The prevalence of French culture in St. Louis led to the presence of what Conrad described as "some strange old customs." One was the chivaree, described by him as "a mock or masquerade ceremony of greeting to a newly married couple," especially "when there was something disproportionate in the union," such as a large age difference between the partners to the marriage. Crowds of revelers making lots of noise would gather at the new-lyweds' house and create "a racket," "[t]he object [of which] was to enforce from the newly married pair a present for some public purpose, the church or the poor."

The French chivaree tradition remained alive in Missouri, and even ex-tended to the isolated and homogenous German Osage County community of my childhood more than a century later. I recall fondly a chivaree held in 1957, soon after local resident Leonard Burchard, a lifelong bachelor, age 59, married a young woman more than two decades his junior. The horn-honking, pot-banging, tin can clattering revelry involved left a life-long impression on an eight-year-old boy.

There were boosters aplenty in Missouri during the late territorial period, all of them encouraging potential immigrants to come to the state, to up-root themselves and move west of the Mississippi River. One of the earliest and most vociferous of these was the St. Louis newspaper publisher, Joseph Charless. A native of Ireland who immigrated to the United States in 1795, Charless worked his way from Pennsylvania to Kentucky and then to St. Louis, arriving in 1808. He became Missouri's first printer soon after his arrival in St. Louis, and on July 12, 1808, he produced the first issue of the *Missouri Gazette*, the territory's first newspaper. Over the course of the next dozen years, and especially after the end of the War of 1812, Charless used the pages of his newspaper to promote Missouri as a paradise for newcom-ers, especially farmers. He advertised the high prices that could be obtained for growing wheat in Missouri, but also proclaimed Missouri's fertile soil and suitable climate as conducive to growing cotton, tobacco, grains other than wheat, and fruit. Additionally, Charless advertised Missouri's mineral wealth, including its rich deposits of coal, lead, salt, flint, and other miner-als. He also promised jobs aplenty for would-be laborers who did not want to farm or mine. There was a need in Missouri, he wrote, for blacksmiths, gunsmiths, wagon makers, brick makers and stonecutters, carpenters, and many, many other trades.

By 1820, the influence of French control over St. Louis could still be felt in local architecture, food, customs, and even language, although by this time the French men and women were already far outnumbered by their old-stock American counterparts. The latter group, most of them

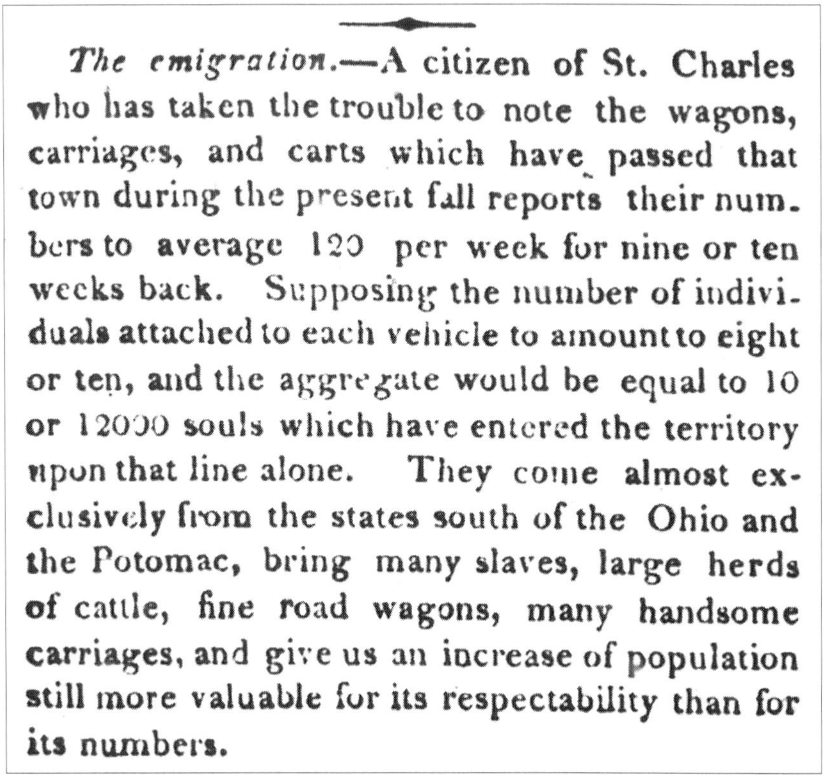

> *The emigration.*—A citizen of St. Charles who has taken the trouble to note the wagons, carriages, and carts which have passed that town during the present fall reports their numbers to average 120 per week for nine or ten weeks back. Supposing the number of individuals attached to each vehicle to amount to eight or ten, and the aggregate would be equal to 10 or 12000 souls which have entered the territory upon that line alone. They come almost exclusively from the states south of the Ohio and the Potomac, bring many slaves, large herds of cattle, fine road wagons, many handsome carriages, and give us an increase of population still more valuable for its respectability than for its numbers.

Fig. 6: This article, describing the large number of immigrants to Missouri passing through St. Charles, appeared in the *St. Louis Enquirer*, November 10, 1819. Credit: State Historical Society of Missouri.

Upland Southerners, had, as mentioned, begun to trickle into the Missouri Territory after the region was acquired by the United States in the Louisiana Purchase (1803). The trickle became a flood after the War of 1812 ended in the defeat of the British and the firm establishment of American control over the territory.

Among the Americans who lived in St. Louis on the eve of statehood were a relatively large number of African Americans, nearly seven hundred persons, most of them enslaved. They served primarily as maids and body servants to the wealthy merchants who called St. Louis home. As historian Kristen Epps has written, "The Chouteaus [and other wealthy, well established St. Louis families] relied on bondspeople not only for their business enterprises, but also for subsistence agriculture and personal comfort."

Slavery was seen as the solution to the labor shortage in St. Louis and the rest of Missouri leading up to the period of statehood and beyond. It was also viewed as the key to the social, political, and economic control of African Americans, the subjugation and exploitation of whom were essential to the growth and maturation of the region.

The popular St. Louis newspaper of the period, the *Missouri Gazette and Public Advertiser*, successor to the *Missouri Gazette*, regularly carried ads announcing slaves for sale and solicitations for slave labor, either in the form of an outright purchase or in the "hiring out" of one or more slaves on a temporary, or per job, basis.

Examples abound. Rufus Easton and Rufus Pettibone, two land speculators in St. Louis on the eve of statehood, offered land for sale in and around St. Louis, "for cash or good likely negro men and boy slaves." Future Missouri governor, Lilburn W. Boggs, a native of Lexington, Kentucky, who moved to St. Louis in 1816 and opened a store, offered for sale, "One Negro Woman about 25 or 28 years of age." In the ad he placed in a newspaper, he described the woman as "an excellent cook and washer."

Joseph Charless, the aforementioned Irish immigrant who fled his native land for the United States in 1795 and settled in Pennsylvania, Ohio, and Kentucky before moving to St. Louis in 1808, served both as a broker and solicitor of slaves. A few years after his arrival in St. Louis, and aware that he had "friends in Kentucky and Ohio intending to remove to Missouri and Illinois," he announced through his newspaper, "I have opened BOOKS for the registry of Lands, Town Lots, and slaves." A few years later, Charless himself was in search of slave labor, although he wanted to hire rather than purchase a slave. In February 1819 he took out a newspaper ad, announcing that he wanted to hire a servant: "I will give generous wages by the month or year, for a negro girl of from 14 to 18 years of age." Hiring someone else's slave allowed an individual to acquire the use of a slave's labor without making the substantial cash investment necessary to purchase a slave. Hiring meant one could acquire a slave's services for the period that they were needed, without having to worry about feeding, housing or clothing the slave during slow times, when there was little or no work to do. Thus, in July 1817, a St. Louis resident placed an ad in the *Missouri Gazette and Public Advertiser*, announcing his desire to hire "Two negro men, or well grown boys, capable of driving a team, chopping wood, mowing and curing hay." The prospective hirer promised, "Liberal wages will be given for servants of the above description." The wages, of course, went to the slaves' owners, not the slaves themselves.

It was common to advertise the skills of slaves who were being sold or hired out. One seller in 1816 took care to note that the woman he offered for sale with her child was "well adapted for a farmer being accustomed to live in the country." He also noted that the woman was "sober and honest," both highly prized qualities among those who sought to acquire or use slave labor. Yet another person advertising in the *Missouri Intelligencer* in 1819 offered "A Liberal price in Cash . . . for an active Negro girl, from 18 to 25 years of age, one that could be recommended as a good trusty house servant."

Another important consideration for those who sought to hire instead of purchasing a slave was that hiring was usually less risky. Newspapers of the time regularly reported on slaves who had run away and on owners' efforts to offer rewards for the safe return of their slaves. In 1816, a slave owner advertised in the *Missouri Gazette* for the return of his runaway slave, Jemima, aged about 23, "of a brown complexion, not very tall and inclined to be fleshy, and when spoken to has a dejected countenance." The owner noted, "it is highly probable her intention is to go to Kentucky, (Union county) from whence she was brought about seven weeks ago, and is now lurking about the town of St. Louis, or its vicinity, until a safe opportunity offers for her escape." The mistreatment of many of these runaway slaves is documented in identifying characteristics noted by advertisers: "He has been badly whipped and has had sore legs," "scar on his chin," "with a scar on his under lip," and more. Indeed, the prevalence of such comments in newspaper advertisements evidences the reality of slavery's harshness in Missouri, despite the arguments of some that it was less brutal than was the case farther south.

A disproportionate number of lawyers lived in St. Louis during the early nineteenth century, many of them drawn there by the lucrative business created by the confusion over land titles that emerged after the brief time that the Spanish government controlled the region (1762–1803). Lawyers, and the people they represented, spent significant amounts of time and large amounts of financial resources litigating competing claims of land. It was not unusual for a single piece of property to be claimed by multiple persons: one, say, made by a Frenchman who asserted that the French government had granted him or his ancestors the land; another who laid claim to the land by virtue of a Spanish land grant; and a third who insisted that the U.S. government had given him claim to the land, perhaps through a "New Madrid claim," which was a certificate to public land in the territory made available to those individuals displaced by the New Madrid earthquake of 1811–1812.

In addition to St. Louis, there were other communities along the Mississippi River, most notably Ste. Genevieve, some sixty miles south of St. Louis. Ste. Genevieve was roughly half the size of St. Louis, with perhaps 1,500 to 2,000 people in 1820. Older than St. Louis by a generation, Ste. Genevieve retained much more of its French character, most of its citizens engaged either in farming or lead mining. They were assisted in these endeavors by a relatively large number of African American slaves whose numbers represented perhaps 20 percent of the village's total population.

Yet another concentration of population along the Mississippi River on the eve of statehood was a community known as "the Barrens," in and around the modern-day site of Perryville, in Perry County, about thirty miles south of Ste. Genevieve. The Barrens ran along Cinq Hommes Creek and attracted a good number of Catholic families from Maryland, by way of Kentucky, during the last decade of the eighteenth century. Geographer Walter Schroeder described the area as being "an excellent one for clear-field agriculture. . . . Farms could be started immediately with no necessity to wait for time-consuming tree felling and stump removal."

The Barrens Settlement, as it came to be called, was a distinctly homogenous community of people who married within their own group and transferred land to other group members, often using the leverage of land ownership as a way of encouraging their children and grandchildren to remain in the community. In 1818, Catholic residents of the Barrens offered Catholic Bishop William Louis DuBourg a 640-acre tract of land and $750 to build a church and seminary there. They also offered to help in the construction of seminary-associated buildings, pledging the labor of their slaves as well.

Bishop DuBourg accepted their offer. The subsequent building of the seminary and the continued presence of one or more priests attracted an influx of more Kentucky Catholics. By 1821, the area had grown sufficiently to warrant the separation of the southeast part of Ste. Genevieve County into a new county: Perry County. A new town, Perryville, which also served as the new county seat, sprang up about a mile and a half from the seminary, on fifty-one acres of land donated by Bernard Layton. Smaller settlements of Anglo-Americans existed farther south along the Mississippi River at Cape Girardeau (incorporated in 1808), its neighboring community of Jackson (incorporated in 1814), and New Madrid.

Another place of population concentration in Missouri Territory in 1820 was the lead mining region of the state, in and around modern-day Potosi in Washington County. Named in honor of the region of modern-day Bolivia that once boasted highly productive silver mines, Potosi, founded by "the lead king" of Missouri, Moses Austin, was platted in 1814 and quickly became the most important smelting center in the territory. In 1818, Austin and Potosi were visited by the New York native Henry Rowe Schoolcraft, who traveled to the region to conduct a scientific study of Missouri lead mining. Working out of space in Austin's home, Durham Hall, described by historian Floyd Shoemaker as "the most impressive private residence" in the territory, Schoolcraft described Potosi and neighboring Mine a Breton in an 1819 book titled *View of the Lead Mines*. Potosi and its neighboring community had approximately eighty buildings at the time, according to Schoolcraft, and perhaps as many as five hundred inhabitants. Buildings included a courthouse, a jail, an academy, two distilleries, two grist mills, a sawmill, and nine lead furnaces, plus a shot tower and sheet-lead factories.

North of St. Louis, also on the Mississippi River, were the aborning towns of Louisiana, founded in 1816 by John Walter Basye and named for his daughter, and Hannibal, founded in 1819 by Moses Bates.

Yet another town with a strong French influence in the Missouri Territory was St. Charles, located just across the Missouri River from St. Louis. Like St. Louis, a community rapidly becoming "American," St. Charles had a population of between five hundred and one thousand residents in 1820. In 1819–1820, Major Stephen H. Long traveled through Missouri on a federal government-sponsored expedition from Pittsburgh to the Rocky Mountains. Long and his party began their ascent up the Missouri River on June 21, 1819. He described St. Charles as a town of about 100 houses, with "two brick kilns, a tan yard and several stores."

Beyond St. Charles, in the interior of the Missouri Territory, the largest town was that of Franklin, where the Binghams chose to settle. By 1820, this Missouri River community had a thousand or more people and served largely as a trading center for what was referred to as the "Boonslick country."

Old stock American migrants, largely from Virginia, North Carolina, Kentucky, and Tennessee, began to populate this region after the sons of famed frontiersman Daniel Boone blazed a trail to modern-day Saline County and opened a salt work operation at one of the many saline springs in the area as early as 1806. Salt was indispensable for preserving and seasoning a variety of food items in the days before refrigeration.

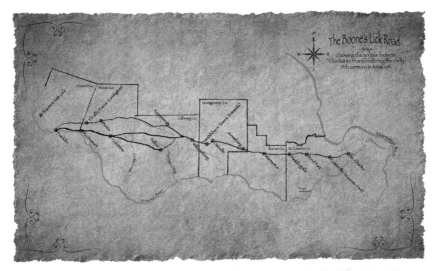

Fig. 7: Map of the Boone's Lick Road, showing the routes from St. Charles to Franklin in the early nineteenth century. Credit: Lisa Heffernan Weil.

The trail established by the Boone brothers extended from St. Charles to Saline County and soon came to be called the Boone's Lick (or Boonslick) Trail, and the area around the trail as the Boonslick Region. An early description of the Boonslick, which appeared in the *Missouri Intelligencer* on August 27, 1819, located the region as extending along "both sides of the Missouri [River} from the mouth of the Osage [River] [near the modern-day village of Osage City, about twelve miles east of Jefferson City] to the western Indian boundary, a distance of about 200 miles."

One of the factors that contributed greatly to the settlement of the Boonslick region was the ending, or at least greatly diminishing, of the violent conflict between Indigenous peoples and settlers in the region. During the War of 1812, most, although not all, of the Native nations in Missouri had sided with the British against the Americans, the latter of whom were rightly perceived as being a threat to the Natives' occupancy and ownership of Missouri Territory land. It is important to remember that when the French "sold" the Louisiana Territory to the Americans in 1803, they were selling land they did not own. The land belonged to the Indigenous peoples, until the American squatters stole or otherwise forced the Natives to relinquish their ownership.

In the wake of continuing violence between Native nations and whites in Missouri during the spring of 1815, violence prompted by Indigenous peoples' efforts to maintain control of their land and expel the white squatters, President James Madison appointed three commissioners to negotiate a peace agreement with the Indians. Accordingly, the three commissioners— Missouri Territorial Governor William Clark, Illinois Territorial Governor Ninian Edwards, and St. Louisan Auguste Chouteau—summoned representatives from various Indian nations in the region for a general council, the purpose of which was to find a way to end the long-standing conflict between Natives and white interlopers. As a consequence, some two to three thousand Indians assembled at Portage De Sioux, a strip of land between the Mississippi and Missouri rivers in St. Charles County.

The conversations and negotiations went on for months, and although the final result left parties on both sides of the negotiations less than satisfied, the outcome was obvious. As early Missouri historian William E. Foley concluded, "for the careful observer of the events during the summer of 1815, the message was clear: the Indians' days in the Missouri Territory were numbered." Despite Native efforts to retain ownership and occupancy of their land in Missouri, white power and greed doomed the desire of Natives to retain ownership and possession of their ancestral lands. American greed and land hunger prevailed over Native desires and rights.

In November 1816, Governor William Clark reported to the U.S. Secretary of War Relative to Indian Affairs that slightly fewer than five thousand Native peoples remained in Missouri, with the largest group, the Great Osages, numbering roughly 1,600, or about one-third of all the Indian peoples still living in Missouri Territory, most of the Osages concentrated along the Osage River. Additionally, there were approximately 1,300 Shawnees in multiple locations, including near Cape Girardeau, St. Louis, and on the St. Francis River. Other tribes with members living in Missouri in 1816 included the Piankashaw, Delaware, Peoria, Ioway, Sac, and Fox.

White encroachment on Native nations' lands during the decade after the War of 1812 was relentless, ruthless, and exploitative. A brief effort at

LE SOLDAT DU CHENE,

AN OSAGE CHIEF.

PUBLISHED BY F. W. GREENOUGH, PHILAD.ᵃ
Drawn Printed & Coloured at I.T. Bowen's Lithographic Establishment Nᵒ 94 Walnut St.
Entered according to act of Congress in the Year 1838 by F. Greenough in the Clerks Office of the District Court of the Eastern District of Pen.

Fig. 8: Le Soldat du Chene (The Soldier of the Oak) also known as "Big Soldier," an Osage Chief in central Missouri who was active in many treaties and negotiations during the early nineteenth century. Born, ca. 1773, died, 1844. Credit: State Historical Society of Missouri, from Thomas McKenney and James Hall, *History of the Indian Tribes of North America* (1836–1844).

transplanting Delawares, Kickapoos, and others from east of the Mississippi River into the southwestern Missouri and northern Arkansas Ozarks after 1818 was short lived. As Foley has summed up the situation, "Within little more than a decade after statehood, the final contingents of Missouri's original inhabitants had left the state."

Migration to the Boonslick region picked up after the war of 1812 and the ending of hostilities with Native Americans, and increased even more after Missouri entered the Union in 1821. Indeed, migration to the Boonslick was so great during the 1820s, according to geographer Carl O. Sauer, that it delayed settlement into the interior of other parts of the state. Recently, historian Robert Lee has demonstrated conclusively that "Boon's Lick ballooned [in population growth] by over 3,000 percent between early 1815 and late 1818." "Boon's Lick was the most intensely growing settlement in the United States after the War of 1812."

What attracted this migration to the Boonslick? Access to salt, of course, was one reason. As historian Lynn Morrow has written, "Salt not only sustained and promoted concentrated frontier settlements, as it did in the Boonslick region, it was mandatory to cure animal skins for the Indian trade, to transport salted meat, and everyone needed it to sustain livestock and their own human diet." There were other reasons as well. The mystique surrounding the famous Boone name played a role. So, too, did the familiarity of the landscape. Most of the migrants to the area came from Virginia and Kentucky. The Boonslick, as geographer Walter Schroeder described it, lay at "the farthest west extension along the Missouri River of the continuous forest environment of the humid American East from which settlers were coming." The settlers found in the Boonslick the same kinds of gentle, sloping land with an abundance of forests, a landscape that felt like home to them. They wanted land with trees, which they used in building and as fuel. The prairie lands of western Missouri did not hold out the same appeal to them; they were too flat, treeless, in short, too unfamiliar.

The fertility of the soil also made the Boonslick desirable. According to historian Perry McCandless, "In 1820 approximately 85 percent of the Missourians reported agriculture as their major economic activity." The Boonslick region featured "extensive deep loess" along with an abundance of fresh water thanks to the many streams and springs. Also, the Missouri River valley featured many valuable "rushes" that provided a ready supply of food for animals until crops could be planted and harvested.

It would be impossible to overstate the pull of the eagerness to own land that drove these early migrants to Missouri. As historian Hattie M. Anderson commented in 1939, "many [immigrants] believed with Jefferson that the way to perpetuate republican liberties and the republic itself, was to give each man land and thus enable him to acquire a home and rear a family." Land sales in the territory boomed in 1818 and 1819 as migrants rushed to Missouri. Timothy Flint, a New England missionary who came to St. Louis in 1816 to "Christianize the West," reported seeing one hundred migrants in St. Charles in one day, "joyously moving on to the promised land in the Boone's Lick region or on Salt River. . . ." The *St. Louis Enquirer* of November 10, 1819, reported that "120 wagons had passed through St. Charles each week for the past nine or ten weeks. . . ." *Enquirer* editor, the future U.S. senator from Missouri, Thomas Hart Benton, encouraged the purchase of land, claiming that those who owned their own land and cultivated the soil were "the chosen of good [God], and their occupation the most fruitful in the production of good patriots and good Christians."

One of the people Benton encouraged to move to the Boonslick during this period was Dr. John Sappington, a native of Maryland who lived in Nashville and Franklin, Tennessee, before moving to Missouri in 1817. Like Henry Bingham, Sappington had scouted the Missouri Territory for land on the advice of his good friend and neighbor, Thomas Hart Benton. Indeed, according to historian Lynn Morrow, Benton loaned Sappington his slave, Jim, as a guide and also provided him with letters of introduction to his Missouri friends. When Sappington finally moved his large family to Chariton in Howard County in September 1817, Benton loaned him $950 to facilitate the move. By 1819, Sappington, whom Morrow described as "a westering entrepreneur . . . in the vanguard of commerce on the fringe of a distinctly southern frontier society," had invested in seven thousand acres in the Boonslick.

Thomas Shackelford, yet another Tennessee transplant, was born in Virginia in 1776 and moved first to Kentucky and then to Nashville before setting out for Missouri in 1819. According to his granddaughter's memoir, Shackelford arranged for his wife and two daughters to be driven to Missouri by carriage, while he "loaded his household goods in flat boats and with the help of his slaves poled the boat down the Ohio to the Mississippi River and up the Missouri River to a small place called Old Jefferson—not far from Miami in Saline County." Subsequently, Shackelford purchased "a large farm—about 1000 acres" near modern-day Gilliam, also in Saline County.

Yet another early Boonslick settler was John Hardeman, a native of Virginia born in 1776, the year of national independence. The son of a westering wanderer, Hardeman followed his father to Howard County, Missouri, after sojourns in North Carolina and Tennessee. In 1817, Hardeman purchased land in Howard County five miles above Franklin. He used the slaves he brought with him to clear the land and establish what he called Fruitage Farm. Over the course of the next decade, Hardeman engaged in agricultural experimentation that allowed him to turn eleven acres of his land into an exotic "English garden" that attracted many visitors, including Henry Shaw, who would later establish his own famous garden in St. Louis. In addition to his work in agriculture and botany, Hardeman also held interest in a general merchandise store in Franklin.

Fig. 9: Exterior front of Van Bibber Tavern, built in 1821 in Montgomery County by Isaac Van Bibber. Credit: State Historical Society of Missouri, Harris B. Dickey Photographs, Collection No. P0683.

The Boonslick trail quickly became dotted with small, insubstantial buildings erected at strategic points, aimed at providing supplies and services to travelers, and an opportunity for financial gain to their owners. As early as July 1818, James Audrain opened a "house of entertainment," or tavern, about fourteen miles west of St. Charles, at Peruque. Other taverns also sprang up along the route, including the more substantial Van Bibber Tavern, located on the east bank of the Loutre River, about sixty miles west of St. Charles, near the modern-day town of Mineola. Establishments such as these provided opportunities for travelers to refresh themselves and their animals before proceeding on their journey. In December 1818, the Reverend John Mason Peck found Nicholas Coontz in a tavern the latter had opened on the trail just west of St. Charles. Rev. Peck described Coontz as "rough, wicked and yet hospitable."

The initial destination of many of the migrants was, as has been indicated, the small town of Franklin, on the north bank of the Missouri River, roughly 125 miles west of St. Charles. Franklin was established in 1817 and soon became the site of a federal government land office, where settlers could go to stake claims to and purchase land. According to economic historian Hattie Anderson, "In Franklin in January, 1819, land was said to be selling enormously high . . . from $4 to $12 per acre."

Stephen Long's description of Franklin in 1819 is one of the earliest accounts of the town. According to Long, "This town, at present, [is] increasing more rapidly than any other on the Missouri. . . . It then contained one hundred and twenty log houses of one story, several frame dwellings of two stories, and two of brick, thirteen shops for the sale of merchandise, four taverns, two smith's shops, two large steam mills, two billiard rooms, a courthouse, a log prison of two stories, a post office, and a printing press issuing a weekly paper." According to Long, "The price of labor was seventy-five cents per day."

Where did the money come from for the purchase of land in the Boonslick? Largely from credit! There was a widespread belief that Missouri was the quintessential land of opportunity where a would-be farmer could acquire a profitable piece of fertile land with little or no outlay of cash and pay down the debt with the fruits of his labor and the proceeds from his crops over the course of a few years. Writing in 1920, on the 100th anniversary of the Missouri Compromise, historian Jonas Viles noted "the Booneslick was the El Dorado of the immigrants following the Ohio westward, the tangible manifestation of cheap land and boundless opportunity."

Such unbridled optimism had already led to an economic panic and depression in other parts of the country by 1819. But Missourians were assured that a depression would not happen to them. On June 25, 1819, the *St. Louis Enquirer* assured Missourians that Missouri remained prosperous, even if other parts of the country were in trouble:

> Its rich and beautiful prairies are rapidly taking on the aspect of cultivated fields; farms are opening, houses are being built; towns and villages are spring[ing] up in all directions. [Missouri's] rivers are enlivened with commerce, with immigrants, and with troops moving to the frontiers. . . . [T]he whole community [is] animated with the consciousness that all the comforts of life lay within the reach of every industrious man.

Five months later, the *Franklin Intelligencer* reported that "Immigration to this country and particularly to this county during this season, exceeds almost belief."

Alas, prosperity was destined not to last. In the first months of 1819 the whole nation succumbed to a credit crisis and severe downswing in the economy that came to be known as the Panic of 1819, what some historians now call the nation's "First Great Depression." The effects of the downturn reached Missouri, where, as in many other places, the land bubble burst. Gold and silver disappeared. Landowners could not pay their mortgages. Banks could not pay their depositors. Stores could not sell their wares. According to Glen Holt, a historian of early- nineteenth-century St. Louis, between forty and fifty stores operated in that city in 1818; by the winter of 1821–1822, only nineteen remained in operation.

By late 1820, migrants stopped coming to the Boonslick, at least for a while. Merchants were going bankrupt, Missourians were developing a deep distrust of banks, and farmers who were still on their land could not find buyers for their agricultural products. The air was heavy with financial anxiety, an atmosphere that led one Boonslick resident, William Becknell, to make a desperate move. He took out an ad in the July 25, 1821, issue of the *Missouri Intelligencer* that read, in part, "An article for the government of a company of men destined to the westward for purposes of trading for Horses and Mules, and catching Wild Animals of every description that we think advantageous to the company." Becknell called for each man who wished to accompany him to bring with him $10 worth of trade goods. The group of five men crossed the Missouri River at Arrow Rock, in Saline

County, on September 1, 1821, headed southwest for Santa Fe, New Mexico, approximately 800 miles away. Santa Fe, at the time, was under Mexican rule, having only the month before escaped the repressive rule of the Spanish, who were suspicious of and hostile toward visitors from the United States. Roughly ten weeks later, on November 16, Becknell recorded, "arrived at Santa Fe and were received with apparent pleasure and joy." The trip was regarded as a great success. Years later, the son of a witness to the scene noted: "My father saw them [the five men] unload when they returned [in late January 1822], and when their rawhide packages of silver dollars were dumped on the sidewalk [presumably in Franklin] one of the men cut the thongs and the money spilled out clinking on the stone pavement and rolled into the gutter." Thereafter, the Santa Fe Trail, first blazed by Becknell and company, would be a critical trade route for Missourians.

The Becknell trip marked a turning point for the Missouri economy. Over the course of roughly the next five years, Santa Fe Trail travelers took approximately $250,000 worth of goods to Mexico via the trail. From 1838 to 1843, the amount of merchandise marketed to Mexico reached $200,000 each year.

One consequence of this trade was a call by Missourians, who benefitted from it, for federal assistance in the form of protection by federal soldiers from attacks by Indians as they travelled to and from Santa Fe. Thus, even in the early days of statehood, as Missourians were battling the federal government over the circumstances under which they might come into the union, at least some Missourians found themselves in the peculiar position of seeking the help of the federal government that was so much reviled. This practice of seeking out and soliciting the help of the government, while simultaneously harboring hostility toward it, would become a hallmark of Missouri life for the next two centuries.

The Santa Fe trade helped Missourians to escape the clutches of the early-decade depression, both by opening new markets and by adding to the supply of specie in the state. Still, life was very hard for the first generation of settlers in the new state of Missouri.

The extent of this hardship can be seen in contemporary accounts of these early immigrants' lives in Missouri. Philander Draper, whose family settled in north-central Missouri in 1815, reported that his family relied heavily on hunting deer and turkey to survive their early years there. Fortunately for them, game was readily available at the time.

Similarly, Stephen H. Long, who traveled through central Missouri in 1819 as a leader of the first federal-government-sponsored scientific expedition into the Trans-Mississippi West, reported that the hunting was so good that one man could provide food for himself and his family for two years just by hunting.

Rose Philippine Duchesne, a Catholic nun, arrived in St. Charles from France in late 1818 to establish a school. In one of her first letters back to her mother superior in France, Duchesne commented, "Divine Providence has brought us to the remotest village in the United States." She, too, noted that she and her fellow nuns relied on game: "During the hunting season, which we are in now, we can procure venison and ducks. . . ." In December of that year, she indicated, "I do not know how to describe the place in which we live. . . . We have had the privilege of doing without bread and water. I had expected the former privation, but I never dreamed that on the banks of the Missouri we should lack water with such an abundant flow of it in sight." The Missouri River had frozen over.

Building a house and clearing the land were major challenges to early-nineteenth-century settlers in Missouri. Trees were killed by girdling them, i.e., cutting a circle around the tree, through the bark. Underbrush and small trees were cut with axes. Dead trees were often left standing until they rotted and fell. Historian Clarence Danhof has estimated that ten to fifteen acres of land could be cleared in this way during the first year of settlement.

The amount of land that could be cleared, and the time it took to clear it, was largely determined by how many people were engaged in the process. In a 1930s article, historian Hattie Anderson praised the early settlers as self-reliant men who tamed the wilderness by themselves. The reality was quite different. Far from being "self-reliant," these early male settlers were highly dependent upon the labor of their wives, their children, and their slaves, if they could afford the latter. Similarly, more than a century later, farmers' wives and children joined husbands as farmers in the fields of Osage County and other Missouri farm communities. Farm work was a shared family responsibility.

Once the land was cleared, corn became the principal crop raised by early settlers, "the universal grain raised practically wherever there was farming," according to historian Paul W. Gates. Historian Jeff Bremer noted that "One person could raise about ten acres [of corn]," and that corn "yielded four times more food per acre than wheat" and was easy to grow. Early farmers raised hogs to supplement their food supply.

By 1820, Missouri settlers were ready for the next stage of life in their new homes—overwhelmingly, they wanted their territory to become a state. That process was destined to be far more difficult and complicated than any of them imagined.

SUGGESTED READINGS

There are a number of first-person accounts of life in the Missouri Territory, ca. 1820. "The Road West in 1818, The Diary of Henry Vest Bingham," edited by Marie George Windell, was published in the *Missouri Historical Review* 40 (October 1945): 21–54. Additionally, John Mason Peck's memoir, *Forty Years of Pioneer Life: A Memoir of John Mason Peck, D. D.*, is still useful. This volume appeared first in 1864 and was edited by Rufus Babcock. Southern Illinois University Press reprinted the original in 1965.

Thanks to the magic of digitization, there are a number of early-nineteenth-century newspapers available through Newspapers.com that provide unparalleled insight into life in Missouri Territory on the eve of and following statehood. I have found the following newspapers especially helpful: *Missouri Gazette* [St. Louis], and its successor, *Missouri Gazette and Public Advertiser*, *St. Louis Enquirer*, *Missouri Intelligencer* [Franklin] and *Missourian* [St. Charles].

As Missouri approached its centennial of statehood in 1920–1921, the *Missouri Historical Review* featured a number of articles about the people of the territory on the eve of statehood. Among the most useful are "Missouri in 1820," by Jonas Viles, *Missouri Historical Review* 15 (October 1920): 36–52. John Adams Paxton's *The St. Louis Directory and Register, Containing the Names, Professions, and Residence of all the Heads of Families and Persons in Business, Together with Descriptive Notes on St. Louis, 1821*, was published in 1821. It has been digitized and is available without cost at the Washington University digital gateway: digital.wustl.edu/c/ccr/browse_cty.html.

The reliance of the Chouteaus and other prominent St. Louisans on slavery during the early nineteenth century is taken up in Kristen Epps, *Slavery on the Periphery: The Kansas-Missouri Border in the Antebellum and Civil War Eras* (2018), published by the University of Georgia Press. St. Louis in the early years of statehood is the subject of a number of works, including James Neal Primm, *Lion of the Valley, St. Louis, Missouri* (1981), Pruett Publishing Company.

The history of St. Charles is addressed in Kate L. Gregg, "The Boonslick Road in St. Charles County," *Missouri Historical Review* 27 (July 1933): 307–14. It should be supplemented by Steve Ehlmann, *Crossroads: A History of St. Charles County, Missouri* (2011), Lindenwood University Press.

Bonnie Stepenoff, *From French Community to Missouri Town: Ste. Genevieve in the Nineteenth Century* (2006), published by the University of Missouri Press, documents life in Ste. Genevieve during the early statehood period. Henry Rowe Schoolcraft's journal recounting his 1818–1819 journey to and through the Ozarks is available in an edition with an Introduction, Maps, and Appendix by Milton D. Rafferty. Titled *Rude Pursuits and Rugged Peaks*, this book was published in 1996 by the University of Arkansas Press. Also useful is Walter A. Schroeder, *Opening the Ozarks: A Historical Geography of Missouri's Ste. Genevieve District, 1760–1830* (2002), published by the University of Missouri Press, and "'I Well Remember': David Holmes Conrad's Recollections of St. Louis, 1819–1823," Part 1, edited by James W. Goodrich and Lynn Wolf Gentzler, *Missouri Historical Review* 90 (October 1995): 1–37; Part 2, *Missouri Historical Review* 90 (January 1996): 124–65.

The settlement of the Boonslick is the subject of Walter A. Schroeder, "Spread of Settlement in Howard County, Missouri, 1810–1859," *Missouri Historical Review* 63 (October 1968): 1–37; and Stuart F. Voss, "Town Growth in Central Missouri, 1815–1880: An Urban Chaparral," *Missouri Historical Review* 64 (October 1969): 64–80. Also useful are two articles by Lynn Morrow: "Dr. John Sappington: Southern Patriarch in the New West," *Missouri Historical Review* 90 (October 1995): 38–60; and "Boone's Lick in Western Expansion: James Mackay, the Boones, and the Morrisons," *Boone's Lick Heritage Quarterly* 13 (Fall–Winter 2014): 4–34; and Michael Dickey, *Arrow Rock: Crossroads of the Missouri Frontier* (2004), published by Friends of Arrow Rock. Older works that remain useful include essays by Hattie M. Anderson: "Missouri, A Land of Promise," *Missouri Historical Review* 30 (April 1936): 227–53; and "Missouri, 1804–1828: Peopling a Frontier State," *Missouri Historical Review* 31 (January 1937): 150–80; and Raymond D. Thomas, "Missouri Valley Settlement—St. Louis to Independence," *Missouri Historical Review* 21 (October 1926): 19–40.

General works that cover this period of Missouri history include Lewis E. Atherton, "Missouri's Society and Economy in 1821," *Missouri Historical Review* 65 (July 1971): 450-77, Stephen Aron, *American Confluence: The Missouri Frontier from Borderland to Border State* (2006), published by Indiana University Press; and Jeff Bremer, *A Store Almost in Sight* (2014), published by the University of Iowa Press. A recent volume, *A Firebell in the Past: The Missouri Crisis at 200*, Vol. 1, Western Slavery, National Impasse, Studies in Constitutional Democracy, edited by Jeffrey L. Pasley and John Craig Hammond, contains a number of useful essays, including one by Robert Lee, referenced in this chapter. This book was published by the University of Missouri Press (2021).

Chapter Two

Missourians' Struggle for Statehood

"But the agony is over and Missouri is born into the Union, not
a seven months baby but a man child; his birth no secret in the
family, but a proud and glorious event, proclaimed to the nation
with the firing of cannon, the ringing of bells and illumination of
towns and cities."

St. Louis Enquirer, March 29, 1820

"MISSOURI," WITH ITS unclearly defined borders and uncertain political and
economic systems, was destined to be a state in the Union from the time of
the Louisiana Purchase in 1803. Indeed, the purchase document specified
that the residents of the trans-Mississippi west "shall be incorporated in the
Union of the United States and admitted, as soon as possible, according
to the principles of the Federal Constitution, to the enjoyment of all the
rights, advantages and immunities of citizens of the United States."

Migration across the Mississippi River and into what would become
Missouri Territory increased in the wake of the Purchase, but it remained
slow until after the United States defeated the British in the War of 1812.
Thereafter, the trickle of migration became a steady, sometimes raging,
stream. A contemporary preacher, the Reverend John Mason Peck, wrote
in his memoir, "The newcomers, like a mountain torrent, poured into the
country faster than it was possible to provide corn for bread-stuff. Some
families came in the spring of 1815; but in the winter, spring, summer and
autumn of 1816, they came like an avalanche."

By the fall of 1817, the Missouri Territory had become a prospering, productive region whose residents numbered more than 60,000, the minimum
population requirement for statehood. Dissatisfaction with the territorial
government was growing, and the inability of the territory's delegate to vote
in Congress was unpopular. An increasing number of Missouri residents

thought they had waited long enough for the territory to become a state. Petitions to Congress urging Missouri's admission to the Union as a state began to circulate in the territory.

On January 8, 1818, a petition for statehood from the "sundry inhabitants of the Territory of Missouri" was presented to Congress. Less than a month later, Missouri's delegate to Congress, John Scott of Ste. Genevieve, presented a similar petition. Like so many other Missourians, Scott was a Virginia native. A Princeton graduate, he had moved to Ste. Genevieve in 1804, the year after the Louisiana Purchase. He served as attorney general for the Missouri Territory in 1808 and 1809 and as the U.S. attorney for the territory from 1813 to 1817. Well-steeped in both the politics and aspirations of the region, he was elected a delegate to Congress in 1816. As such, he stood in the forefront of Missouri's struggle for statehood, from its inception to the realization of that dream.

The petition presented by Scott was followed by others, all of which languished in Congress for months. On November 13, 1818, the Missouri territorial legislature tried to nudge the process along by adopting a resolution calling for Congress to take up the statehood petition. The resolution offered three arguments for Missouri statehood: 1) the population of the territory was approaching 100,000 persons, and growing rapidly; 2) the territory comprising Missouri was too large to govern effectively under the existing structure; 3) the territorial system deprived residents of their full citizenship rights as U.S. citizens. In December 1818, Speaker of the House Henry Clay of Kentucky presented this resolution to Congress.

The Missouri statehood bill was finally reported out of committee and taken up by the full House on February 13, 1819, after extensive prodding by John Scott. The process took on an unexpected level of intrigue and complexity when Congressman James Tallmadge Jr. of New York introduced an amendment to the bill. Tallmadge's amendment stipulated, first, that "the further introduction of slavery or involuntary servitude [in Missouri would] be prohibited." The Tallmadge Amendment also called for the children of slaves born in Missouri after statehood to be freed when they reached the age of twenty-five. Taken together, these two measures would, eventually, have led to the abolition of slavery in Missouri.

Tallmadge was a lawyer, a native of New York, a state in which Blacks could vote, and a fierce opponent of slavery. He introduced his amendment at a time of great tension between the states that allowed slavery and those

Fig. 10: This petition for statehood began circulating in Washington County in the Missouri Territory in late 1817 as part of the effort to persuade Congress to admit Missouri to the Union. Among the petition signatories was future Missouri governor, Daniel Dunklin. Credit: State Historical Society of Missouri.

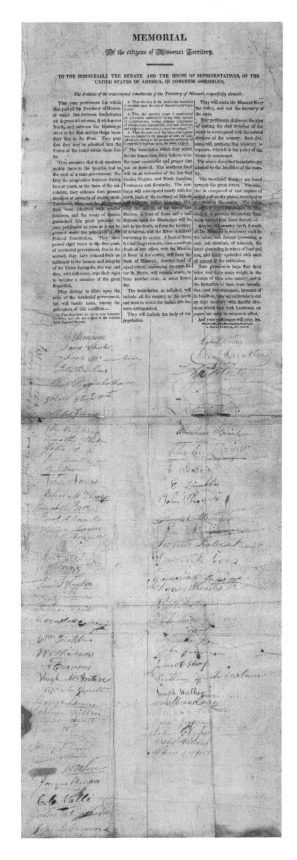

that prohibited it. When the Missouri petition for statehood came before Congress, there were an equal number of slave and free states in the Union. The admission of Missouri threatened to undo that balance, thereby giving primacy to one or the other faction, depending on whether Missouri came in slave or free. Moreover, the notion that Congress could prohibit slavery in a new state was seen by many Southerners as a crucial first step in the process of possibly abolishing slavery anywhere in the United States.

Thus, the issue of slavery delayed Missouri's entry into the Union. Already by the last years of the second decade of the nineteenth century, Americans were deeply divided over the issue of slavery, a division that would threaten the very existence of the Union some four decades later. Ironically, the question of slavery, and the associated issue of race, bedeviled the nation and the aborning state from the very beginning; indeed, the issue of race continues to confound the nation and the state two centuries later.

Three days after proposing his amendment to the Missouri statehood bill, Tallmadge delivered an impassioned speech in support of his amendment and of abolitionism generally. The House voted that same day to support the amendment, but the Senate rejected it. The bill languished in Congress until that body adjourned on March 3, 1819, without having taken action on Missouri's request for statehood.

Missourians, with a few notable exceptions, were outraged over the notion that Congress thought it could decide whether slavery should be allowed in Missouri. That question, they thought, was one that Missourians should be allowed to decide for themselves. Moreover, many Missourians, who came from states that already allowed slavery, worried that prohibiting slaves in the new state would stifle immigration from older slave states such as Virginia, Kentucky, Tennessee, and North Carolina. During the Congressional recess, the matter festered, and over time a deep hostility toward Congress and the federal government took hold in Missouri.

Missouri's Congressional delegate, John Scott, felt compelled to draft a message, "To the People of Missouri Territory," and have it circulated throughout the territory, including in the *Missouri Intelligencer*, published in Franklin. Scott explained that the statehood bill had been brought up in Congress and "was progressing through the House with as much unanimity and success as could be expected, when an unanticipated amendment on the subject of slavery was offered, which produced a greater sensation in Congress than was almost ever witnessed before. . . ." Although it seems likely that the Talmadge amendment was not quite the surprise that Scott claimed it was, the consequence was "the total loss of the bill."

Scott's circular was, in part, an attempt to defend himself and to show that he had done all that he could do to get the statehood bill passed. But he also wanted to make the argument that slavery was not really the issue. "I regret as much as any person can do the existence of slavery in the United States," he wrote. "I think it wrong in itself." More important, however, Scott saw himself as "the advocate of the people's right to decide on this question . . . for themselves." He continued: "I consider it, not only unfriendly to the slaves themselves to confine them to the south, but wholly incompetent for Congress to interfere upon the subject . . . the state of Missouri has a clear right to decide for herself, as every other state has done."

Most Missourians agreed. Over the course of the summer and fall of 1819, countless meetings and gatherings were held in Missouri that provided Missourians with the opportunity to vent their frustrations with and anger toward Congress. It was as if Missourians were simultaneously laying the groundwork for rebellion and resistance against a government they were trying to join! As historian Walter B. Stevens pointed out many years ago: "The grand jury of every county went on record in most formal protest against the attitude of Congress toward Missouri."

Examples of what Stevens refers to abound. The *Missouri Gazette and Public Advertiser* [St. Louis] of July 14, 1819, carried an account of a recent meeting of a grand jury in St. Charles County. The twenty jurors met on July 6, 1819. The group asserted its "privilege and duty to take notice of our grievances of a public nature." Their complaint was "that the Congress of the United States at the last session," was "attempting to restrict the people of Missouri, to the exercise and enjoyment of their rights as American Freemen." The jurors claimed that the Congressional effort to restrict slavery in Missouri was unconstitutional and "a direct attack and infringement on the sacred rights of state sovereignty and independence. . . ."

Similarly, residents of Washington County held a town hall meeting in Potosi on July 20, 1819, "for the purpose of expressing their opinion as to the powers of Congress to impose conditions or restrictions on the people of Missouri, in the formation of a constitution for their state government." After electing Major John Hawkins as president of the meeting, the group passed eight resolutions, including one that asserted that Congress had no constitutional right "to impose any other condition on admission of any state in the Union."

Interestingly, the second resolution agreed to by the group not only declared the effort to restrict the introduction of new slaves into Missouri, and to free children when they reached the age of twenty-one, violated the state's right of self-determination, but it also "was contrary . . . to the welfare of the slaves themselves." African American slaves, it was implied, would be better off in servitude in Missouri than in a more Southern state, just as, in the opinion of many whites, African Americans were better of as slaves in the United States than they were on the barbaric, uncivilized, unchristian continent of Africa.

Over the course of the following summer, resentment toward Tallmadge and the federal government grew in Missouri, as residents of the territory nurtured a sense of outrage that Congress or its members could or would try to tell them what they could or could not do. At a gathering in Franklin, called to commemorate the arrival of the first steamboat in that Missouri River town, speaker after speaker lashed out at the federal government, articulating resentment toward its overreaching interference with state's rights that would become a hallmark of Missouri history for the next two centuries. A series of toasts reflected the sentiment of those present. Duff Green, a Kentucky-born land speculator and politician who had moved to Howard County in 1816, led off with the toast, "The Union—It is dear to us but liberty is dearer."

Other toasts of defiance toward the federal government followed, with Stephen Rector, surveyor general for Illinois, Missouri, and Arkansas, introducing a militant tone into his toast: "May the Missourians defend their rights, if necessary, even at the expense of blood, against the unprecedented restriction which was attempted to be imposed on them by the Congress of the United States."

Clearly, the attempt by Congress to decide the issue of slavery in the proposed new state rubbed many Missourians the wrong way. A grand jury meeting in St. Louis referred to the effort "by the Congress of the United States to restrict us in free exercise of our rights in the formation of a constitution and form a state government for ourselves is an unconstitutional and unwarrantable usurpation of power over our inalienable rights and privileges as a free people."

Thomas Hart Benton, the St. Louis newspaper publisher and future U.S. senator, became one of the fiercest opponents of "restriction," as it was known, arguing that Missourians needed "to make a fair and regular stand against the encroachment of Congress upon the sovereignty of the States."

The opposition in Missouri to Congressional efforts at restriction did not go unnoticed in the rest of the country, especially in the Northeast. While Missourians planned in the summer of 1819 to go forward with new petitions for statehood, a kind of "Anti-Missouri Crusade" began to emerge in the North, beginning in New Jersey in the summer of 1819. Among the national figures involved in this movement were Bostonian William Tudor, editor of the *North American Review*, and U.S. senator from New York, Rufus King, whose 1819 essay "Observations on the Exclusion of Slavery from the State of Missouri" elaborated on the restrictionist views he had earlier articulated on the floor of the Senate in late February 1819. Indeed, Alexander McNair, Missouri's future governor, would subsequently complain that this conflict seriously stifled immigration to Missouri: "While the future character of the State, and the tone of our municipal policy remained doubtful, and our very existence as a sovereignty was questioned abroad, the tide of emigration ceased to flow into our country, and we were left to depend on our own crude resources without the aids on which new countries ordinarily rely."

McNair's judgment notwithstanding, migrants did continue to pour into Missouri from slaveholding states. Late in 1819, *The St. Louis Enquirer* carried the following notice: "[T]he emigration to Missouri is astonishing. Probably from thirty to fifty wagons daily cross the Mississippi at the different ferries, and bring in an average of four to five hundred souls a day. The emigrants are principally from Kentucky, Tennessee, Virginia and the states further south. They bring great numbers of slaves, knowing that Congress has no power to impose the agitated restriction, and that the people of Missouri will never adopt it."

When the Sixteenth Congress reconvened in early 1820, the House once again endorsed the idea of trying to restrict slavery in Missouri as a condition of statehood. This time, however, circumstances were even more muddied. Members of the Senate wished to facilitate the creation of the state of Maine out of Massachusetts. It was readily accepted that Maine would come in as a free state, laying the groundwork for Missouri to come

Fig. 11: Alexander McNair was Missouri's first governor, serving from 1820 to 1824. Credit: State Historical Society of Missouri, Art Collection, Collection No. 013377.

in as a slave state without destroying the equal balance of slave and free states in the Senate and the Union. Two amendments were added to the bill early in 1820, one authorizing Missourians to draft a constitution without restricting slavery, and the second a provision stipulating that slavery would be forever prohibited in new states north of the line of 36 30', excepting Missouri. Despite this latter restriction on the expansion of slavery, enough Southern states supported it to allow the bargain, which became known as the Missouri Compromise, to be struck.

Finally, on March 6, 1820, President James Monroe signed the enabling legislation authorizing Missourians to draft a constitution without restriction as to slavery and to establish a government. It took weeks for the news of the passing of the legislation to make its way back to Missouri. According to Benton's *St. Louis Enquirer*, word of the passage of the bill reached St. Louis on March 25, 1820. "A handbill announcing the happy intelligence . . . was immediately issued from this office amidst the ringing of the bells and the firing of cannon and the joyful congratulations of the citizens." Four days later, Benton's *St. Louis Enquirer* carried the following announcement: "But the agony is over and Missouri is born into the Union, not a seven months baby but a man child; his birth no secret in the family, but a proud and glorious event, proclaimed to the nation with the firing of cannon, the ringing of bells and illumination of towns and cities."

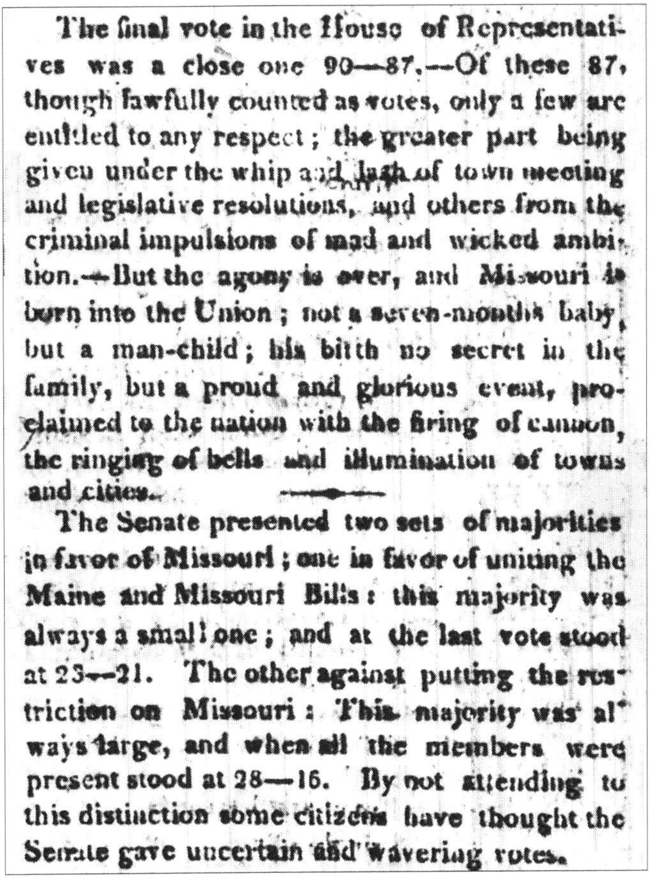

The final vote in the House of Representatives was a close one 90—87.—Of these 87, though lawfully counted as votes, only a few are entitled to any respect; the greater part being given under the whip and lash of town meeting and legislative resolutions, and others from the criminal impulsions of mad and wicked ambition.—But the agony is over, and Missouri is born into the Union; not a seven-months baby but a man-child; his birth no secret in the family, but a proud and glorious event, proclaimed to the nation with the firing of cannon, the ringing of bells and illumination of towns and cities.

The Senate presented two sets of majorities in favor of Missouri; one in favor of uniting the Maine and Missouri Bills: this majority was always a small one; and at the last vote stood at 23—21. The other against putting the restriction on Missouri: This majority was always large, and when all the members were present stood at 28—16. By not attending to this distinction some citizens have thought the Senate gave uncertain and wavering votes.

Fig. 12: Congressional Vote on Missouri Statehood as Reported in *St. Louis Enquirer*, March 29, 1820. Credit: State Historical Society of Missouri.

St. Louis followed up with a much more elaborate celebration on March 30, 1820. The April issue of the *Enquirer* noted, "The town was illuminated on Thursday evening." The celebration was one theretofore unrivalled in the city. The *Missouri Gazette and Public Advertiser* reported, perhaps apocryphally, that the public celebrations of statehood featured a representation of "a slave in great spirits, rejoicing at the permission granted by Congress to bring slaves into so fine a country as Missouri."

Not everyone was celebrating. Among those bothered by the intense debate over the Missouri question was the aging third president of the United States, Thomas Jefferson. The debate over Missouri's admission to the Union, and the rancor over the issue of slavery between North and South, caused Jefferson to fear for the future of the nation. Prophetically seeing the debate as a harbinger of things to come, on April 23, 1820, Jefferson wrote to Senator John Holmes of Maine, one of the architects of the compromise: "this momentous question, like a fire bell in the night, awakened and filled me with terror. I considered it at once as the knell of the Union."

The next step toward statehood for Missouri was for the residents of the territory to select delegates to a constitutional convention, the members of which were charged with drafting a state constitution. Elections were to be held during the first week of May. Forty-one delegates were to be chosen from the territory's fifteen counties. Voting was open to all white males, aged twenty-one years and older, who had resided in the territory for at least ninety days prior to the election.

As the delegate election approached, the issue of slavery loomed over the process. Would Missourians choose delegates who favored or opposed the existence of slavery in Missouri? One of the outspoken supporters of restriction was Benjamin Lundy, from the Jefferson County town of Herculaneum. Lundy was a Quaker, a religious group known for its fiercely antislavery sentiments. Born in New Jersey in 1789, he was apprenticed as a young man to a saddler in Wheeling, Virginia, in 1808. He married in 1815, and he and his wife moved to Saint Clairsville, Ohio, where he joined with a number of like-minded individuals to form an antislavery association. In 1820, he moved to St. Louis, where he began publishing an antislavery newspaper. In the run-up to the delegate election, Lundy chaired a committee that prepared an address to Jefferson County voters, urging them to elect an antislavery candidate, labeling African American slavery a "dangerous system of cruelty and injustice."

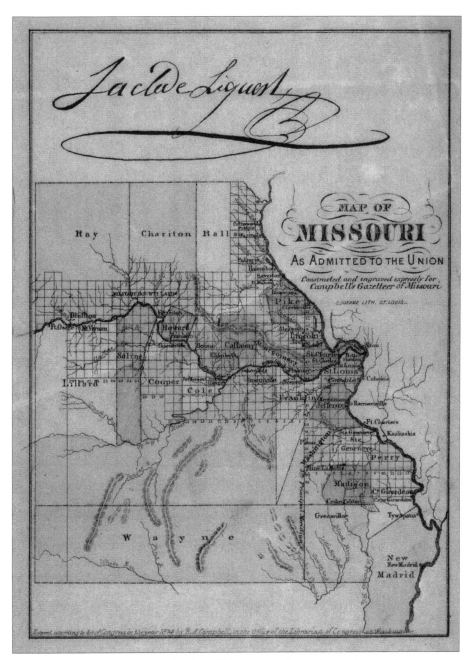

Fig. 13: This map indicates the borders of Missouri and the state's counties when it was admitted to the Union in 1821. Created by R. A. Campbell and Charles Juehne, ca. 1874, lithograph. Credit: State Historical Society of Missouri.

Without doubt, the two most prominent "restrictionists" in the debate over whether slavery should be allowed in Missouri were St. Louisans Joseph Charless and John Baptiste Charles (J. B. C.) Lucas. Ironically, both men owned slaves.

Lucas, a native of Pont-Audemer, France, immigrated to the United States in 1784, at the age of twenty-six. He and his wife settled first in western Pennsylvania, where they took up farming. Travel in search of trade took him to the upper Mississippi River valley in the 1790s. In 1805, he moved his family to St. Louis, after being appointed a justice to the territorial superior court and a member of the board of land commissioners for the newly created Louisiana Territory. Over the course of the next several years, Lucas managed to anger many of the territory's large land owners who traced their land claims to grants made by the Spanish government (during its stewardship of the territory), for he was convinced that many of those claims were fraudulent.

In 1820, Lucas declared his candidacy as a member of Missouri's constitutional convention. He advocated for a restriction on the number of years slaves could be imported into the state. According to historian William E. Foley, for Lucas, "the issue was economic, not moral. He touted the advantages of free labor in promoting the new state's long-term economic development."

Similarly, Joseph Charless, an Irish immigrant who fled his native Ireland in 1795, also supported the restriction of slavery in Missouri. Like Lucas, Charless first settled in Pennsylvania before moving to Kentucky and then on to St. Louis in 1808, where he became a printer and the publisher of the territory's first newspaper, the *Missouri Gazette*, in July 1808. Indeed, as the debate over whether slavery should be restricted or unrestricted in the new state of Missouri, battle lines were drawn in the pages of the *Gazette*, with Charless making it clear which side he supported. Perhaps the best expression of the restrictionist position came in the form of several letters published in the *Gazette* under the byline of "A Farmer of St. Charles." In a letter published in the paper on April 7, 1819, the "Farmer of St. Charles" summarized his position by noting that "slavery is at once a most sacred right, and a most flagrant wrong."

Ultimately, according to historian Perry McCandless, 7,000–11,000 people participated in the selection of delegates to the constitutional convention. Forty-one individuals were chosen to draft the state's first constitution. This group was dominated by businessmen and lawyers who had already established themselves as influential participants in territorial politics. More than half of the delegates had attended college and a disproportionate number were from St. Louis, a reality that bothered many residents of rural, outstate Missouri. Even before the state's first government was elected, an urban-rural split emerged that would bedevil Missouri politics for the next two centuries.

David Barton presided over the convention. Born near Greenville, North Carolina, in 1783, Barton attended Greenville College before studying law with a Tennessee judge and gaining admittance to the bar in the Volunteer State. He, too, took up residence in St. Louis, where he established a successful law practice and began laying the groundwork for a political career.

Barton endeared himself to Territorial Governor William Clark, who appointed him attorney general in 1813 and first district judge of the Northern District of Missouri in 1815. Barton held the latter position only briefly, before resigning to practice law. In 1818 he returned to politics as a member of the territorial House of Representatives. That body chose him as its Speaker, signaling Barton's growing political prowess.

Barton's influence on the first constitutional convention was so great that some historians have referred to the document it produced as the "Barton Constitution." That constitution was a conservative document, much like the men who wrote it. Influenced by several existing state constitutions, most notably those of Illinois, Alabama, and Kentucky, the Missouri constitution called for a popularly elected governor and lieutenant governor, each of whom was to serve a four-year term. The governor could serve no more than one term. An adjutant general, auditor, attorney general, and secretary of state were all to be appointed by the governor. The state treasurer was to be elected semiannually by the legislature.

While the governor had the authority to veto legislation, his veto could be overridden by simple-majority votes in the state House and Senate. The judicial branch of government was to be independent and was intended to be a strong check on the legislature.

Not surprisingly, the constitution protected the rights of slaveholders to their human property. It forbade the legislature from freeing any slave without the slave owner's permission, and it denied lawmakers the authority to prohibit any slaveholder the right to bring slaves into the state. In a further attempt to protect the institution of slavery, the constitution denied "free

[N]egroes or mulattoes" the right to enter or settle in the state. This provision was driven largely by the contemporary fear that free Blacks threatened to incite discontent and even rebellion among enslaved persons.

Unfortunately for Missourians, this constitutional provision against free Negroes ran afoul of the Congress's intent and launched yet another round of conflict between Missourians and the federal government. That conflict would require what became known as the Second Missouri Compromise before Missouri would be recognized as a state by the federal government.

Meanwhile, Missourians assumed that their territory had become a state, and they moved forward with holding elections and establishing a government. They held their first election on Monday, August 28, 1820. The man chosen to serve as the state's first governor was Alexander McNair, a native of Pennsylvania who immigrated to Missouri in 1804, the year after the completion of the Louisiana Purchase. A close associate of the governor of the Northwest Territory, General William Henry Harrison, McNair held a succession of public offices in St. Louis during the territorial period, including that of town trustee when St. Louis was first incorporated. In the years running up to statehood, McNair held the important position of registrar of the U.S. Land Office in St. Louis.

McNair was elected as an "anti-restrictionist" member of the 1820 constitutional convention, although he appears not to have been one of the gathering's main activists. He seems to have emerged as an opponent of the convention's "lawyer delegates," and soon after the new constitution went into effect on July 19, 1820, he surfaced as a leading candidate for governor in opposition to the lawyers' candidate, Territorial Governor William Clark.

The gubernatorial campaign lasted little more than a month, with surrogates of each candidate criticizing their opponent. McNair defeated Clark by a 4,020-vote margin out of 9,132 votes cast, in what historian Stephen Aron argues was a transformational election, one that signaled the decline in power of the St. Louis French merchants who had previously dominated state politics. McNair's election, according to Aron, represented the beginning of a Missouri tradition, by which "many more Missourians became engaged in politics, rejecting older ideals about deferring to their betters and demanding that their voices be heard and heeded."

The first legislature met in St. Louis on Monday, September 18, 1820. At 4:00 p.m. the next day, McNair and Lieutenant Governor William Ashley took their oaths of office, and the new governor delivered a brief inaugural address. In it, McNair made clear that he considered the statehood issue as settled. He referenced the "happy change which has just taken place in our political affairs. From a dependant [sic] condition of a Territorial government, we have passed into a sovereign and independent state. . . ."

But the statehood issue was not settled. The constitution that the Missourians had drawn up was considered by Congress in November 1820. Once again, strong opposition to Missouri's entrance into the Union as a slave state surfaced in that body. And once again, the battleground was in the Northern-dominated House of Representatives.

A number of lawmakers took issue with the provision in the Missouri constitution aimed at prohibiting free Negroes and mulattoes from entering the state. Opponents argued that free Blacks were U.S. citizens and the Missouri provision violated the U.S. constitution's provision guaranteeing "all Privileges and Immunities of Citizens in the several States." Thus, to deny free Blacks from other states the rights and privileges afforded to them in their home states would be a violation of the U.S. Constitution.

In February 1821 another effort to force Missouri to provide for the gradual emancipation of its slaves as a condition of statehood emerged in the U.S. House of Representatives. It failed to get the requisite number of votes. Still, the measure's strong support (it had garnered sixty-one votes) represented a clear statement of Northerners' unhappiness with the Missouri Compromise. This effort once again raised the hackles of Missourians and fueled their anger toward those interests that challenged Missouri's effort to determine its own destiny.

Once again, Kentuckian Henry Clay, the Speaker of the House, emerged to forge a Second Missouri Compromise, much as he had done the previous year with the first. His proposal, which passed the House by a narrow margin of 87 to 81, allowed Missouri's admission into the Union with the promise by the Missouri legislature that it would never deprive any U.S. citizens of the privileges and immunities of U.S. citizenship.

Missourians did not like this response, and bristled at the notion that Congress was once again trying to tell them what to do. They knew they had to comply to achieve statehood. Still, they could not restrain themselves from asserting their rights in the face of Congressional authority: the Missouri legislature passed an act reminding Congress that Missouri had already agreed to abide by all the provisions of the U.S. constitution, but asserting that the Missouri constitution could not be changed except by the provisions contained in that document. And then, in what can only be seen as an act of defiance, the Missouri General Assembly declared, "such declaration will neither restrain, or enlarge, limit or extend the operations of the constitution of the United States, or of this state, but the said constitutions will remain in all respects as if the said resolution had never passed."

The Congress accepted this less-than-complete surrender to federal authority on June 26, 1821, and on August 10, 1821, President James Monroe signed the legislation making Missouri the twenty-fourth state in the Union.

Meanwhile, the Missouri General Assembly moved forward with the task of creating a government and establishing the institutions and practices needed to move forward as a state. One of these challenges was establishing the location of the state's permanent seat of government.

The constitutional convention had taken up the question of the location of the new state's capital the previous year. Although St. Louis interests wanted their city to be so designated, the heavy immigration of settlers into the Missouri interior, especially the Missouri River Valley, over the previous few years prompted delegates to lean toward a more centrally located site.

The first draft of the constitution presented to the convention on July 10, 1820, called for the permanent seat of government to be located on the Missouri River, within forty miles of the mouth of the Osage River, and to sit on four sections (2,560 acres) of unclaimed land or at least land whose ownership was not contested. These specifications acknowledged the importance of river traffic to the future of the aborning state. Ultimately, the convention assigned the final selection of a capital site to the first General Assembly. The legislature authorized a five-person commission to select the site. The site chosen would not become the permanent seat of government until 1826, giving ample time, it was thought, to adequately develop it. Meanwhile, after considerable wrangling over multiple possible sites, including the mining town of Potosi, the convention chose the city of St. Charles to serve as the temporary site of Missouri government.

After Governor McNair approved the legislative proposal of a five-member commission to select a site for the permanent seat of government on November 16, 1821, he appointed the five commissioners, who began work immediately.

Fig. 14: This building in St. Charles served as Missouri's temporary state capitol between 1821 and 1826, while a permanent capitol was being planned and erected in Jefferson City. Credit: George McCue Photograph Collection, State Historical Society of Missouri, Collection No. S1116-435.

Their first choice for the permanent site of the capital city was a place called Cote Sans Dessein, a village of a few hundred people on the north side of the Missouri River in Callaway County. Named for Captain James Callaway, a grandson of Daniel Boone, Callaway County was organized on November 25, 1820. Cote Sans Dessein was conveniently located just across the Missouri River from the mouth of the Osage River. The surrounding soil was quite fertile, capable of sustaining a large population, and the settlement already boasted a few established businesses.

Although the commissioners liked the choice of the Cote San Dessein site, two nagging concerns left them unsettled. One was the area's susceptibility to flooding. More important, the land surrounding the village was fraught with contested ownership claims, making it unlikely that the commissioners would be able to guarantee clear title to a full four sections.

Ultimately, the site the commissioners chose was one they thought the least desirable—the site of the modern-day City of Jefferson. Indeed, one commissioner described it as a place that would "not support any considerable population or extensive settlement." The terrain was hilly and there was little arable land nearby. Still, it was readily accessible, being on the Missouri River, within forty miles of the Osage River. In addition, it was seemingly uncontested land, to which it was thought clear title easily could be obtained. In that regard, the site ultimately chosen was one relatively easy to get to, but to which few people had wanted to go.

The site was located at the mouth of "Weir's Creek" about twelve miles above the mouth of the Osage. The legislature approved the selected site on December 31, 1821, and Governor McNair signed the bill into law the next day. On January 11, 1822, the governor directed the commissioners to begin laying out a town and selling lots, the first of which were sold on May 5, 1823. On that same day the town trustees called for bids for the first state building to be erected in the new capital city. The building was to be a combined residence for the governor and meeting house for the legislature.

Adequate accommodations for the new state government would not be available in the City of Jefferson until the fall of 1826. The legislature convened there for the first time on November 20, 1826. At the time there was but one hotel in town, directly across the street from the legislature's meeting place. It was called the House of the Rising Sun and was not large enough to accommodate all the lawmakers newly arrived. So, during the state's first legislative session, many of the legislators were forced to board with the town's few residents, while still others had to sleep in tents. Calvin Gunn, publisher of a Jefferson City newspaper called the *Jeffersonian Republican*, summed up the town's appearance in the paper's first issue in 1826, when he wrote that it featured "a series of promontories," separated by "intervening dells . . . [that] render the appearance of the place some-what fatiguing [sic]."

Throughout the remainder of the nineteenth century, many people, lawmakers included, continued to think of the City of Jefferson (known widely as "Jefferson City" almost from the beginning) as an inadequate state capital. In 1828, Joseph Shriver, a young civil engineer from Maryland, was engaged by the federal government to complete a survey for an extension of the Cumberland Road from Indianapolis to Jefferson City. Begun more than twenty years earlier in Baltimore, this road was conceived of as a major thoroughfare connecting the Middle Atlantic States to the West.

By the summer of 1829, Shriver and his party were in central Missouri, within "10 or 12 miles of Jefferson City," a destination he hoped to reach within a few days. Writing to his brother back East, Shriver commented on the passing of a steamboat on the Missouri River, which he labeled "a cheering sight in this wild region." In early August, Shriver and his party arrived at Jefferson City, the capital of Missouri. He noted, "We entered it with no small share of interest and disappointment." The growth of the city had been slow and halting. "'Tis a rough looking city indeed," Shriver wrote his brother, "and one which does not bid fair to become of much importance." According to Shriver, there were about thirty houses in the town, some of them brick, "and about 200 inhabitants." Despite multiple efforts to move the capital of the state to a more welcoming and appealing site, the City of Jefferson was destined to remain the state's capital for the next two centuries.

The early Missouri government faced many challenges, the most significant of which was that of financing improvements to life in a state with limited financial resources. In a message to a special session of the legislature on June 4, 1821, Governor McNair laid out the difficulties they faced. First, the governor complained about Missouri's difficulty in becoming a state, commenting that the struggle for statehood had caused many would-be immigrants to avoid the state: "Our unsettled political condition has already prevented thousands from making our country their home." Had those immigrants come to Missouri, they "would have divided and diminished the burden of taxation." Additionally, he took note of the "depression into commerce and credit" that had hit Missouri and the nation, noting it "has been severely felt throughout the continent."

To address these problems, McNair laid out a plan of action that would, arguably, come to dominate the thinking of state governmental officials for the next two centuries. "As we expect to increase in wealth and numbers by the accession of citizens from other states," he noted, "it is our true policy to remove every obstacle and hold out every inducement to emigration." A key element of this effort would require "the establishment of a rigid economy in every department of the state, and the retrenchment of every unnecessary expense. . . ." In short, if state government could hold expenses down and keep taxes low, more people would immigrate to Missouri, and those new immigrants would "divide and diminish the burden of taxation." The challenge over the next few decades, indeed, over the next two centuries, would be to devise a way to provide the governmental services that citizens of the state expected while limiting the amount of taxes charged them.

SUGGESTED READINGS

The starting point for understanding this period of Missouri history are two important works published by the University of Missouri Press: William E. Foley, *The Genesis of Missouri: From Wilderness Outpost to Statehood* (1989); and Perry McCandless, *A History of Missouri, 1820–1860* (1971). There are older works that still provide insight into Missouri's struggle to become a state. They include Floyd C. Shoemaker, *Missouri's Struggle for Statehood* (1916), published by the Hugh Stephens Printing Company. An essay by Shoemaker that sheds light on the formative years of Missouri statehood is "The First Constitution of Missouri," *Missouri Historical Review* 6 (January 1912): 51–63. Also helpful are Walter B. Stevens, "The Travail of Missouri for Statehood," *Missouri Historical Review* 15 (October 1920): 3–35; and F. H. Lehmann, "The Constitution of 1820," *Missouri Historical Review* 16 (January 1922): 239–46.

The classic book on Missouri's struggle to become a state remains Glover Moore, *The Missouri Controversy, 1819–1821* (1953), published by the University of Kentucky Press. It should be supplemented by David D. March, "The Admission of Missouri," *Missouri Historical Review* 65 (July 1971): 427–49; Alfred Lightfoot, "Henry Clay and the Missouri Question, 1819–1821," *Missouri Historical Review* 61 (January 1967): 143–65; Robert Pierce Forbes, *The Missouri Compromise and Its Aftermath* (2007), published by University of North Carolina Press; and John R. Van Atta, *Wolf by the Ears: The Missouri Crisis, 1819–1821* (2015), published by Johns Hopkins University Press. Other works that are worth consulting include Richard H. Brown, "The Missouri Crisis, Slavery, and the Politics of Jacksonianism," *South Atlantic Quarterly* 65 (Winter 1966): 55–72; Joshua M. Zeitz, "The Missouri Compromise Reconsidered: Rhetoric and the Emergence of the Free Labor Synthesis," *Journal of the Early Republic* 29 (Fall 2000): 447–85; and, Sean Wilentz, "Jeffersonian Democracy and the Origins of Political Antislavery in the United States: The Missouri Controversy Revisited," *Journal of the Historical Society* 4 (Fall 2004): 375–401. The most recent scholarship on the debates over Missouri's admission to the Union is a book edited by William S. Belko, *Contesting the Constitution: Congress Debates the Missouri Crisis (1819-1821)*, published by the University of Missouri Press (2021).

Biographical sketches of Missouri's first governor, Alexander McNair, can be found in Walter B. Stevens, "Alexander McNair," *Missouri Historical*

Review 17 (October 1922): 3–21; and Kenneth W. Keller, "Alexander McNair and John B. C. Lucas: The Background of Early Missouri Politics," *Bulletin of the Missouri Historical Society* 33 (July 1977): 231–45. It is also helpful to read early messages delivered by McNair and other Missouri governors in *The Messages and Proclamations of the Governors of the State of Missouri*, ed., Buel Leopard and Floyd C. Shoemaker (1922).

The election of Missouri's first two U.S. senators is addressed in Monas N. Squires, "A New View of the Election of Barton and Benton to the United States Senate in 1820," *Missouri Historical Review* 27 (October 1932); 28–45.

The events surrounding the selection of a site for Missouri's permanent seat of government are covered in Jonas Viles, "Missouri Capitals and Capitols," *Missouri Historical Review* 13 (January 1919): 135–56; and Perry S. Rader, "The Location of the Permanent Seat of Government," *Missouri Historical Review* 21 (October 1926): 9–18.

Chapter Three

Settlement and Civilization in Post-Frontier Missouri

"My recent tour through the state afforded me the high gratification of witnessing the onward march of Missouri, toward that proud pre-eminence which ere long she is destined to occupy among her sister republics."

Governor Thomas Reynolds, November 18, 1840

ON NOVEMBER 18, 1840, Missouri Governor Thomas Reynolds delivered his inaugural address to the members of the state's General Assembly. A native of Bracken County, Kentucky, and a lawyer, Reynolds moved to Illinois at a young age before migrating to Howard County, Missouri, in 1829. By 1840, he had become a prosperous farmer who owned eleven slaves. Reynolds was the seventh governor to lead the state of Missouri. By the time he assumed the office, Missouri's population had grown from 140,455 in 1830 to 383,702 persons in 1840, a growth rate of more than 200 percent. Indeed, over a twenty-year period, from 1820 on the eve of statehood, Missouri's population had grown nearly six-fold, from 66,557 in that year to 383,702 in 1840. The boosters had been right—Missouri was a place to which people wanted to come.

Missouri was also a far different place in 1840 than it had been in 1820, or even 1830. Governor Reynolds remarked on this when he commented after a "tour through the state" in 1840 that he had witnessed "the onward march of Missouri, toward that proud pre-eminence which ere long she is destined to occupy among her sister republics." The governor also pointed out that "regions that just a few months past were covered with the deep shade of the unbroken forest, or presented the more monotonous, but not less solitary aspect of the uncultivated prairie, are now blooming with the fruits of civilization, and affording sustenance and wealth to an industrious and intelligent population."

What, one might ask, were these tangible fruits of civilization? Growth in educational institutions and opportunities, for one. What historian Perry McCandless called "the first significant state effort to launch an organized system of public schools" began during the administration of Governor Daniel Dunklin (1832–1836). In 1835, the legislature created a State Board of Commissioners for education and tried to designate a statewide curriculum and a standard six-month school term.

Before those plans could be implemented, the legislature passed the Geyer Act (1839), providing for a comprehensive educational system for all Missouri students, from the primary grades through the college and university levels. The location of the University of Missouri, the first public university in the former Louisiana Territory, in Columbia was orchestrated primarily by a young and newly elected legislator from that town, James Sidney Rollins. He persuaded county residents to donate more than $100,000 to attract the university to Columbia. He also donated the land upon which the campus would be built. Rollins was a slaveowner, as were a number of the other early supporters of the university. Indeed, slave labor, and the profits from slave labor, helped to build and sustain the University of Missouri throughout its early history.

Although the Geyer Act laid out a plan for public education in Missouri, its plan went largely ignored, with no concrete steps taken toward establishing a public-school system for the state's youth. The problem lay in the difficulty of financing highly centralized, ambitious plans for public education. The principal revenue for public schools remained the proceeds from public land sales, but the revenue land sales generated was never sufficient and there was no appetite for taxing Missourians to expand and support the school system. Plus, Missourians thought of public education as a local function, a predilection that would inform, and arguably hinder, the state's educational policies for the next two centuries.

Whatever public funds that were available for education during this period went largely to elementary schools in the state. The first public high school in Missouri was not established until 1852, with the opening of one in St. Louis. At the time, most Missourians did not think that a high school education was something that should be paid for out of the public treasury. Widespread support for publicly funded high schools would not develop until much later in the state's history.

Fig. 15: James Sidney Rollins, Boone County, Missouri, Legislator, sponsored the 1839 legislation creating the University of Missouri. Credit: State Historical Society of Missouri. Collection No. P0020.

One mark of a maturing Missouri was, however, the effort on the part of an increasing number of Missourians to improve residents' ability to communicate and trade with each other and the rest of the country. Many such proponents of these "internal improvements" looked to their state government to fund them, although this position was by no means universally held.

Governor Lilburn W. Boggs, a native of Kentucky who immigrated to St. Louis in 1816 before moving across the state to Jackson County in 1826, had extensive experience in the fur trade business. He knew well the importance of effective and affordable transportation to traders and other

Missourians. As governor, he called legislators' attention to the need for state-supported internal improvements in his First Biennial Message to the General Assembly, on November 22, 1836. "...[W]e must adopt a system of internal improvements," he declared ".... [N]ow is a suitable time for us to commence; and the sooner we begin . . . the sooner will be developed those resources which nature has so bountifully lavished upon us."

Fig. 16: *Watching the Cargo*, an 1849 painting by Missouri artist George Caleb Bingham, reflects the artist's unhappiness with the state and federal governments' failure to support the financing of internal improvements. Credit: State Historical Society of Missouri.

River travel was a principal means by which residents of the young state could connect with each other and with the state's population centers at St. Louis, Ste. Genevieve, St. Charles, and Franklin, the latter of which was more than 100 miles upstream, in the heart of the Boonslick. The state's rivers, especially the Missouri and the Mississippi, were also important trade routes, by which farmers could ship their surplus goods downstream to New Orleans and from there to urban markets along the eastern seaboard, or even to European or Asian destinations.

For years, river travel was largely a one-way proposition—downstream, on raft-like structures propelled by the river currents. Upstream traffic, largely in keelboats powered by human effort, was much more difficult, and as a result slower and more expensive. As mentioned, that all began to change with the introduction of steam-powered boats on Missouri's rivers on the eve of statehood.

The first steamboat to venture into Missouri Territory was the *Zebulon M. Pike*, named for the early explorer and War of 1812 hero. The *Pike* arrived in St. Louis on August 2, 1817, having made the 160-mile journey up the Mississippi River from Louisville, Kentucky, in six weeks. The boat's arrival at the foot of Market Street attracted a large crowd of curiosity-seekers and well-wishers, most of whom recognized that the event represented a transformational moment in the history of St. Louis and Missouri. Henceforth, travel to and from St. Louis, by both people and cargo, would be quicker and more affordable than ever before.

The first steamboat trip up the Missouri River, into the Boonslick country, elicited similar excitement. The steamboat *Independence*, also out of Louisville, became the first of its kind to enter the Missouri River on May 15, 1819. It arrived in the central Missouri town of Franklin, population roughly one thousand, thirteen days later, on May 18, 1819. The local newspaper, the *Missouri Intelligencer*, announced "the elegant steamboat[']s" arrival "With . . . pride and pleasure," noting that the boat was filled "with passengers and cargo of flour, whiskey, sugar, iron castings etc." The editor of the paper took the arrival of the *Independence* as a welcome sign "that steamboats can safely navigate the Missouri."

The golden age of the steamboat, made possible by more powerful and shallower-drafted vessels, began in 1837. By 1839, a Jefferson City newspaper, the *Jeffersonian Republican*, boasted that, thanks to the steamboat, one could make the 300-mile round trip from Jefferson City to St. Louis in less than four days. Within two years, that time had been reduced by more than half, to thirty-six hours. Still, the residents in Missouri continued to experience a pronounced "news lag." When, for example, President William Henry Harrison died on April 4, 1841, it took the news of his death thirteen days to reach Jefferson City from the nation's capital.

Regular steamboat traffic on the Missouri River, into the interior of the state, provided farmers and merchants with ever-expanding opportunities to market their goods beyond their local communities. During

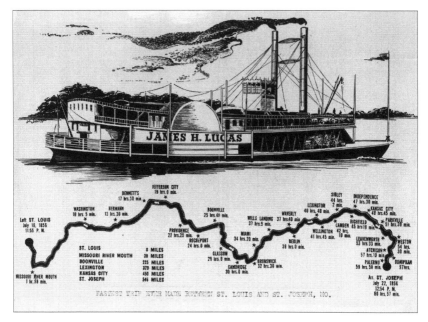

Fig. 17: Advertisement for *James H. Lucas* steamboat, for "Fastest Trip Ever Made Between St. Louis and St. Joseph, Mo." Credit: State Historical Society of Missouri, E.B. Trail Collection, Collection No. C2071.

the 1840s, for example, Captain N. J. Eaton of the *Iatan* regularly made two dozen trips during a season between St. Louis and the Howard County town of Glasgow. Glasgow's principal export item during this decade was tobacco, planted, nurtured, and harvested by Howard County's large slave population. Other significant export items included hemp, corn, bacon, and ham. Glasgow and Howard County, on the other hand, were regular importers of sugar, coffee, and salt.

By 1847, Missouri's capital city decided it could benefit financially by brokering trade between ship owners and their captains and the persons who wanted to purchase their wares. The city authorized the construction of a 228-foot wharf along the Missouri riverbank and constructed a city-owned warehouse. The city began collecting $2 for every regular packet landing, $1 more for landings by transient boats, 50 cents for flatboats, and a nickel for each cord of wood.

Steamboats and steamboat traffic had a dramatic effect on the lives of all Missourians. Steamboats changed people's ideas of time and space, of possibilities and prospects, by connecting people and products to each other across long distances in ways that had been all but unimaginable only a few years before.

But there were some unintended consequences of this new interconnectedness of places and increased ease of travel. One was the spread of disease. Cholera was an especially dreaded disease in Missouri and the nation during the decades leading up to the Civil War, in large part because there was no understanding that it was caused primarily by a bacteria transmitted through contaminated food and water, or exposure to sewage, and, thus, there was no possibility of a treatment or a cure for its deadly consequences.

Reports of cholera became especially frequent in Missouri newspapers in late 1848 and early 1849 and were of special concern in communities along the Missouri River. On July 12, 1849, the *Glasgow Weekly Times* reported that St. Louis had established a "Quarantine Station" several miles below the city, "where all boats having cholera, ship fever, or other malignant diseases among her passengers, have to land such passengers." The newspaper alleged that in St. Louis "a great portion of the fatality in cholera cases occurs among emigrants [sic] from foreign countries," thus anticipating a future propensity on the part of native residents to blame immigrants for the spread of disease. St. Louis reported 283 deaths for the week ending June 11, 1849, 191 of them the result of cholera. By late July, the weekly cholera death toll in St. Louis reached more than 600. Among the victims of the insidious infectious disease that summer was a member of St. Louis's founding family, Pierre Chouteau, Sr. In hindsight it's easy to see why cholera ravaged St. Louis that year. By that time, it was a city of 75,000 people, the streets and sewers of which had not been modernized to keep pace with the city's rapid population growth.

Cholera reappeared in Missouri in 1850 and once again caused death and heartache, despite the availability of widely advertised "remedies," such as Capt. C. T. Paynter's Egyptia Cure for Asiatic Cholera and Diarrhea, "prepared by himself," in his St. Louis business. Capt. Paynter claimed, without evidence, that his concoction "has been generally used in St. Louis, with great success." In 1852, Jefferson City mayor Jason Harrison urged the liberal use of lime to prevent the spread of cholera, also to no avail, much as twenty-first-century victims of COVID-19 would seek quick fixes and remedies in untested drugs such as hydroxychloroquine.

The success of steamboat traffic notwithstanding, Missourians continued to try to improve methods of travel, especially into the interior of the state, throughout the antebellum period. Some thought canals connecting Missouri's plentiful rivers would be a good approach, but Governor Boggs urged the building of railroads instead. "Railroads," he argued, "would not only shorten and cheapen transportation, but render it less hazardous." He urged the legislature to consider three possible railroad routes: the first one he proposed would extend from Missouri's western border, "on the south side of the Missouri river, passing through the intermediate counties to Boonville, and to the City of Jefferson, thence through the mineral region, to terminate at some point on the Mississippi river, below where that stream is usually blocked with ice." Boggs hoped such a rail line might hook up with others that could eventually extend to Cincinnati on the Ohio River, and even to South Carolina on the southeastern Atlantic coast.

Boggs proposed a second railroad route that paralleled the Missouri River on its north side, running through Howard County's Fayette, on to St. Charles and St. Louis, and then down to lead-rich Potosi, in Washington County. The third route he proposed would be a north-south line that bisected the state "passing the rich country of Salt River," a Mississippi River tributary that flowed through twelve eastern Missouri counties, including Pike and Monroe. This railroad would ultimately intersect with the two east-west roads also proposed by the governor.

The problem with all of Boggs's proposals was that despite lawmakers' general desire to see railroads built, they balked at the thought of public funding for such ventures. In 1836–1837, the Missouri General Assembly voted to charter eighteen railroad companies in the state, but provided no state funding or financial incentive for any of them. Perhaps it was just as well, given that another economic depression hit the nation in 1837, and the situation would have been worse in Missouri had the state recently taken on increased public debt through the financing of railroads.

Parallel to the discussion of railroad building in the state during the 1840s and 1850s was what one historian described as a "mania" for all-weather plank roads, made, as the name implies, by laying planks of native hardwoods, usually two and a half inches thick and wide enough to accommodate farm wagons and carriages, across existing dirt roads. Beginning in 1849 and running through the 1850s, the state of Missouri chartered

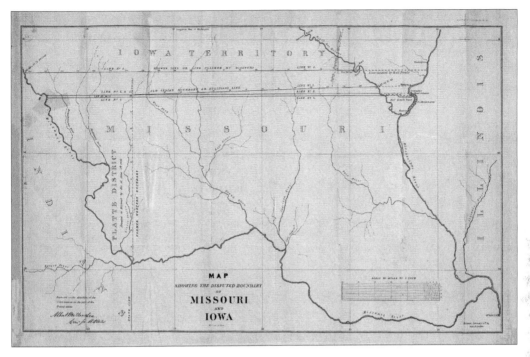

Fig. 18: This map shows the Platte Purchase, 3,149 square miles of land acquired in 1836 from Indigenous Peoples in northwest Missouri, extending the state's borders. Credit: State Historical Society of Missouri, Map850UN3 (1839).

nearly fifty companies that submitted proposals for the building of plank roads, mostly to and from towns near the Missouri and Mississippi rivers. The shortest of these proposed roads was only 1.75 miles; the longest, more than 150 miles. Some, such as the Versailles Plank Road, aimed to connect county seats, such as the Morgan County town of Versailles, to railroads, such as the Missouri Pacific. In 1851, William Switzler, editor of Columbia's weekly *Missouri Statesman*, proposed building a plank road from Howard County's Glasgow all the way to St. Louis, some 165 miles away.

Transportation advancements aside, life was hard on the Missouri frontier, as the men and women who settled there did their best to ameliorate the harsh conditions in an attempt to secure their families' existence, even as they tried to transport the "civilized" lives they had left behind in the eastern United States or Europe. A series of letters written by a young German immigrant woman to her brother back in Germany, beginning during the mid-1830s, reveals the hardships and trials of life in mid-Missouri during the second decade of statehood.

Henriette Geisberg Bruns was a young wife and mother in her early twenties when her physician-husband, fifteen years her senior, decided that he wanted to move to America and become a farmer. Henriette arrived in the aborning community of Westphalia, located at the western edge of what was then Gasconade County (in 1841, this part of Gasconade County became Osage County). Soon after arriving in Westphalia and bemoaning the loss of her comfortable home in Oelde, Germany, she wrote, "Our first shelter was in the middle of a field, a simple log cabin with two bed steads, one table, four chairs, and one bench." This "shelter" was home to Henriette, her husband, their son, two of her brothers, and a brother-in-law.

The next year, the Bruns family began to build a new, larger house. Progress on the new house was slow, but the family decided to move into it before it was completed, as winter was setting in: "There was still no gable, no chimney, no floor. Neither windows nor doors." It was a long, hard winter.

To her regret, Henriette soon realized that her life on the frontier would largely be one of suffering. As her husband knew little about farming, hunger and deprivation haunted the family. Henriette was homesick, missed her friends and family back in Germany, and was lonely. The vagaries of life on the frontier only intensified when, in 1838, a friend and neighbor, "young Mrs. Huber," who "was not twenty years old" was severely burned in a fire of uncertain origin. The young mother of two suffered horribly for two weeks before dying, something which profoundly affected Henriette.

As the 1830s gave way to the new decade, Henriette struggled to learn the English language, continued to miss her friends back in her homeland, as well as its culture. In 1840 she allowed her frustration to spill over in a letter to her brother: "Here, how lonely I am," she wrote. "[T]here is not another congenial female being with whom I could exchange now and then my feelings when I need some relief and [to] forget the daily worries and cares and set these aside for a short time."

Nothing, however, could prepare her for the pain she experienced in the fall of 1841, when three of her children died of dysentery. Daughter Johanna was the first to pass, on September 13. Six days later, son Max lost his grip on life. On October 2, 1841, nine-month-old Rudolf perished. "I myself sewed him his shroud," she wrote her brother.

Henriette Bruns was only one of thousands of new migrants to Missouri who sought opportunity and a better way of life during the first generation after statehood. The Early Republic period seemed to many to offer an open and fluid society that beckoned to adventurers and dreamers. Unfortunately, as historian David Rothman has noted, the openness and fluidity were fraught with potential danger. Migration took people away from the traditional stabilizing forces in their lives: extended family members, churches, and other long-established social anchors in the communities from which they moved. Left with inadequate institutional structures and aborning social institutions, migrants were susceptible to failure, poverty, even criminality and insanity.

Above all, early-nineteenth-century Americans believed in the perfectibility of mankind, and the idea that social and environmental factors determined character. Belief in this notion led them to the conclusion that old ways of dealing with deviancy, such as corporal punishment, were no longer acceptable. Thus, they began to advocate for replacing prisons with "penitentiaries," an American invention that promised a place where deviants could be reformed through reflection, learning new habits of work and discipline, and exposure to moral instruction. At the heart of this notion was the belief in what one historian called "the profitable utilization of convict labor." As early as 1830, Governor John Miller spoke out in favor of the building of a state penitentiary: "Individuals whose characters are disgraced by corporal punishments, beyond the hope of reparation, might otherwise by confinement to hard labor be made useful citizens." As an aside, the governor argued for building the penitentiary in the capital city, noting that such an action might help to quiet the movement to move the permanent seat of government elsewhere. The more public buildings that could be erected in Jefferson City, he reasoned, the less likely the capital would be moved.

Miller's idea came to fruition, but the newly constructed Missouri State Penitentiary, which received its first inmates in 1836, quickly challenged the state government's ability to fund its operation. A fiscal conservative, Miller had made the following remarks when he delivered his "First Biennial Message" to the legislature years before, in 1826: "The fact that our revenue has decreased since 1821, while the population and taxable property of the state has greatly increased in the same period, is the highest evidence of an imperfect and defective system." Forsaking "reform" for financial solvency, state officials subsequently came up with an enterprising new "system" to operate the penitentiary: they leased out the institution to two businessmen (William S. Burch and John C. Gordon) who paid the state for the right to run the penitentiary at their own expense in exchange for the privilege of hiring out the labor of inmates for their personal profit.

Burch and Gordon hired prisoners out all over the city, a practice that led to frequent escapes by inmates. In one twenty-month period in 1843–1844, fifty inmates escaped, an incredible twenty-eight percent of the 178 persons confined. Understandably, this raised the ire of city residents, even leading to threats of vigilante action if the high rate of escapes continued.

Equally troubling to city residents was the problem of local jobs lost to convict labor. As early as 1842, the editor of the *Jeffersonian Republican* asserted that "the [convict lease] system is a bad one, in every respect, and particularly as regards the interest of the State, and calculated moreover, to produce the most withering influence upon the prosperity of our City." "Where," the editor asked, "are the many industrious mechanics that formerly gave our town life and prosperity?" He answered, of course, that they had been "driven away, for want of employment." The newspaper expressed concern that the penitentiary threatened local economic stability and growth.

The challenge of dealing with female felons was no less confounding. When the state penitentiary was built in the mid-1830s, no consideration was given to the thought of incarcerating women. The prevailing, if chauvinistic, sentiment seemed to be that since women were morally superior to men, their naturally pious, angelic characters would preclude them from committing serious crimes.

This attitude notwithstanding, Missouri women did indeed commit crimes, the first woman to be sentenced to the penitentiary in Missouri being Rebecca Hawkins, who was found guilty of poisoning her husband in 1841. Governor Thomas Reynolds pardoned Hawkins before she arrived at the penitentiary, in part because of evidence that her husband had abused her ("she had borne his cruelty as long as it was sufferable") and in part because there was no one available to care for the couple's eight dependent children should their mother be incarcerated in Jefferson City.

The first woman confined in the Missouri State Penitentiary, Ann Amelia Eddy, an Irish immigrant, arrived at the prison on May 28, 1842. She remained behind bars only two weeks, until pardoned on June 11, 1842.

Governor Reynolds set Eddy free because he realized the inadequacy of prison facilities to house women.

Less fortunate, Martha Casto arrived at the Missouri State Penitentiary from Barry Country slightly more than a year later, on August 10, 1843, to serve a five-year sentence for murder. Since the penitentiary still had no facilities for women, Casto worked outside the prison walls, in the homes of Captain Ezra Richmond and Judge James Brown, the prison lessees. Reportedly, Brown's wife mistreated Casto and she ran away, only to be recaptured and placed in solitary confinement in the penitentiary for a short while. Soon thereafter, prison officials discovered that Casto was pregnant; the following fall she gave birth to a baby, who lived in a cell with her.

Soon thereafter, no doubt embarrassed by having a baby confined to an unheated cell in the state penitentiary with winter approaching, fifty-five persons, including a number of prominent legislators and former Missouri Governor Lilburn W. Boggs, petitioned Governor John C. Edwards to pardon Casto. He did so on December 6, 1844.

Although there were calls to build a separate women's prison over the next several years, penurious legislators failed to appropriate the necessary funds. Instead, throughout the 1840s and 1850s women sentenced to the Missouri State Penitentiary remained locked in their cells twenty-four hours a day to keep them away from the male prison population and male guards. Indeed, the prison physician reported in 1857 that female inmates were not even allowed out of their cells when they fell ill, as fear for their personal safety precluded their treatment in the prison hospital. Although multiple governors and the Board of Inspectors called repeatedly for the building of a separate facility for female felons, legislators would not fund the construction of a separate cellblock for women prisoners until the eve of the Civil War. And a new prison facility, specifically designed for women in Missouri would not be realized until the last decade of the twentieth century, when the Women's Eastern Reception, Diagnostic and Correctional Center was opened in Vandalia in 1998.

My own interest in the state of Missouri's arguably unsuccessful effort at dealing with deviant behavior accelerated during the mid-1970s, when I began teaching a course each semester at the Missouri State Penitentiary in Jefferson City through a degree program offered to inmates through Lincoln University. This was, of course, the same penitentiary established by the state in the 1830s.

Over the course of a decade, I taught at MSP, and experienced on a regular basis the consequences of a century and a half of the inadequate funding for inmate education and training. I witnessed the challenges associated with recruiting, training and adequately paying a professional staff, not to mention the many ways in which inmates were demoralized on a daily basis. I also saw firsthand the consequences of institutional racism that prevailed in the facility, along with the rampant violence that pervaded the place. It became obvious and demonstrable to me that the problems of the penitentiary in the late twentieth century were rooted in and understandable only from the perspective of the previous century and a half of the institution's history.

Meanwhile, governmental officials also tried to address the issue of mental illness in the maturing state, a condition that contemporaries also considered a result of mobility and social dislocation. As with the creation of a penitentiary, addressing the needs of the "insane" and "feeble-minded" seemed to be a mark of civilization that early Missourians hoped to attain. The need to treat mental illness came to the fore in the wake of Governor Thomas Reynolds's suicide in the Governor's Mansion in Jefferson City on February 9, 1844. His successor, Meredith Miles Marmaduke, a Saline County planter, was deeply troubled by this "melancholy occurrence." In his "First Biennial Message" to the General Assembly, delivered on November 18, 1844, Marmaduke told lawmakers that he felt it "to be my duty to recommend to your serious consideration, the erection of a lunatic asylum in this State." He bemoaned the fact that Missouri made no provision for the insane other than confinement "in our county jails where they seldom if ever receive any of those soft and kind attentions that have been found so necessary for their recovery and restoration to society." In short, the "fruits of civilization" referenced earlier by Governor Reynolds included providing an adequate facility for the insane, a place where they could be treated, healed, and returned to society as contributing citizens.

In January 1845, legislators began debating a bill "to provide for the erection of a Lunatic Asylum," but the proposition faced two major challenges. The first was how to pay for the construction of the new asylum (the projected cost stood at $30,000). The second had to do with the location of the proposed asylum. Governor Marmaduke wanted it built in Jefferson City, but in 1846 the legislature received a petition signed by hundreds of St. Louisans who wanted the facility in their city.

Ultimately, the legislature decided to borrow the money to build the asylum, and in 1847 it formed a three-person committee to determine the asylum's location. The enabling legislation directed that the facility must be built in one of eight mid-Missouri counties: Boone, Callaway, Chariton, Cole, Cooper, Howard, Moniteau, or Saline. Eager to reduce the cost to the state of establishing the facility, the legislature instructed the commissioners to solicit pledges of land and money from those communities hoping to become the asylum's home. The pledges had to include offers of from 100 to 500 acres of free land, the hope being that at least some of the asylum inmates would be able to work the land and produce food for their own consumption, or maybe crops in quantities that could be sold, thereby further mitigating the outlay of public funds required to operate such an institution.

Ultimately, Callaway County submitted the winning proposal, offering 500 acres of land and $11,500 in cash. One of the commissioners described the site chosen in glowing, uninhibited terms, as "a rich, fertile and healthy county . . . [with] lands . . . well adapted to the growth of corn, wheat, grass, vegitables [sic], etc., together with a great abundance of timber . . . as well as a great abundance of stone coal of a fair quality." "The town of Fulton," he added, "is a beautiful village, containing a population of about 700 souls. . . ."

The erection of the asylum was, however, further delayed, as the project incurred both increased and unexpected costs. A good deal more legislative haggling naturally ensued before the structure was finally completed in 1851, at a cost of approximately $50,000. The first two patients arrived at the institution in December 1851. By November 1852, less than a year after its opening, the Fulton Lunatic Asylum had seventy residents. The majority of the asylum's patients were individuals committed there by actions of county courts. Counties that sent patients to the asylum were obligated to pay the cost of transporting them to Fulton, as well as a weekly charge of $1.50 to cover the costs of their housing and care. The rules of the institution were strict and the lifestyle highly regimented, the hope being that structure, discipline, and good habits would "cure" the patients and allow them to return to mainstream society. A contemporary physician, Dr. R. W. Wells, explained that work "Soothes the patients, and prevents that everlasting brooding over their misfortunes or supposed misfortunes, which caused and continued their insanity."

At the same time that the Fulton Lunatic Asylum was being readied to receive patients, another state facility was opened in Fulton to care for yet another group of vulnerable Missourians: the "Asylum for the Education for the Deaf and Dumb." Located on forty acres adjacent to the Lunatic Asylum, the new school operated out of an old farmhouse.

The man placed in charge of the Asylum for the Deaf and Dumb was William Dabney Kerr, who arrived in Fulton in the summer of 1851 from Danville, Kentucky. That same year, in November, Kerr, his wife, and their three children welcomed the school's first student, a fifteen-year-old boy named John Isaacs from St. Louis.

By the end of its first year of operation, the school had seventeen students, ranging in age from nine to thirty-five. The farmhouse no longer adequate, in 1853 a new building was erected on a hilltop nearby, designed and built by the same St. Louis architect, Solomon Jenkins, who envisioned and crafted the Lunatic Asylum.

Kerr and his wife Susan ran the school much as a couple might have run a large household. Kerr noted as much in his first report to the General Assembly, when he wrote, "The government exercised over the Asylum is thoroughly parental in character." As the school's historian, Richard D. Reed, has written, "the male pupils were employed in cutting wood, working in the garden, etc. The female pupils were also employed . . . in needlework and in attending to the lighter duties of housekeeping."

Kerr wanted the students to learn self-reliance so that they would not become public charges. In his report to the General Assembly, he explained why he insisted that all students, regardless of their social class, learn how to perform routine tasks: "Habits thus formed will qualify them to perform with credit, in after days, these necessary duties, growing out of their position in society, and in their families."

If there was a downside to the early law that provided for the education of hearing-impaired students at public expense, it was that it provided for only three years of publicly financed education per student. Pupils who wished to remain at the asylum beyond three years were required to pay for their continued education, although there is evidence that Superintendent Kerr sometimes paid the bill for those students who couldn't afford to do so. In 1855, he succeeded in getting the legislature to expand the term to five years, although the law was amended to allow only indigent students to attend the asylum free of cost to them. By 1861, the enrollment at the asylum reached sixty-one students.

And how were the poor cared for during the early years of Missouri statehood? As early as 1815, even before Missouri became a state, the territorial legislature laid the groundwork for poor relief when it decreed that each county "shall relieve, support and maintain its own poor, such as the lame, blind, sick and other persons, who from age and infirmity are unable to support himself or herself. . . ." Poor relief recipients had to be without resources to support themselves for at least nine months.

Over the next few decades, the law was revised in some details, but the responsibility of poor relief remained with each county, whose court was given wide latitude in determining who was deserving of relief and what form the relief should take. Not surprisingly, treatment of the poor varied greatly from county to county.

The economic depression of the late 1830s increased the number of dependent paupers and prompted the state legislature to pass a law in the early 1840s which, according to historian David March, "empowered the county courts to purchase up to 160 acres and to erect a poorhouse on the land. . . ." Over the next half century, 95 of Missouri's 114 counties operated poor farms to care for the indigent, the hope being that the poor would be able to work on the farms and help to pay the costs of their own confinement.

The most vulnerable Missourians, the tens of thousands of African Americans who were subjected to enslavement, were the least protected and cared for. Slavery was an indispensable part of the Missouri experience dating back to the colonial period, to and through the period of Missouri's admission to the United States and beyond. During the early days of statehood, few whites in the state questioned the legality or morality of some white people holding Black people in bondage. Few Missourians recognized the abolition of slavery as a condition of an advancing civilization.

Indeed, little debate about the morality of slavery and whether the institution should be abolished emerged in Missouri until abolitionist petitions began to be introduced in the U.S. Congress during the mid-1830s. A small but growing antislavery sentiment in Missouri was abetted by the growing presence of German immigrants in the state, many—though not all—of whom had left Europe to live as free persons and were fiercely opposed to slavery on both economic and moral grounds.

German immigrants began arriving in Missouri in ever-increasing numbers by the mid-to-late 1820s, driven in large part by promotional literature that painted the state as a romantic paradise for farmers. No one played a more important role in this effort to attract Germans to Missouri than Gottfried Duden, a new arrival to Missouri who settled in present-day Warren County in 1825 and in 1829 published his *Report of a Journey to the Western States of North America*. Wildly popular in his home country, Duden's book portrayed Missouri as a place of temperate climate where a would-be farmer could make a better living for himself and his family with far less effort than was required in Germany. By 1860, Missouri's German-born population had grown dramatically, totaling 88,487 and ranking the state sixth in the nation among states with German-born residents. As historian Steven Rowan has pointed out, ". . . [S]lavery was seen [by the Germans] to be harmful because it provided inordinate power to a small elite and undermined the value of free labor. . . . The existence of slavery discouraged immigrants, degraded labor and craftsmanship, and subsidized a few agrarian industries (hemp, tobacco) that were of little intrinsic profit to Missouri."

On February 1, 1837, the Missouri General Assembly sought to stifle any antislavery sentiment in the state by making it illegal to distribute abolitionist literature or to "disrupt" the institution of slavery. Lawmakers emphasized the seriousness of this action by allowing for life sentences in the Missouri State Penitentiary for third-time offenders.

Arguably, one of the most dramatic challenges to this 1837 law occurred in Marion County in 1841, when a trio of would-be abolitionists crossed the Mississippi River from Quincy, Illinois, and tried to entice a group of slaves to flee their masters and the state. The abolitionists were caught, tried, and convicted of violating Missouri law and sentenced to twelve-year terms in the state penitentiary. One of the men, George Thompson, subsequently became famous through the publication of a book he wrote about his experiences in being arrested, tried, convicted, and confined in prison. Although Thompson and his co-conspirators were all sentenced to long terms in prison, they were pardoned by Governor John C. Edwards in 1846, less than halfway through their terms of incarceration.

Some of the Missourians who believed in the abolition of slavery tied the notion of the freeing of slaves to their forced removal from the state. This was the idea behind the formation of the Missouri Colonization Society in 1839, although the supporters of the Colonization Society tended to be slaveholders, not abolitionists.

Missourians' long-standing trade connections with New Mexico, extending back to the early days of statehood, meant that they would take a more than casual interest in the Mexican War (1846–1848). This war followed the American annexation of Texas in 1845, some nine years after Texas declared its independence from Mexico.

Soon after Congress declared war on Mexico, on May 13, 1846, Missouri Governor John Edwards called for Missouri volunteers to join an expeditionary force being created by Gen. Stephen W. Kearny to head out on the Santa Fe Trail to try to capture Santa Fe. Attorney and politician Alexander W. Doniphan, of Liberty, Missouri, one of Kearny's officers, played a key role in the capture and subjugation of the city that had been so important to a generation of Missouri traders. In the fall of 1846, another thousand or more Missourians under the command of Chariton County planter and politician Sterling Price joined the fight against the Mexican government that eventually saw the Americans prevail in the conflict.

The defeat of Mexico by the United States and the signing of the Treaty of Guadalupe Hidalgo on February 2, 1848, brought the question of the expansion of slavery into the forefront of public discussion nationally. In Missouri, the Democrats, who held control of politics in Missouri, tended to favor the expansion of slavery into the vast territory acquired from Mexico, while the Whigs, Missouri's minority political party, tended to oppose slavery's expansion beyond the places where it already existed. The issue was a contentious one and ended up dividing Missouri Democrats. A "Free Soil" faction of the party emerged in St. Louis, under the loose leadership of newspaper publisher Frank Blair and long-time U.S. Senator Thomas Hart Benton, a former slave owner, turned opponent of slavery expansion.

In opposition stood Democratic Party leaders led by a group of Boonslick region landholders and slaveholders known as the "Central Clique," which resolved to nip the so-called free-soil movement in the bud. Thus, after a long period of dormancy, the question of slavery's expansion into U.S. territory re-emerged in the wake of the Mexican War, invoking memories of the fiery debates in Congress and among the American public that had occurred during the "Missouri Crisis," the three years leading up to Missouri's entrance into the Union.

In December 1848, Central Clique leader, State Representative Claiborne Fox Jackson, a Saline County planter and slave owner, persuaded Missouri lawmakers to pass a series of resolutions directing the State's Congressional delegation—Senator Benton included—to oppose any effort by the Congress to limit slavery in the territories. Instead they were directed to allow the residents of the individual states to decide for themselves whether they were going to allow slavery within their borders. Benton defied this directive, increasingly fearful that the fight over slavery would lead to the dissolution of the Union. His position, which was unpopular back home in Missouri, ultimately led to his losing the senatorial seat in 1850.

By that time (1850), there were 87,422 slaves in Missouri, roughly a 50 percent increase over the 57,891 enslaved persons residing in the state a decade earlier. Most Missouri slaves lived and worked in the rich farmlands of the Missouri River valley, especially in the Boonslick. In addition to serving as field hands, they worked as valets, butlers, handymen, carpenters, common laborers, maids, nurses, and cooks. As historian Diane Mutti Burke has written, "Slavery was central to Missouri's economy and labor system. . . ."

Slavery proved to be as capricious and dangerous an institution in Missouri as it was in other slave states, a fact graphically illustrated in the life of a young Callaway County slave named Celia. Born in the late 1830s in neighboring Audrain County, Celia was sold at a slave auction in 1850 to a moderately successful farmer from Callaway County named Robert Newsom. At the time he bought Celia, Newsom owned a number of other slaves who worked his farm.

All the available evidence suggests that Newsom purchased Celia primarily to satisfy his sexual desires, his wife having died the previous year. Newsom built a brick cabin for Celia near the farmhouse he shared with two adult daughters and two grandchildren. Over the next few years, Newsom fathered two children by Celia, having forced her to submit to his sexual demands and continuing unabated in his predatory behavior.

In 1854, Celia began a relationship with a male slave on the Newsom farm, a man named George. Aware of Celia's relationship with the master, but powerless to exercise control over Newsom's behavior, George placed the burden of terminating the relationship on Celia who, by this time was experiencing a third, and difficult, pregnancy.

Celia tried multiple ways to get Newsom to end his sexual abuse of her, including talking to his adult daughters, imploring them to try to persuade their father to cease molesting her. When these attempts failed, Celia determined to take matters into her own hands, arming herself with a club.

One night in June 1855, Newsom came to Celia's cabin, demanding sex, but she warned him to stay away from her. When he refused to do so, angrily advancing toward her, she struck him with the club, and continued to beat him to death out of fear that if she did not do so he would manage to rise and kill her. Having ended the life of her tormentor, Celia dragged her dead master into the fireplace and stoked the flames until they consumed his corpse.

For days, no traces of Newsom were found, until George, her lover, turned on Celia and implicated her in the killing, apparently fearful that he too might be implicated in their master's death. After local officials threatened her with harm to her children, Celia confessed to killing Newsom. Subsequently, she was tried by an all-white jury of men, half of whom were slave owners. The impossibility of Celia's circumstances were revealed in the fact that she was not allowed to testify in her own defense at the trial and her court-appointed attorneys' argument that she was only defending herself against an attempted rape was squelched by the judge. Simply put, the ugly reality was that there was no such crime in Missouri (and most likely all other slave-holding states) at the time as that of the rape of an enslaved woman. Her body was not hers, but the property of her owner. If there was a crime involved with the rape of a slave, the crime was that of trespassing on the master's property, and had been committed against the master, not the victim of the sexual assault. Since Newsom legally owned Celia, in the eyes of the law he had never committed a crime, as a master could hardly be said to have trespassed on his own property. Celia was found guilty of capital murder and hanged on December 23, 1855.

There is at least some evidence to suggest that many Callaway County residents were bothered by Celia's circumstances on the Newsom farm. Still, Celia's killing of her master in one of Missouri's largest slave-owning counties could not be allowed to go unavenged, lest other slaves get the idea that they could attack their masters with impunity. The need for slave owners to retain absolute and total control over their slaves demanded that Celia pay for her "crime" with her life. So, while many Missouri slave owners in the years leading up to the Civil War claimed that in Missouri slavery was more humane than it was in the states of the Deep South, no degree of kindness, whether imagined or real, undid the fact that some people held other people as chattel property.

Not only does Celia's case reveal the heinousness of the slave system, but it also reveals the tremendous anxiety that existed over the issue of slavery in Missouri. That anxiety was especially strong in the mid-1850s, in the wake of the debates and activities surrounding the passage of the 1854 Kansas-Nebraska Act. The roots of the Kansas-Nebraska Act lay in the emerging question in the early 1850s of the future settlement of the Nebraska Territory, the land immediately west of Missouri. Although the federal government had reserved this territory for some time for Native American settlement, politicians and entrepreneurs increasingly hoped to open the region to white settlement. A driving ambition for some, including Missouri's Thomas Hart Benton, was to build a transcontinental railroad through the Nebraska Territory that would connect St. Louis to San Francisco, something Benton called "the Great Central Route."

A major problem associated with opening the Nebraska Territory to settlement was the Missouri Compromise agreement that, except for Missouri, prohibited slavery above the line of 36° 30' north latitude. This meant that if the Nebraska Territory became a state, it would have to enter the Union as a free one. Missouri slave owners greatly feared that prospect, for it would mean that Missouri would then be surrounded on three sides (Illinois, Iowa, Nebraska) by free states, dramatically increasing the prospect of Missouri slaves escaping to freedom.

In subsequent Congressional deliberations, spearheaded by U.S. senator from Missouri, David Rice Atchison, the Nebraska Territory was split into two prospective states—Kansas and Nebraska. The Kansas-Nebraska Act, passed into law on May 30, 1854, repealed the Missouri Compromise restriction on slavery and instituted the doctrine of popular sovereignty to determine whether Kansas would enter the Union as a slave or free state. In short, the people of Kansas would determine for themselves whether slavery would be allowed in the new state.

Atchison, a native of Kentucky and a college classmate of the future president of the Confederate States of America, Jefferson Davis, was a slave owner and tireless defender and promoter of slavery. Fearful that Kansans would vote to outlaw slavery and unwilling to leave it to chance, Atchison led a group of heavily armed proslavery Missourians into Kansas to vote in the November 1854 election. Running gun battles between proslavery Missourians and Kansas Free Soilers followed, the worst of which began on May 21, 1856, when Atchison and his followers attacked the Kansas town of Lawrence. This "Sack of Lawrence" resulted in the destruction of a newspaper office and the home of Free Soiler Charles Lawrence Robinson. It also resulted three days later, in retaliation by the vigilante abolitionist John Brown. Along with his four sons and two other accomplices, Brown came upon a group of five proslavery settlers at Pottawatomie Creek in Kansas and brutally murdered them with guns and broadswords. Thus began the Border War of Bleeding Kansas. Atchison, by the way, supported and campaigned for John C. Breckinridge, the secession-supporting candidate for the presidency in the 1860 election that, to the horror of slaveholders in the nation, was won by the candidate of the newly formed Republican Party, a U.S. senator from Illinois named Abraham Lincoln. When the Civil War broke out in 1861, Atchison chose to support Missouri's secessionist governor, Claiborne Fox Jackson and the Southern cause.

Meanwhile, another discussion around the issue of slavery arose in the 1850s, one that put the national spotlight back on Missouri. The issue at hand was the debate emerging over the status of Dred Scott, a formerly enslaved man who now made a legal claim for his freedom, a claim the proslavery forces steadfastly renounced.

Dred Scott was a Virginia-born slave who moved to St. Louis with his master, Peter Blow, in 1830. Blow subsequently sold Scott to Dr. John Emerson, an army surgeon who took Scott with him to live in Illinois and the Wisconsin Territory, both of which were free of slavery. Years later, in 1846, Scott and his wife Harriet, whom he had met and married in the Wisconsin Territory, sued their owner, Irene Emerson, for their freedom. The basis of their suit was that they had lived for a period of years in free territory, a practice which had long been accepted as a legitimate basis for a freedom suit.

The case went to trial in St. Louis on June 10, 1847. Technical challenges delayed a decision until January 12, 1850, when the court rendered the predictable verdict: Dred Scott was granted his freedom.

By this time, Irene Emerson had transferred her interest in the case to her brother, John F. A. Sandford, who appealed the St. Louis court's decision to the Missouri Supreme Court. The state's highest court reversed the lower court decision, and on March 22, 1850, rendered what legal scholar Walter Ehrlich called a "blatantly . . . extreme proslavery" verdict, overturning the "once free always free" precedent and ordering Dred Scott returned to slavery.

Ultimately, the case ended up in the U.S. Supreme Court. On March 6, 1857, Chief Justice Roger B. Taney delivered the court's opinion that Dred Scott still was and must remain a slave. Taney went further than that, further than he needed to go. He proclaimed for the court that slaves were not American citizens and as such had no individual rights. They were, Taney maintained, the property of white people, whose right to own them was enshrined in the U.S. Constitution. Moreover, that right could not be restricted, as the Congress had done in 1820 when it struck the Missouri Compromise, which of course had outlawed slavery in states above the 36° 30' line. Thus, Taney's assertion had rendered the Missouri Compromise as null and void.

By this time, however, battle lines were being drawn in both the state and nation, as slavery supporters and their opponents moved ever closer to a shooting war. Cautionary voices on both sides tried to warn Americans of the immensity of the impending crisis. Their warnings went unheeded. Henceforth, Missouri and Missourians would be at the center of the greatest conflict Americans would ever be engaged in—the Civil War.

SUGGESTED READINGS

The starting point for understanding the period leading up to the Civil War in Missouri is Perry McCandless, *A History of Missouri, 1820–1860* (1971), published by the University of Missouri Press. Although dated, Claude Phillips's essay, "A Century of Education in Missouri," *Missouri Historical Review* 15 (January 1921): 298–314, provides a useful survey of education in the state prior to the Civil War. This essay was published in commemoration of Missouri's centennial of statehood in 1921. Also helpful is David L. Colton, "Lawyers, Legislation, and Educational Localism: The Missouri School Code of 1825," *Missouri Historical Review* 69 (January 1975): 121–46.

Frank F. Stephens's *A History of the University of Missouri* (1962) remains useful. It was published by the University of Missouri Press. It should be supplemented with an essay by James C. Olson, "A Turbulent Half-Century: The Early Years of the University of Missouri," *Missouri Historical*

Review 84 (October 1989): 1–22. More recently, Zachary Dowdle has documented the role of slavery in the early years of the university in his essay, "Preventing a 'School of Nullification': Politics, Slavery, and the Presidency of the University of Missouri, 1839–1856," *Missouri Historical Review* 114 (January 2020): 79–104.

Among the helpful works on early steamboating in Missouri are Louis C. Hunter's *Steamboats on the Western Rivers* (1949), published by Harvard University Press; and Lawrence Everett Giffen, *Walks in Water: The Impact of Steamboating on the Lower Missouri River* (2001), published by Giffen Enterprises. More recently, William E. Lass's *Navigating the Missouri: Steamboating on Nature's Highway, 1819–1835* (2008) was published by Arthur H. Clarke Co.

The toll that cholera took in Missouri generally and St. Louis specifically is chronicled in Christopher Alan Gordon, *Fire, Pestilence, and Death: St. Louis, 1849* (2018), published by the Missouri Historical Society Press. Cholera is also treated extensively in Eldon Hattervig, "Jefferson Landing: A Commercial Center of the Steamboat Era," *Missouri Historical Review* 74 (April 1980): 277–99. More recently, Linda A. Fisher's "A Summer of Terror: Cholera in St. Louis, 1849," *Missouri Historical Review* 99 (April 2005): 189–211, is also helpful. Plank roads are the subject of Paul C. Doherty, "The Columbia-Providence Plank Road," *Missouri Historical Review* 57 (October 1962): 53–69.

The remarkable story of German immigrant Henriette "Jette" Bruns is told in her own words in *Hold Dear, As Always: Jette, a German Immigrant Life in Letters* (1988), edited by Adolf E. Schroeder and Carla Schulz-Geisberg, and translated from German by Adolf E. Schroeder. This book was published by the University of Missouri Press. A very different perspective on antebellum life, this time from the Boonslick, can be gleaned from "Personal Memoirs of Ida Shackelford Hemenway," edited by James M. Denny, *Boone's Lick Heritage Quarterly* 18 (Fall 2019): 4–18.

The challenges of operating the Missouri State Penitentiary during its early years are documented in an essay by Gary R. Kremer and Thomas E. Gage, "The Prison Against the Town: Jefferson City and the Penitentiary in the 19th Century," *Missouri Historical Review* 74 (July 1980): 414–32. Kremer's essay, "Strangers to Domestic Virtues: Nineteenth-Century Women in the Missouri Prison," *Missouri Historical Review* 84 (April 1990): 293–310, is also useful. The story of the beginnings of Missouri's efforts to deal with mental health issues is told in Richard L. Lael, Barbara Brazos and Margot Ford McMillen, *Evolution of a Missouri Asylum: Fulton State Hospital, 1851–2006* (2007), published by the University of Missouri Press. How Missouri dealt with its poor is the subject of David D. March, "Missouri's Care of the Indigent Aged," *Missouri Historical Review* 78 (January 1984): 202–18.

Although more than a century old now, Harrison A. Trexler's *Slavery in Missouri, 1804–1865* (1914) is still useful. It was published by Johns Hopkins University Press. More recently, Diane Mutti Burke's *On Slavery's Border: Missouri's Small Slaveholding Households, 1815–1865* (2010) is very helpful. It was published by the University of Georgia Press. Also useful is R. Douglas Hurt's *Agriculture and Slavery in Missouri's Little Dixie* (1992), published by the University of Missouri Press.

The tragic story of Celia is told by Melton McLaurin in *Celia, a Slave* (1991), published by University of Georgia Press. Through the years, there have been several local studies of slavery in Missouri. Among the most useful are the following: Philip V. Scarpino, "Slavery in Callaway County, Missouri: 1845–1855," Parts 1 and 2, *Missouri Historical Review* 71 (October and April 1976–1977): 22–43, 266–83; and James William McGettigan Jr., "Boone County Slaves: Sales, Estate Divisions and Families, 1820–1865," Parts 1 and 2, *Missouri Historical Review* 72 (January and April 1978): 176–97, 271–95.

The fight over the so-called Jackson Resolutions and the spread of slavery into western American territories is told in Christopher Phillips, *Missouri's Confederate: Claiborne Fox Jackson and the Creation of Southern Identity in the Border West* (2000); and Ken S. Mueller, *Senator Benton and the People: Master Race Democracy on the Early American Frontiers* (2014). The former was published by the University of Missouri Press, the latter by the Northern Illinois University Press.

The background to the famous Dred Scott case is told in Anne Twitty, *Before Dred Scott: Slavery and Legal Culture in the American Confluence, 1787–1857* (2016), published by Cambridge University Press. Also useful are Walter Ehrlich, *They Have No Rights: Dred Scott's Struggle for Freedom*, published by Greenwood Press (1979); and two books by Lea VanderVelde, *Mrs. Dred Scott: A Life on Slavery's Frontier* (2009); and *Redemption Songs: Suing for Freedom before Dred Scott* (2014), both published by Oxford University Press.

Abolitionism, and the role played by German immigrants in opposing slavery, is the subject of Kristen Layne Anderson, *Abolitionizing Missouri: German Immigrants and Racial Ideology in Nineteenth-Century America* (2016), published by Louisiana State University Press. Also helpful are Walter D. Kamphoefner, *The Westfalians: From Germany to Missouri* (1987), Princeton University Press, and Steven Rowan, *Germans For a Free Missouri: Translations from the St. Louis Radical Press, 1857-1862.* Selected and translated by Steven Rowan, with an Introduction and commentary by James Neal Primm. Published by the University of Missouri Press (1983).

Chapter Four

Turbulence in Civil War Missouri

"Slavery dies hard. I hear its expiring agonies and witness its contortions in death in every quarter of my district."

General Clinton B. Fisk, U.S. Army, March 1865

NO EXPERIENCE BEFORE or since has more bitterly and deeply divided Missourians than the American Civil War. When Missouri Governor Claiborne Fox Jackson, a Saline County planter and the owner of nearly fifty slaves, delivered his inaugural address on January 3, 1861, he proclaimed that he wanted Missouri to stand by her sister slave owning states of the South, the ones that had only days earlier decided to secede from the Union. Many Missourians, although certainly not a majority, agreed with him. But even among those who opposed secession, there was a widespread support of slavery and a virulent racism present that supported the notion of white supremacy.

Four candidates vied for the presidency of the United States in the 1860 election, leading up to the Civil War. Stephen A. Douglas of Illinois was the candidate of the Northern Democrats, and the candidate who carried Missouri. He favored allowing states to decide the issue of slavery for themselves, an idea that many Missourians had been advocating since the statehood struggle. John Bell of Tennessee, a slave owner, represented the Constitutional Union Party. Douglas and Bell were considered the moderate candidates. Most Missourians sided with them. Douglas carried Missouri with 35.5 percent of the vote. Bell trailed closely behind him, with 35.2 percent of the vote. Abraham Lincoln, the Illinois Republican who opposed the expansion of slavery into the territories, and John C. Breckinridge, the Kentuckian who supported it, were regarded by their opponents as "extremists." It is instructive to remember that Lincoln, the ultimate victor in this race, came in a distant fourth in Missouri, carrying only Gasconade and St. Louis counties, and the latter just barely. His vote totals in those two counties came overwhelming from German immigrants, who tended to oppose slavery.

By contrast, Breckinridge, the unabashed defender and supporter of slavery, and the candidate who carried all the future Confederate states, outpolled Lincoln in Missouri by a two-to-one margin. Breckinridge carried twenty-one counties to Lincoln's two, including the county of Cole, location of the capital city.

Governor Jackson rejected President Lincoln's call to raise troops in Missouri (and other Union states) to assist in suppressing the rebellion of the Confederate states. Instead, Jackson began to raise his own force of Missouri State Guard soldiers, who, he hoped, would repel a Union "invasion."

Hoping that he could persuade a majority of Missourians to side with the Confederacy and secede from the Union, Governor Jackson called for a state convention to decide the issue and asked for legislative support to strengthen the State Guard.

Over the course of the early months of 1861, Missourians debated and discussed the relative merits of supporting the Confederacy versus the Union. Ultimately, delegates were chosen for a convention that met for eighteen days in St. Louis, the home of many German immigrants, who were almost universally opposed to slavery and to secession. The Germans were not the only opponents of secession; ultimately, the convention, dominated by Unconditional and Conditional Unionists, decided by a vote of 98 to 1 on March 19 that Missouri should remain with the Union.

This was a tense time for all Missourians. Writing a letter in April 1861 to her brother back in Germany, from a house across the street from the Capitol in Jefferson City, German immigrant Henriette Bruns summed up the situation with an understatement: "We are living in very stirring times." She added, "At present, almost no business is carried on," adding, "at our place," a general merchandise store owned by her and her husband, "we sell only for cash and consequently business is not worth mentioning." "The people have no money," she continued. "One has to wait and not use anything."

The first bloodshed of the war in Missouri occurred early in May 1861. The battleground was the hastily built "Camp Jackson" in St. Louis. The camp was controlled by Confederate-sympathizing supporters of Governor

Jackson who were challenged by newly mustered-in Union soldiers under the command of General Nathaniel Lyon. Lyon's forces far outnumbered the Southern supporters they opposed, but as the former arrested the latter and began marching them to Jefferson Barracks, some ten miles away, a fight broke out between onlookers and the Union soldiers. When the fighting was over, twenty-eight persons lay dead. As it turned out, in Missouri and elsewhere in the nation, the killing and dying would continue for four more years.

Governor Jackson's response to this event was to redouble his efforts to expand and strengthen the Missouri State Guard. He named popular former governor and military hero of the Mexican War, Sterling Price, also a slaveholder, as the guard commander.

On June 11, 1861, Governor Jackson and General Lyon had a heated confrontation in the Planter's House hotel in St. Louis. Lyon told Jackson that his attitude and actions meant that he was at war with the state of Missouri and the United States of America.

Jackson and his coterie of followers hightailed it back to Jefferson City by train. Knowing that Lyon and his forces would soon be coming after them, they burned at least two railroad bridges behind them.

On June 13, 1861, Lyon and two thousand U.S. Army soldiers arrived in Jefferson City aboard four steamboats, rather than by railroad. Almost all these soldiers were German-speaking immigrants from the St. Louis area. At the time, Jefferson City had a population of just over three thousand people, and its citizens, not including the German immigrants, had a reputation for being strongly supportive of the Confederacy.

Realizing that he faced imminent capture, Jackson rode out of town ahead of Lyon, who left a couple of hundred of his men in the capital city to secure the Missouri state government for the Union cause. Concerned that they might be attacked by local secessionist sympathizers, the soldiers barricaded themselves in the State Capitol, the largest public building in the city. To aid in their self-defense, they impressed dozens of prisoners from the nearby Missouri State Penitentiary to build earthen works around the building to help fortify it.

Meanwhile, Lyon and the remainder of his men chased the governor, finally catching up with him at a spot near Boonville where, arguably, the first battle of the Civil War in Missouri occurred. The twenty-minute-long "Battle of Boonville" ended in a Union victory, with Jackson and his supporters retreating to the southwest Missouri town of Neosho to set up a rump government. Jackson continued to live in exile another eighteen months, claiming until his death in Little Rock, Arkansas, in 1862 to be the legitimate governor of Missouri.

Meanwhile, the same state convention that had decided that Missouri would not leave the Union reconvened in Jefferson City on July 22, 1861, and declared the office of governor, as well as the offices of elected officials who had supported him, to be vacant. They created a "provisional government" and selected Hamilton R. Gamble, a native of Winchester, Virginia, as governor. Gamble had become a lawyer in Virginia in 1817 before moving to Missouri in 1818. He practiced law in Franklin and St. Louis before winning election to the Missouri Supreme Court as a Whig in 1846. A slave owner himself for many years, Gamble served as Chief Justice of the Missouri Supreme Court in 1852, when that body decided against Dred Scott's quest for freedom in the famous *Dred Scott* case of that year. For his part, Gamble dissented from the majority opinion and argued that Scott was indeed free by virtue of his having been taken into free territory years earlier.

The 1861 Missouri state convention further removed from office all elected officials in both the executive and legislative branches and called for new elections to replace them. To ensure loyalty to the provisional government and the Union, Missouri citizens were required to swear allegiance to both before they were allowed to vote. Failure to take the oath led to disfranchisement and the label of being a Confederate sympathizer. Imposition of the oath engendered anger and resentment among many who were sympathetic to, if not necessarily supportive of, the Confederate cause.

In August of that year, Governor Gamble proclaimed martial law in the state, meaning that military rule superseded civilian rule throughout the remainder of the war. A provost marshal general was appointed for the entire state, with district provosts and their deputies assigned to oversee virtually all matters for the different regions of the state. Provost marshal officials could arrest anyone whom they deemed to be a threat to the state or nation. Unsurprisingly, this system lent itself to great abuses of individuals' basic civil rights.

A major reason for the imposition of martial law in Missouri was the widespread guerrilla warfare that was occurring throughout the state. When early efforts to take the state into the Confederacy failed, many Southern

sympathizers turned to guerrilla activity and began to try to recruit supporters to the Southern cause and to surreptitiously try, by any means including
violence, to thwart the Union war effort. According to historian Michael
Fellman, "Almost all Missouri guerrillas were very young men. All fought
outside of regular military units, roaming the countryside in shapeless, temporary groups, lurking, striking, vanishing and terrorizing everyone they
considered their enemies. . . ."

For the remainder of the summer of 1861, indeed for the remainder of
the war, Jefferson City residents, regardless of their sympathies, including
newly chosen Provisional Governor Gamble, lived in fear of a military attack by Southern forces aimed at bringing Missouri into the Confederacy,
something that deposed Governor Jackson worked to make happen. In late
July he travelled to Richmond, Virginia, where he met with Confederate
President Jefferson Davis. On August 5, Jackson issued a proclamation of
independence for the state of Missouri. In return, the Confederate congress
appropriated one million dollars for Missouri troops who supported the
Confederate cause.

In August 1861, General Ulysses S. Grant was sent to Jefferson City
to command Union troops there and to repel an expected attack on the
capital city by Confederate General Sterling Price. Meanwhile, Price's army

Fig. 19: General Ulysses S. Grant speaks to soldiers under his command, 1863, Lookout
Mountain, Tennessee. Credit: State Historical Society of Missouri, Ruth Rollins Westfall
Photograph Collection, Collection No. P0020.

of roughly fourteen thousand men clashed with Lyon's force half that size on August 10 at Wilson's Creek, near Springfield. Ordered by his superior, General John C. Fremont, to retreat, Lyon instead engaged Price and his men in what would be the first major Civil War engagement fought in Missouri. Lyon's decision cost him his life in a fiercely contested battle that resulted in a victory for the Southern forces.

Following the Battle of Wilson's Creek, General Sterling Price moved north and west along the Missouri-Kansas border, hoping to thwart Kansan Jim Lane's incursions into Missouri, attract more Missouri recruits to the rebel cause, and, ultimately, to free the Missouri River from Union control. His travels took him to Lexington, Missouri, on September 11, 1861. At the time, Lexington was a town of about four thousand people and the county seat of Lafayette County, located at the western end of what one could call the Missouri Black Belt, as nearly one out of every three residents of the county was an enslaved Black person. Not surprisingly, there were many Southern sympathizers in Lexington and the rest of Lafayette County.

One of them was Susan A. Arnold McCausland, a native of Lynchburg, Virginia, who was twenty-two years old in 1861. According to federal census returns for 1860, she and her husband owned eleven slaves. In a late-life reminiscence about the Battle of Lexington, McCausland recalled that Confederate flags were ubiquitous in Lexington in the spring and early summer of 1861. Union Colonel Charles G. Stifel arrived in Lexington "at the head of a regiment of foreigners, some of whom spoke English not at all." The Confederate flags disappeared, all save one that flew in front of McCausland's father's house. McCausland refused to surrender that flag until forced to do so by Stifel's troops.

On September 17, McCausland and other town residents were warned to abandon their homes and their town as fighting seemed imminent. Fighting did indeed commence on Wednesday, September 18, with General Price's force of some fifteen thousand men attacking approximately 3,500 Union soldiers holed up on the campus of Mason College. McCausland was among the town's residents who refused to evacuate. Instead, she took up a "post of operation" in the middle of Third Street, and watched the battle unfold. On Thursday September 18, she reported, "a ceaseless sharp cracking of rifles went on throughout the day. The possessors of those squirrel rifles hidden behind every available tree, stump, or elevated ground did deadly work whenever a human target . . . appeared within range. Some of this was done from the vantage of tree limbs, which many men climbed and sat at ease to watch their opportunity."

McCausland also watched "the men of the hemp bale strategy" roll bales toward the line of Union forces, firing their weapons from behind their mobile ramparts. "On they came," she recalled, "crawling, as implacable as fate, and when the day was run on towards the morning's close, the end came. The Confederates were inside the defenses, the white flag of surrender was run up over the citadel, and a shout to reach the heavens was shouting from a thousand throats." The Confederates had won the battle, thereby bolstering their confidence in their cause, and, at least for the time being, their control of the Missouri River Valley in that part of the state.

Guerrilla warfare continued throughout the early years of the war. Two of the most dangerous early guerrillas in Missouri during this period were Joseph Porter and William Clarke Quantrill. In October 1862 Porter and his group of as many as 400 men attacked the Marion County town of

Fig. 20: "Paw Paw" Militia, a home guard unit commanded by Colonel Odon Guitar, standing in formation in St. Joseph, 1862. Credit: State Historical Society of Missouri, North Todd Gentry Photograph Collection, Collection No. P0166.

Palmyra in northeast Missouri. During the attack, Porter captured and carried off a Union supporter, Andrew Allsman, whom he and his men presumably killed. A local military commander retaliated by ordering ten Confederate soldiers to be executed if Allsman was not returned in ten days. When the ten days passed without the return of Allsman, ten Confederates, most of them local guerrillas, were executed by firing squad. This incident became known as the Palmyra Massacre and only intensified feelings of animosity among both Rebel and Union sympathizers. For the remainder of the war, according to historian Andrew William Fialka, guerrillas remained especially effective at targeting federal and military garrisons in the state.

The year 1863 witnessed a series of transformational events in the war experiences of many Missourians. The changes began with President Abraham Lincoln's Emancipation Proclamation, issued on January 1, 1863. The proclamation announced the freeing of all slaves residing in states that were officially in rebellion against the Union. This order did not directly impact Missouri slaves, since the state was not officially in rebellion. Still, the president's action suggested that the institution of slavery might not survive a Union victory. Even slaveholders in the border state of Missouri had to acknowledge the likelihood that slavery throughout the nation would likely come to an end if federal forces prevailed.

Knowledge of the president's action, and its obvious redirection of the war's purpose, emboldened many Missouri slaves to abandon their masters and move to towns and cities where they hoped to find security in numbers, especially in places where Union troops were garrisoned.

This migration of African Americans away from the rural Missouri countryside was abetted by an ancillary provision of the Emancipation Proclamation, namely President Lincoln's call to enlist slaves into the Union army as part of the effort to suppress the rebellion.

As Union officers began to travel up and down the Missouri River corridor recruiting Black slaves into the army in mid-to-late 1863, many whites, especially slave owners, were enraged. They began to use violence and the threat thereof against Blacks, hoping to intimidate slaves who might be considering joining the army not to do so and to punish those who had enlisted.

The enslaved women these newly enlisted African American soldiers left behind often encountered great difficulty, bearing the brunt of white hostility toward their self-emancipated husbands. Such was the case of a

Mexico slave woman named Martha Glover who wrote to her husband, Richard, in December 1863, when he was stationed at Benton Barracks. "I have had nothing but trouble since you left. You recollect what I told you how they would do after you was gone. They abuse me because you went & say they will not take care of our children . . . and beat me scandalously the day before yesterday." Martha told her husband he "ought not to left me in the fix I am in."

According to historian Sharon Romeo, this harsh treatment of the wives of Black soldiers was all too common. It led to many Black women fleeing their masters, often with children in tow, for Union military outposts and towns where Union troops were garrisoned. Without exception, the Union army was unequipped and unprepared to handle these Black refugees. In March 1864, General Egbert B. Brown, Commander of the District of Central Missouri, wrote to Major O. D. Greene, Headquarters, Department of the Missouri, telling him that approximately 2,000 women, children, and old men had descended upon military outposts in the District. Sedalia's provost marshal commented at about the same time, "We have a large number of Black women and Children, many of them are the wives of soldiers, that have been enlisted in my District. . . ."

Guerrilla activity in the large slaveholding counties of the Boonslick (especially Howard, Cooper, Saline, Boone, and Callaway counties) dramatically increased, with guerrilla leaders such as Boone County's Jim Jackson and others whipping, beating, and even lynching Black males of military age who threatened to leave their masters to join the Union Army. Consequently, the number of Blacks fleeing to towns such as Jefferson City, where thousands of Union soldiers were quartered, increased.

Contemporary newspapers document this migration of Black refugees. In May 1863, for example, the Jefferson City *Missouri State Times* reported that "A sable stream of contrabands [the terms used to describe Blacks who fled to Union lines] have been flowing into this city and neighborhood, [sic] for the last few weeks." According to the paper, the "contrabands" came "principally from Boone and Callaway counties." The paper continued: "Saturday and Sunday nights appear to be the most favored time for their travel, and as many as fifty have crossed the Missouri [R]iver of a night."

By the summer of 1864 the large influx of African Americans into the capital city had become a matter of official concern, and Black refugees were being blamed for all sorts of offenses against the local citizenry. On

August 18, 1864, the minutes of the city's board of aldermen reported that a "Mr. Miller" had "called the attention of the Board to the very annoying condition of the city deriving from the great increase of Colored people who are every day congregating from other parts of the country who are bent on nothing but thieving and stealing from innocent people whose lives and property are now at risk." After a discussion, the board voted to ask the mayor to write to General William Rosecrans, Commander of the Department of Missouri, about the situation and to inquire if a decision on their part to remove African Americans from the city would be regarded as interference with military prerogatives. No effort to remove Blacks from the city resulted.

As the winter of 1864–1865 approached, the Republican *Missouri State Times* expressed fear that there was a human tragedy in the making. Under the title, "The Colored People in Jefferson City and Vicinity—What is to Become of Them," the *Times* asked, "How are the colored people here, (who are mostly women and children) to live through the coming winter?" The paper acknowledged that many of them "occupy little out-buildings which are too small and too open to live in during cold weather," and it called for "some public provision to be made to send them where they can procure labor, and where subsistence is more abundant." The paper made clear that its motives lay in large part in freeing white residents from the burden of providing for Black refugees when it asked: "Should not measures be taken at once to ascertain where they can be sent . . . [to] benefit them, as well as relieve this community of a large number of consumers who will find the procurement of labor impossible." The challenge of dealing with Black refugees played out in other Missouri cities where African Americans sought shelter, sustenance, and an escape from white violence.

Meanwhile, pro-Confederate guerrilla leader William Quantrill was leading an effort along the Missouri-Kansas border to stop Union troops stationed in Missouri and Kansas from attacking Missouri farms, towns, and villages along the interstate border. In the summer of 1863, Union General Thomas Ewing sought to damage the guerrilla cause by arresting a number of women known to be supporting the guerrillas, including a sister of Quantrill. Ewing imprisoned the women in a Kansas City house that subsequently collapsed from overcrowding, which resulted in the death or injury of several of the occupants. An enraged Quantrill sought revenge almost immediately. On August 21, he led a raid on Lawrence, Kansas, killing as many as 150 men and boys and damaging or destroying more than $2 million worth of property.

Determining that he could not allow the "Sack of Lawrence" to go unpunished, on August 25, 1863, four days after Quantrill's raid, Union General Thomas Ewing, commander of the District of the Border, with headquarters in Kansas City, issued Order No. 11, requiring all the inhabitants of the western Missouri counties of Jackson, Cass, Bates, and part of Vernon not living within one mile of specified military posts, to vacate their homes by September 9, with no provision made for where they might go or be received. Those who refused to go were turned out of their homes at gunpoint by Union soldiers and their grain and hay destroyed. This edict, called by historian Albert Castel "the harshest treatment ever imposed on United States citizens under the plea of military necessity in our nation's history," was aimed at putting an end to the civilian support given by pro-Southern sympathizers to guerrillas operating in the area.

Whatever the goals of Ewing and his superiors, the immediate consequence of Order No. 11 was terrible suffering and loss among the people living in the counties impacted by the order. Colonel Bazel Lazear, a Union officer stationed at Lexington, reported to his wife, "It is heart sickening to see what I have seen. . . . A desolated country and women & children, some of them almost naked. Some on foot and some in old wagons. Oh, God." H. B. Bouton, a Unionist from near Kansas City in Jackson County, reported many "poor people, widows and children, who, with little bundles of clothing, are crossing the river to be subsisted by the charities of the people amongst whom they might find shelter." And George Caleb Bingham, the artist, who was also a Unionist, wrote of "barefooted and bareheaded women and children, stripped of every article of clothing except a scant covering for their bodies," being "exposed to the heat of an August sun and compelled to struggle through the dust on foot."

Bingham was in fact among the harshest critics of Ewing and Order No. 11. Subsequently, he produced a dramatic painting named for the order, portraying Ewing and his hated supporters, self-described as Kansas Redlegs, as callous killers of Missouri civilians and shameless destroyers of their personal property. If Ewing's actions had sought to stifle local residents' support of guerrilla activity, he missed his mark badly. Instead, his action

Fig. 21: *Order No. 11*, an 1868 painting by George Caleb Bingham that reflects the artist's hostility toward a wartime order issued by Union General Thomas Ewing, vacating several western counties in the state. Credit: State Historical Society of Missouri.

seemed to have had the opposite effect, creating a greater sympathy for Southern supporters in the region as well as a hard-edged hostility toward the Union army, and, indeed, the federal government it represented.

Although we know through hindsight that Missouri's capital city was never invaded, much less occupied, by Confederate forces during the war, residents of the city lived in fear that war might come to their doorsteps. And if Confederate forces could conquer the state capital, perhaps they could force Missouri state governmental officials to join the rebellion.

In September 1863, Confederate General Sterling Price sent General Jo Shelby north from Arkansas to attack Missouri's capital city. Shelby entered Missouri on September 23, 1863, the one-year anniversary of President Lincoln's "preliminary Emancipation Proclamation," a statement and warning of what he intended to do three months hence. Shelby and his men rode around Missouri for weeks, cementing his reputation as a legendary Confederate cavalryman and the basis of a legacy that would persist into the twenty-first century. By October, Shelby got as close to the Capitol as Tipton, less than forty miles away, but then abandoned his mission after learning that federal troops under the command of General Egbert B.

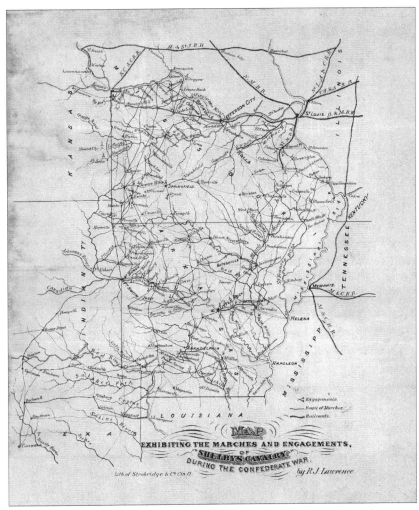

Fig. 22: Map Illustrating General Joseph O. "Jo" Shelby's Missouri "Marches and Engagements" during the Civil War. Credit: State Historical Society of Missouri, Map 850L438 n.d.

Brown were being rushed there to defend the city. Notwithstanding this decision, residents of Jefferson City were terrified.

One year later, in October 1864, General Sterling Price made a last-ditch effort to bring Missouri into the Confederacy. By that time, the war was going badly for General Robert E. Lee and his forces. Desperate Confederate leaders hoped that if they captured Missouri, specifically St. Louis and Jefferson City, they could use both river cities to block the transport of war material to the Union army. They also might be able to influence Northern voters to support Union General George B. McClellan, who advocated for a negotiated peace, in the 1864 presidential election. If McClellan could defeat Lincoln, a negotiated peace would be tantamount to victory for the South.

General Sterling Price assumed command of this effort, despite the dim view of him held by many Confederate leaders. Price, a former Missouri governor, was still quite popular in the state. Riding with Price, as an aid to General Jo Shelby, was Thomas C. Reynolds, who in 1860 had been elected Missouri's lieutenant governor and who claimed to be the state's legitimate governor in the wake of Governor Claiborne Fox Jackson's death in exile in Arkansas in late 1862. If Price were to succeed, Confederate leaders hoped to install "Governor" Reynolds into office after taking Jefferson City.

General Price planned to take St. Louis first, where he hoped to stock up on arms; some contemporary reports claimed that half of his men had no weapons. In addition, Price thought his presence in Missouri could attract as many as twenty thousand additional soldiers for the Confederate cause. He seems to have thought that he could capture Missouri with relative ease, first because the majority of Union forces were concentrated in the eastern theater of the war, and second because he thought most Missourians would perceive him as a great liberator arrived to rescue them from the Union's tyrannical control. Neither of those suppositions turned out to be true.

Price and his forces departed from Pocahontas, Arkansas, on September 19, 1864, headed to St. Louis. A few days later, after conferring with three of his generals (Jo Shelby, John Sappington Marmaduke, and James Fagan) Price decided enroute to St. Louis that he would attack the much-hated General Thomas Ewing Jr. and his men at Fort Davidson, near Pilot Knob in Iron County, Missouri. Price's army outnumbered Ewing's by at least ten to one.

Although heavily outmanned, General Ewing held off Price's forces for two days. During that period, Price lost 1,200 men to Ewing's 73. Convinced, however, that he could not hold out much longer, Ewing led his men on a tactical retreat from the fort under cover of darkness, blowing up the fort's powder magazine behind him. Price's failure to capture the fort, its occupants, and their arms was a colossal blunder.

Price's army of three divisions split up and headed west toward the capital city, attacking, looting, and pillaging small towns along the way. On October 4, 1864, Marmaduke's troops attacked the largely German-American town of Hermann and subsequently destroyed a bridge over the Gasconade River at the town of Gasconade. Shelby and his men "stormed" the Osage County town of Linn, where they claimed to have taken one hundred prisoners before moving on to the village of Westphalia. Of Westphalia, Shelby wrote on October 6, 1864, "I find that this settlement is Catholic and composed of Southern sympathizers," a curious comment, given that Westphalia was made up overwhelmingly of German immigrants who tended to oppose slavery. Shelby further wrote, "I have done all in my power to protect them. . . ."

Curiously, more than a century and a half later, the "German Heritage Corridor" through which Price and his troops travelled became one of the areas of the state in which rebel battle flags could be readily seen, flown from the pickup trucks, front porches, and yards of descendants of those Germans attacked by Confederates who marched with Price. By 2021, many locals had forgotten for which side their ancestors had fought, and why.

Price and his men crossed the Osage River at multiple places southeast of Jefferson City and advanced toward the capital, carrying on a running battle with advanced guard Union soldiers enroute. Stopping within sight of the state Capitol, Price apparently received faulty intelligence that there were at least fifteen thousand soldiers ready to defend Jefferson City. Consequently, he decided to forego his intended attack (he feared a repeat of the Pilot Knob disaster) and now headed toward the Missouri-Kansas border. Curiously, decades later, in a celebration of the Lost Cause, members of a local chapter of the United Daughters of the Confederacy placed a marker near the spot where Price was alleged to have made his decision, a memorialization of a battle that never occurred. In late 2020, that memorial was removed from the site by action of the City of Jefferson.

Meanwhile, Jefferson City residents had spent weeks preparing for the impending attack on their city. Although they were heartened by the fact that the attack never came, Price's presence on the doorstep of their city engendered fear and elaborate preparations for the attack that never came. Some idea of the extent to which the threat of Price's raid disrupted everyday life in Jefferson City, and resulted in significant damage and expenses to city residents and their property, can be gleaned from letters and claims filed by local residents with the provost marshal in charge of the region.

Edward L. Edwards, publisher of the Jefferson City *Examiner*, filed a detailed account of the damage done to his property "in preparing for the defence of Jefferson City, previous to the 10th of October 1864." First, he alleged that "between 800 and 1000 fence rails" were taken from his property and used to build "fortifications on the hill east of the graveyard," somewhere near the high ground where the Immaculate Conception Catholic Church now stands, at the intersection of Clark Avenue and East McCarty Street.

Likewise, Edwards claimed damages for a 65–70-foot-long trench cut across his property and eighteen picket fence panels that had been torn down. Additionally, Edwards claimed that hundreds of other crop fences were destroyed. There were more than two thousand claims such as Edwards's from Cole County alone filed with the provost marshal. These claims evidenced widespread disregard for personal property rights by Union soldiers in the face of an attack by Confederate forces. One can only imagine the consequences of miles of fences torn down and used for firewood or breastworks, freeing livestock to roam unchecked through the city and countryside. Even Henriette Bruns wife/widow of the mayor and the resident of a house directly across from the Capitol, filed a claim for damages through her son, Herman L. Bruns. According to the son, "About six hundred feet of her fence . . . were nearly all utterly destroyed or carried away." No doubt many others in the city shared the view expressed in the local newspaper after Price had finally left the state: "May the alligators of the Southern bayous devour Price and his horde of ruffians, rather than that they may be permitted to return to Missouri."

Early in 1865, Missourians finally confronted the slavery issue, which had bedeviled them throughout the war, indeed, throughout the state's history. General John C. Fremont had pressed the issue early in the war when, as Commander of the West, stationed in St. Louis, he issued an order on August 30, 1861, calling for the emancipation of the slaves of all those who had taken up arms against the United States. Fearful that this edict would drive slave owners into the arms of the Confederacy, President

Lincoln urged Fremont to rescind his order. When the latter refused, the president revoked it on his own.

The question of the future of slavery had continued to simmer in Missouri throughout the war, with many Missouri slaves abandoning their masters when they heard of the presence of federal troops in the area. In the summer of 1863, Provisional Governor Gamble called the state convention into session to consider the future of slavery. After much discussion, the convention agreed to abolish slavery in Missouri, effective July 4, 1870. There were, however, varying degrees of apprenticeship associated with what amounted to a gradual process of emancipation, depending on the age of the slave at the time that freedom was granted.

The matter of slavery was taken up anew in January 1865, when a new convention met to begin planning for the state's postwar future. On January 11, 1865, the convention passed an Emancipation Ordinance, declaring slavery to be officially dead. The final vote on the 1865 Missouri ordinance came after an unsuccessful effort by convention delegate William F. Switzler of Boone County to amend the order to allow for the creation of an "apprenticeship system" for freedmen between the ages of twelve and twenty-one. Such a system would have allowed for the virtual enslavement of young African American men and women for an indeterminate number of years. Switzler, a Columbia newspaper publisher, later defended and explained his position in an editorial in his paper, the *Missouri Statesman*. Writing in the patronizing tone characteristic of the slave-owning class, Switzler argued that Missouri slaves were unprepared for freedom. "The solemn truth," he wrote, is that "here in midwinter they are without homes and employment and the means of subsistence." Thus, he saw freedmen as being worse off than they had been as slaves, because they were "thrust . . . from . . . homes without a dollar in money, without an acre of land, or horse or mule or cow or ass or plough or saw with which to earn food or raiment."

Switzler's sentiment notwithstanding, convention delegates rejected his amendment and adopted the emancipation ordinance with only four dissenting votes. Those joining Switzler in opposition included Thomas B. Harris of Callaway County, William A. Morton of Clay County, and Samuel A. Gilbert, also of Clay County. The four opponents of emancipation represented counties which, according to the 1860 federal census, held more than 16,000 slaves on the eve of the Civil War. Reflecting the fear that many whites in Missouri had of freed slaves, Samuel Gilbert called for their forced colonization outside the state's borders, exclaiming in exasperation, "In the name of God, if you are going to free [N]egroes, send them from us."

Word of the passage of the emancipation ordinance reached the State Capitol by telegram shortly after 3:00 p.m. on the afternoon of January 11, 1865. The telegram was read on the floor of the House of Representatives by Speaker *Pro Tem* E. H. W. Johnson of St. Louis. The one-sentence message got right to the point: "The Ordinance of Emancipation has just passed the Convention."

The simplicity of the nine-word message belied its profound significance. More than one hundred thousand African American slaves in Missouri were suddenly legally free, their white masters deprived forever of the right to control their labor or to demand a return on the investment involved in their purchase.

A Jefferson City newspaper reported that the news of the passage of the ordinance was met "with vociferous and prolonged applause." Both houses of the legislature adjourned and reconvened in the "Hall of the House" with "Such of the citizens as heard the news" for a celebration. Large-scale celebrations broke out elsewhere in the state, with perhaps the largest occurring in St. Louis. Slavery, which had existed in the state since its inception, was officially ended.

And what was the consequence of this action? To be sure, many Black Missourians were elated at finally obtaining their freedom. But Switzler was right, in that the institution of slavery had ill-prepared many slaves for life after emancipation. Many freedmen and women had few resources upon which to draw when freedom came. They had little or no money, and few if any possessions. They owned no land and no livestock, and they had little if any education. Some chose to stay with their former masters because of the familiarity of their current lives. Such was the case of Hanna Allen, of Madison County. Hanna was approximately thirty-five years old when freedom came in 1865. Decades later, when she was interviewed for a WPA project during the 1930s, she recalled, "I was paid nothin' after slavery but just stayed with de boss and dey gave me things like a calf, clothes, and I got to go to church with dem and to camp meetings and picnics." Thinking, no doubt, of the circumstances of those freedmen who ended up destitute in towns and villages, Allen commented, "I was better off den de free people."

Others reacted just the opposite, resolved to get as far away from their masters as quickly as they could. William Blake of Hannibal fell into this category. He recalled in a WPA interview, "When we was freed our master didn't give us nothing, but some clothes and five dollars. He told us we could stay if we wanted to, but we was so glad to be free dat we all left him."

Those who left their masters' farms and plantations, as has been pointed out, tended to move to towns and villages. The *Louisiana* [Missouri] *Journal* reported on this phenomenon on January 28, 1865: "Since the era of freedom began there has been a pretty steady stream of loyal Africans flowing into our city, and we are informed that Clarksville has likewise received a considerable accession of this class to its population." The editor of the paper expressed concern about this influx: "The towns are overcrowded already with a population that cannot find employment." The editor continued, "There are no vacant houses in the city now, and in some quarters as many as thirty negroes are huddled together in a single small tenement."

Similarly, in Columbia, there was a high incidence of homelessness, destitution, and death among the freedmen in the immediate post-emancipation period. In a March 3, 1865, article titled "Emancipation and Death," the Columbia *Statesman* reported that more than thirty African Americans had died in the city in recent days.

Equally troublesome was the fact that many whites refused to acknowledge the legitimacy of emancipation. General Clinton B. Fisk confronted this reality in the heart of the Missouri Black Belt in the weeks following the adoption of the emancipation ordinance. Writing in the late winter of 1865, Fisk observed: "Slavery dies hard. I hear its expiring agonies and witness its contortions in death in every quarter of my district." According to Fisk, "In Boone, Howard, Randolph, and Callaway [counties] the emancipation ordinance has caused disruption of society equal to anything I saw in Arkansas or Mississippi in the year 1863." Guerrillas such as the notorious Jim Jackson tried to force Blacks to continue on as slaves, to work for whites, to honor the long-held tradition of Black subservience to whites. Regarding Jackson, Fisk commented, "I have no doubt that the monster, Jim Jackson, is instigated by the late slave owners to hang or shoot every negro he can find absent from the old plantations. Some few have driven their black people away from them with nothing to eat or scarcely to wear.

The consequence is . . . the poor blacks are rapidly concentrating in the towns and especially at garrisoned places."

Although slavery had officially ended, the war was destined to continue for three more months. By January 1865 many thought the outcome was both obvious and inevitable. In many ways, the Civil War ended in Missouri with a whimper rather than a bang. The Missouri state capital was no longer seriously threatened after General Sterling Price's aborted raid on it in October 1864. And Price's decisive defeat by Major General Samuel R. Curtis later in the month at the Battle of Westport ended any serious Confederate threat in Missouri.

On April 8, 1865, the *Missouri State Times* reported what seemed to residents to be an announcement of the end of the war: "The Fall of Richmond—Jefferson City jubilant." According to the article, news of the fall of the capital of the Confederacy arrived by telegram on April 3, 1865, and "the news spread like the flames of a prairie fire." That evening, locals filled the Hall of the House of Representatives in the State Capitol to celebrate the news and to begin thinking about reconstructing their lives and the economic, political, and social life of their city and state. Even in the Callaway County seat of Fulton, folks cheered the war's end, at least according to local resident Margaret Bruin Machette, the Missouri-born daughter of native-Virginian parents, who wrote in a letter on April 12, 1865, "The good people of Fulton have had a good time rejoicing over the taking of Richmond and the surrender of Lee and his army. This night [a] week ago the town was illuminated and there was several speeches. Old Ansel [sic] made a speech in which he said the confederacy was in Hell or something to that amount." The war was over!

Or, was it? As former rebel soldiers returned to the capital city during the spring and summer of 1865, hard feelings persisted. "The usual quiet of the Capital was somewhat disturbed a few days since by the appearance upon the streets of two men who left their homes here at the beginning of the war and went South with the rebel army, where they remained, fighting for their rights till the confederacy caved in," reported the *Missouri State Times*. The paper noted that the presence in the city of these men agitated many residents, some of whom threatened to lynch them. Seemingly sympathetic to that course of action, the paper warned, "We really think the responsible people of Jefferson [City] should take this matter in hand, and give notice to men who have rendered themselves obnoxious by their past bad conduct, that they will not be permitted to live here," adding, "We cannot expect men who have been insulted and robbed by rebels to receive them very kindly on their return."

Some weeks later, in late July 1865, a fight occurred in Jefferson City's Virginia Hotel when several veterans of Sterling Price's army came into conflict with "a recently discharged United States Officer." One of the former Confederates reportedly remarked, "Union men may have the power now, but our day will come before long."

Some Missouri supporters of the Confederacy were downright despondent over the war's outcome. Former and future Missouri Supreme Court Judge William Barclay Napton, a large landowner and slaveholder, recorded his reaction to the South's defeat and the ending of slavery in his private journal in late May 1865: "The type of civilization heretofore existing in the slave states of this Union is now at an end. . . . Thus ends one of the finest types of civilization known to this century. . . ." Others found even more dramatic ways to express their displeasure at war's end. Major General Mosby Monroe Parsons, a native of Charlottesville, Virginia, who moved with his family to Jefferson City during the mid-1830s, refused to surrender. A lawyer by training and a former Missouri state legislator, Parsons and three companions, including his brother-in-law, Austin M. Standish, and former Confederate Congressman, Aaron H. Conrow, fled to the nation of Mexico rather than return to Missouri and live under federal rule. Unfortunately for Parsons and his companions, the four men were attacked and captured by Mexican soldiers on August 15, 1865, near China in the Mexican state of Nuevo Leon, just off the northeastern border of Mexico. Their bodies were never recovered.

How would Missourians who had supported opposite visions of the future reconcile their differences after the brutal and divisive civil war that had pitted parts of the state, and in some cases even friends and family members, against one another? What would become of the newly free African Americans, and how would those who had relied on their forced labor adjust to a free economy? And what, then, did the future hold for the divided state of Missouri? Those were the questions Missourians sought to answer—in some ways still strive to answer—as they moved into the postwar world.

The Civil War in Missouri continues to attract scholars in a way that no other topic does. A good starting point for reading on the subject is William E. Parrish's now-classic work, *Turbulent Partnership: Missouri and the Union, 1861–1865* (1963). Other works by Parrish that illuminate Missouri's Civil War experience include *David Rice Atchison of Missouri: Border Politician* (1961); *A History of Missouri: Vol. III, 1860 to 1875* (1973); and *Frank Blair: Lincoln's Conservative* (1998). All these books were published by the University of Missouri Press.

Christopher Phillips has also produced a number of books that are essential to an understanding of the Civil War in Missouri, including his *Damned Yankee: The Life of General Nathaniel Lyon* (1990); *Missouri's Confederate: Claiborne Fox Jackson and the Creation of a Southern Identity in the Border West* (2000); and *The Union on Trial: The Political Journals of Judge William Barclay Napton, 1829–1883*, co-edited with Jason L. Pendleton, all published by the University of Missouri Press. Phillips's most recent book, *The Rivers Ran Backward: The Civil War and the Remaking of the American Middle Border* (2016) was published by Oxford University Press.

The guerrilla war in Missouri is documented in Richard S. Brownlee II, *Gray Ghosts of the Confederacy: Guerrilla Warfare in the West, 1861-1865* (1958), published by Louisiana State University Press. It should be supplemented by Michael Fellman, *Inside War: The Guerrilla Conflict in Missouri During the American Civil War* (1989), published by Oxford University Press. Other works on guerrillas in Missouri during the war include Joseph M. Beilein Jr., and Matthew C. Hulbert, eds., *The Civil War Guerrilla: Unfolding the Black Flag in History, Memory, and Myth* (2015), published by University Press of Kentucky, Joseph M. Beilein Jr., *Bushwhackers: Guerrilla Warfare, Manhood, and the Household in Civil War Missouri* (2016), published by Kent State University Press, and Matthew M. Stith, *Extreme Civil War: Guerrilla Warfare, Environment, and Race on the Trans-Mississippi Frontier* (2016), published by Louisiana State University Press. Mark W. Geiger's *Financial Fraud and Guerrilla Violence in Missouri's Civil War, 1861–1865* (2010), published by Yale University Press, is a highly original work that ties guerrilla activity in the state to a controversial failed scheme aimed at raising funds to defend the state against Union control.

Other useful biographies of Civil War-era figures include Dennis K. Boman, *Lincoln's Resolute Unionist: Hamilton Gamble, Dred Scott Dissenter and Missouri's Civil War Governor* (2006), published by Louisiana State University Press. In addition, Robert E. Shalhope, *Sterling Price: Portrait of a Southerner* (1971); Norma L. Peterson, *Freedom and Franchise: The Political Career of B. Gratz Brown* (1965); and Marvin R. Cain, *Lincoln's Attorney General: Edward Bates of Missouri* (1965), though dated, remain useful. All three books were published by the University of Missouri Press.

Louis Gerteis's *Civil War St. Louis* (2001), published by the University Press of Kansas, and his *The Civil War in Missouri: A Military History* (2012), published by the University of Missouri Press, also add greatly to our understanding of the war in Missouri.

Sharon Romeo's work, *Gender and the Jubilee: Black Freedom and the Reconstruction of Citizenship in Civil War Missouri* (2016), published by the University of Georgia Press, documents the dangers African Americans in the state faced during the war years, and the resilience and resourcefulness that carried them through.

The Civil War continues to be the most popular topic for article submissions to the *Missouri Historical Review. Review* articles prior to the current year can be accessed through the State Historical Society of Missouri's website: www.shsmo.org/publications/missouri-historical-review. In 2006, and again in 2012, the State Historical Society published anthologies of essays on the Civil War that appeared in the *Missouri Historical Review* during its first one hundred years of publication, from 1906 to 2006. The first of these collections, edited by William E. Parrish, is titled *The Civil War in Missouri: Essays from the Missouri Historical Review, 1906–2006.* That volume contains reprints of twelve essays, plus an introduction by Parrish. The 2012 volume, edited by William Garrett Piston, is titled *A Rough Business: Fighting the Civil War in Missouri.* That volume contains fourteen essays, in addition to an introduction by the editor.

Chapter Five

Post–Civil War Missouri
An Age of Reconstruction and Railroads, 1865–1900

"There are certainly no class of people who more richly deserve
the benefits of an education than the colored people of Missouri."

Howard [Glasgow] *Union*, June 15, 1865

THE FORMAL FIGHTING of the Civil War may have ended with Lee's surrender to Grant at Appomattox on April 12, 1865, but the hard feelings and
destruction wrought by the conflict lingered long after that date. Cyrus
Thompson, who lived in Jefferson City during the period from 1865 to
1875, and initially worked in the office of his brother, State Auditor Alonzo
Thompson, summed it up this way: "So soon after the close of the Civil
war [sic] many of those who were active participants in it on one side or the
other, still retained some of the belligerent spirit and were ready to settle
their differences by harsh measures rather than by arbitration and peaceful
methods."

In the wake of the epic struggle, the challenges Americans faced in trying
to reconstruct the state and nation seemed overwhelming, even insur-
mountable. For starters, people were still trying to cope with the great many
deaths and life-altering injuries incurred during the course of the four-year
war. Additionally, there had been a tremendous disruption of trade and
commerce. Many railroads and other routes of commerce had been damaged or destroyed. Houses, barns, fences, crops, and livestock had been
laid waste. Faith in government at all levels had been shaken. Finally, the
enslavement of African Americans, which to varying degrees had operated
both as a source of labor and a vehicle for social control in America for more
than two hundred years, had abruptly come to an end.

The changes wrought by the war were nothing short of revolutionary.
Indeed, at least two Missouri newspapers used the term "revolution" to
describe the ending of slavery. An editor of the *North Missourian* in the

Daviess County town of Gallatin described the ending as "The Revolution Complete," going on to explain, "it is, in the very fullest sense, a revolution, for it has changed our whole domestic economy, our social relations, our institutions, our ideas, our modes of thought, our policy and our habits."

The paper further proclaimed that Missouri could now embark on a new way of doing business, one that held out the promise of economic growth and prosperity. It predicted that "Free hands shall till our soil hereafter[,] free hands shall delve into our mines and bring our buried wealth to light, free hands shall work our engine and drive our locomotives, free hands shall train our flowers and free hearts sing our songs."

The *Kansas City Daily Journal* employed similar language in proclaiming the emancipation of Missouri's slaves to be the completion of a "revolution," and "dawning upon the State [of] a new era." While the editor of the paper regarded the emancipation of slaves as an act of "simple social justice," he also saw it as an action that would transform the state's economy. "We behold peace once more prevailing, among [the state's] now distracted people." Peace and the ending of slavery would bring prosperity: "We see her fields smiling [illegible] in plenty and fast repairing the wastes of war. Free industry directs the plow, the anvil and the loom."

One major change that dramatically impacted Missouri during the war was that many thousands of its residents fled the state because of the widespread violence that occurred there. Civil War historian William E. Parrish estimated that the state lost as much as one-third of its population between 1861 and 1865.

Not surprisingly, then, there was a great push in the immediate postwar period to bring people back to Missouri as well as to recruit new immigrants to the state. Indeed, as early as February 1865, even before the war had concluded, the Missouri legislature created a state Board of Immigration and authorized the expenditure of funds to send agents to the eastern states and to Europe to try to recruit new Missouri citizens to the state.

Groups promoting migration to Missouri advertised the state's natural advantages. One such group, attempting to entice people to come to southwest Missouri, boasted: "The climate is the golden mean of the temperate zone. Its salubrity is proverbial. . . . Consumption and asthmatic complaints never originate here, and are often cured by the climate."

There was still much good farmland available for homesteading in Missouri immediately after the Civil War. Nearly 250,000 acres of public land in Missouri passed into private hands during the first four months of 1866 alone. More than half of that acreage was claimed under the federal Homestead Act of 1862, which provided lots of 160 acres of land in the western United States to those who paid an $18 filing fee (the equivalent of approximately $460 in purchasing power in 2020), built a home on the land, and stayed on it and improved it for five years. Over the course of the five-year period following the Civil War, Missouri's efforts at recovering its population succeeded: by 1870, the state had increased its population to 1,721,295, having grown by more than a half a million people above the 1,182,012 residents recorded in 1860.

No challenge in the postwar period loomed larger than the problem of accommodating the needs of the roughly one hundred thousand former slaves who had been set free. How would they live, and how would white Missourians adjust to the freedmen's new status? What, indeed, would freedom come to mean for Black Missourians?

In its simplest form, "freedom" to the former slaves meant being able to do those things they could not do as slaves, things most white Americans took for granted: go someplace where and when they wanted, court whom they wanted to and marry should they choose, have children whom someone else could not take away from them, attend or even establish churches of their own choosing, go to or send their children to school, and determine the circumstances of their employment, perhaps even own their own property.

Property ownership was especially important to the immediate postwar generation of freed people. As historian Leon Litwack has noted, "With the acquisition of land, the ex-slave viewed himself entering the mainstream of American life, cultivating his own farm and raising the crops with which to sustain himself and his family. That was the way to respectability in an agricultural society, and the freedman insisted that a plot of land was all he required to lift himself up." Colonel Theodore H. Barrett, the white commander of the 62nd United States Colored Infantry, one of the regimental founders of Lincoln Institute, offered this advice to the Black members of his unit as the group disbanded in January 1866: "I advise everyone to get for himself a piece of land, for a home. . . . It is a great deal better for you to live upon your own land, than to hire land from another, or to work for another."

Land ownership, however, was difficult and unusual for recently enslaved Black Missourians. Joseph Penny of Saline County was a rare exception to this rule. After working as a tenant farmer for a few years, Penny accumulated enough savings by 1871 to purchase eight acres of land on the edge of Saline County's great rolling prairie and within the timbered breaks of Blackwater River drainage. Over the course of the next decade, other Black farmers purchased small tracts adjacent to Penny's, until a freedmen's hamlet named "Pennytown" emerged, giving these Black freedmen and women greater control over their own lives than they had ever had before.

Fig. 23: Joseph Penny (center), a former enslaved person from Kentucky, purchased land in Saline County, Missouri, in 1871. A freedmen's settlement, Pennytown, grew up around his original landholding. Credit: Lynn Morrow Papers, State Historical Society of Missouri. Collection No. R1000.

More common in the postwar period was the experience of Black residents in the not-too-distant Saline County village of Arrow Rock. African Americans made up approximately a quarter of the village's population throughout the generation following the Civil War, but as late as 1880, fifteen years after emancipation, a majority of Blacks continued to live in white households as servants and cooks.

Even among those white Missourians willing to accept the legal end to slavery, there was widespread unwillingness to accept the notion that Blacks and whites could ever live in the same society as equals. As one newspaper summed up the sentiment, "We believe that God, when he created men, made the white man a little better than the red or black." John Fletcher, from the Jefferson County town of De Soto, and a brother of Missouri Governor Thomas Fletcher, made his feelings known as a delegate to the 1865 Missouri constitutional convention, originally called for by the state General Assembly in January of that year: "I am not here for the purpose of giving any rights to the negro further than the right of freedom. I desired to see every slave in the state freed, and I desire to see every slave in the country free, but when they are free, I am done with them." A Lexington newspaper known as the *Weekly Caucasian* was equally blunt. In an 1866 editorial, the paper indicated its hope for the future: "We want to see them all quietly and happily settle in Liberia, where they may enjoy the full blessings of liberty. . . . Here, these blessings can never be enjoyed by the African. . . . The position of the negro is that of vassalage here. . . ."

Newspapers throughout the state competed with each other to draw attention to African American impropriety, criminality, and general immorality by way of demonstrating that African Americans should not be regarded as the equals of whites. In September 1865, for example, the Howard County newspaper, the *Fayette Advertiser*, reported: "On Monday of this week, two negroes were arrested in Fayette for petty larceny." Four months later, numerous Missouri papers carried a story about a "disgraceful scene in the shape of drunken men." In Oregon, Missouri, however, the Holt County *Sentinel* acknowledged that "the negro is to remain in our midst, as one of the peoples of the land." Given that reality, the paper editorialized, Missouri should educate African Americans: "It will be for us to make him better. . . . We can already see, that at no very distant day, he will prove himself worthy. . . . We should make the best of him."

With the latter opinion, African Americans agreed; having been denied access to education by state law during the days of slavery, education was among the most sought-after goals of the freedmen. As the African American historian, W. E. B. DuBois wrote in his classic work, *Black Reconstruction in America*, "[Former slaves] wanted to know. . . . They were consumed with curiosity at the meaning of the world. . . . They were consumed with [a] desire for schools."

Some whites supported the effort to educate freedmen. *The Howard Union* [Glasgow] endorsed a "School for Colored Children" in a June 15, 1865, article, commenting, "there are certainly no class of people, who more richly deserve the benefits of an education than the colored people of Missouri." The paper added, "No one denies a white person, however little or great the mind may be, the right to an education, as high as it is possible to acquire; why then, should the same be denied the colored person." Indeed, at least one white educator, Lincoln Institute Principal Richard B. Foster, argued that whites "owed" the former slaves educational opportunities. In an early form of the "reparations" argument, Foster, speaking to a State Teachers' Association meeting in St. Louis in 1869, proclaimed: "From the first settlement of this State down to 1865, the Negroes were deprived of liberty and incidentally of education. During that period their unremu-nerated labor created a vast amount of the material wealth of the State." As a result, Foster argued, freedmen should be given "the widest possible opportunity for education, to let them have the fullest chance to find out what capacities God has given them. . . ." To illustrate his point, he spoke of his "friend and neighbor," a former slave in Jefferson City named Cyrus Trigg, who "was 68 years old when freedom came." Foster argued that the state of Missouri owed Trigg for decades of lost wages, and that one way to begin paying down this debt was for the state to dramatically increase the amount of money it was spending on educating African Americans.

In the immediate aftermath of the Civil War, the Missouri legislature, dominated by Radical Republicans, who had organized in 1863 around the notions of immediate emancipation, the recruitment of immigrants, and efforts to attract new capital to the state, argued that the rights of citi-zenship must be granted to the newly freed slaves and all Black Americans. They passed a law requiring each township or city board of education in the state to establish and maintain schools for Blacks in jurisdictions where Black school-age children numbered twenty or more. School terms for Blacks were to be equal in length to those for whites, unless attendance dropped below twelve, in which case the Black school could be closed for a period of up to six months. Where there were fewer than twenty Black children in a district, school boards could provide for Black educational needs as they saw fit.

Many communities began to establish schools for Blacks within a year or two of war's end. The *Weekly North Missouri Courier* reported on October 24, 1867, that "The Colored School at La Grange [Lewis County], opened on Tuesday the 8th with a good attendance." The paper added, "Miss Mattie Spencer has been selected as the teacher, and as she is a young lady of educa-tion, an[d] intelligence, and some experience in teaching, the education of the colored children will doubtless progress well and rapidly."

Similarly, the Benton County town of Warsaw opened a "colored school" about the same time. According to a newspaper account, African Americans gave up on waiting for whites to open a school for them: they "have taken the bull by the horns," established a school, and hired a Black teacher, "a dusky son of Ham, a veritable descendant of Canaan."

Many other communities from all over the state established schools for African American children. Still, by 1869, Foster argued that data provided by the state superintendent of schools revealed that only about two thousand of Missouri's thirty-four thousand "colored children 'of educable age'" were enrolled in Missouri's public schools. While some whites supported the establishment of public schools for African Americans, no doubt many others agreed with the man in charge of the Mississippi County schools, when in 1871 he wrote in his annual report to the state superintendent of public schools, "The breed of negroes of this latitude are returning to their primeval state. . . . To attempt to educate them is folly."

In 1869, four years after the ending of the Civil War, state superintendent of schools, the Radical Republican Thomas A. Parker, joined forces with the Freedmen's Bureau, established by Congress in March 1865 to assist freed slaves in adjusting to their new circumstances, and the American Missionary Association, a Protestant-based group begun in New York in 1846 to oppose slavery and to assist freed Blacks during and immediately following the war, to investigate the condition of Black education in the state and advance its cause. They hired as their investigating agent one of the best educated African Americans in the state, James Milton Turner, who had been born a slave in St. Louis in 1839. Freed as a child and educated in clandestine St. Louis schools and at Oberlin College in Ohio, Turner was one of the most visible and widely recognized African Americans in Missouri during the generation after the Civil War.

Turner first came to be recognized by the Radical Republicans by virtue of his involvement with the Missouri Equal Rights League, a Black organization that worked with various white philanthropic groups attempting to advance the rate of assimilation and adjustment of freedmen to their new status.

The Missouri Equal Rights League was part of a larger "convention movement" that took place throughout the former slaveholding states immediately after the war. The organizational meeting of the Missouri Equal Rights League occurred in St. Louis on October 3, 1865. According to the

Tri-Weekly Missouri Democrat, the meeting was called "for the purpose of advancing the rights of the race and promoting the interests of the colored people in the State."

One outgrowth of this meeting was the creation of a 1,700-word *Address to the Friends of Equal Rights*, which was printed and distributed widely throughout the state, both as a broadside and as a newspaper proclamation. The *Address* drew upon one of the American people's most hallowed documents, the Declaration of Independence, and framed the Civil War as a holy battle between good and evil, between an advanced civilization and a relic of barbarism.

The *Address* called especially for Black access to the ballot box, but also, more generally, for assistance for freedmen so that they could control their own destinies without becoming burdens on society. Subsequently, the equal rights movement added access to education for freedmen to their goals, and increasingly turned to their secretary, James Milton Turner, to carry this message throughout the state.

Turner threw himself into this work as only a man on a mission could. He travelled in circles that Black Missourians had rarely before frequented, reporting in September 1869 that he had spoken with the governor about a suspicious murder in Fayette. The former slave, who had spent the bulk of his life living in a state that restricted the movement of even free Blacks, now enjoyed the opportunity to move about the state at will. It was a heady experience.

Turner's work on behalf of Black education led him to an understanding that a shortage of African American teachers was a major stumbling block to his effort to establish schools for Black children. Quite simply, many African American parents did not want their children taught by white teachers.

Turner sought to turn a fledging private school for African Americans in Jefferson City, Lincoln Institute, into a state-supported facility where African Americans could be trained to become teachers. Established in 1866 largely through the financial contributions of former Missouri slaves who served in the U.S. Colored Infantry, Lincoln Institute began receiving state funds in 1871, in the wake of a deal struck between Turner and the Radical Republicans of Missouri. Turner agreed to campaign intensely for the Republicans among newly enfranchised Black voters, beneficiaries of the ratification of the Fifteenth Amendment to the U.S. Constitution in

1870, in exchange for a state appropriation of $5,000 for Lincoln Institute. The school was taken over completely by state government in 1879.

Apart from their search for access to education, many freedmen struggled just to make a living during the generation after the Civil War. Most had little to help them in the transition to freedom: no land, no livestock, no tools or equipment, no family members who could take them in and help them get a new start. In many ways, they were like the refugees of twenti-eth- and twenty-first century wars, cast from their homes with little more than the clothes on their backs and the knowledge and experience of hard work to help them along.

Some former masters were moved to help their former slaves get a new start, either as free laborers within their own households, or as freedmen in new jobs. In a late-life memoir titled *Plantation Life in Missouri*, Berenice Morrison-Fuller, granddaughter of a large Howard County slave owner, remembered the slaves' transition to freedom in a self-serving, paternalistic way. "On the large plantations," she wrote, "or farms, old customs still pre-vailed, and many of the servants, as many as could be cared for, remained, although slavery was a thing of the past." Offering her own assessment that former slaves were neither mentally nor physically prepared to care for themselves, Morrison-Fuller noted, "It was an accepted fact that the Negro could not be turned out into the cold world, of which he had no experience, and left to shift for himself. So the erstwhile master assumed the burden as best he could."

While it is true that some Blacks chose to stay with their former masters and work as free laborers, the circumstances were rarely as beneficent and altruistic as Morrison-Fuller's comments suggest. The truth was that many landowners had neither the labor force nor expertise to continue to produce crops on their own. Writing in 1914, T. C. Rainey, a white man who had arrived in Saline County's Arrow Rock by way of Tennessee and Springfield, Missouri, remembered the dire circumstance he found in that Missouri River community when he got there in the fall of 1865: "The negroes were freed," he remembered, "and the former owner[s] not well trained to hard labor. Farms and fences were neglected, the roads in miserable condition, and the people without capital and discouraged."

While the question of whether to allow African Americans to vote was decided in the affirmative through the Fifteenth Amendment, the question of allowing women the franchise was not. The National Women's Suffrage

Association, founded in 1869, took the position that the Fourteenth Amendment to the United States, which guaranteed all citizens the equal protection of the laws, granted women full civil and political rights. In 1869, NWSA member and St. Louis resident Virginia Minor addressed a national suffrage convention in St. Louis and proclaimed the following: "The Constitution of the United States gives me every right and privilege to which every other citizen is entitled."

In 1872, Minor acted upon this assertion, appearing before the St. Louis registrar of voters to register and vote in the 1872 presidential election. Thwarted by the registrar and denied legal standing because of her gender, Minor sued the registrar, Reese Happersett, through her attorney husband, arguing that Minor's constitutional rights had been violated. She lost her case at the local level, and appealed to the Missouri Supreme Court, where she lost again. Still determined, she appealed her case all the way to the U.S. Supreme Court, which rendered its judgment on March 29, 1875.

Writing for the court in the case of *Happersett* v. *Minor*, U.S. Supreme Court Chief Justice Morrison Remick Waite opined that while women were, indeed, citizens of the United States, citizenship did not automatically confer the right to vote. That right, the court asserted, was to be granted or withheld by individual states. Thus, women would have to wait until the ratification of the Nineteenth Amendment to the U.S. Constitution in 1920 to gain the right to vote. Unfortunately, Virginia Minor, who died in 1894, did not live to see that occurrence.

Whatever measure of animosity toward Southerners and supporters of secession that might have persisted immediately after the war seems to have largely dissipated in Missouri by the mid-1870s. In 1874, for example, Missourians elected Charles Henry Hardin, whose loyalty to the United States had been questioned during the early years of the war, to the state's highest office.

A native of Trimble County, Kentucky, Hardin moved with his family to Columbia, Missouri, as an infant. His father established a tannery there, a business in which the son worked as a boy. Hardin attended school in Columbia before furthering his education in Indiana and Ohio. He returned to Columbia to practice law during the early 1840s. He became involved in politics during the 1850s as a Whig and was elected to the Missouri House of Representatives in 1852, 1854, and 1858. He was elected to the state senate in 1860 and attended the rump legislative session called by exiled, secessionist Governor Claiborne Fox Jackson in October 1861. To his credit, Hardin cast the only senate vote against secession among those senators present. Despite that vote, his presence at the legislative session cast doubt on his loyalty, and he was disenfranchised by the state's Provisional Government. He sat out the war on his farm near Mexico, Missouri, and was returned to the senate by voters in 1872. By that time, Hardin benefitted, in part, from the early 1870s abandonment of the so-called "Test Oath," the war-time measure carried into the postwar period that had required candidates for office to swear loyalty to the Union.

Perhaps more striking was the election in 1875 of Francis M. Cockrell to the U.S. Senate by the Missouri General Assembly. A native of Johnson County, Missouri, Cockrell attended elementary school in his home county and college at Chapel Hill College in Lafayette County. He began the practice of law in Warrensburg in 1855. The 1860 U.S. federal census slave schedules indicate that Cockrell owned two slaves that year: a forty-two-year-old female and a twelve-year-old male, presumably a mother and son. Charles Henry Hardin, by the way, owned four slaves, three males and one female, on his Callaway County farm in 1850.

Cockrell enlisted in the Missouri State Guard in May 1861. This unit was formed earlier by secessionist Governor Claiborne Fox Jackson to try to repel an "invasion" of Missouri by Union forces. By July 1863 he had been appointed brigadier general. He fought in many of the major battles of the war, including Vicksburg, and was wounded five times and captured three! Despite his many efforts to overthrow the government of the United States, he subsequently served as a U.S. senator in the same government for thirty years.

His contemporary in the Senate, George Graham Vest, was also a veteran of the Confederate war effort. A native of Frankfort, Kentucky, and a graduate of Central College in Danville and the University of Transylvania, Vest began practicing law in Missouri in the mid-1850s. A resident of Boonville on the eve of the Civil War, Vest was elected to the Missouri House in 1860 and became an outspoken supporter of secession. He joined the Confederate cause and fought at the Battle of Wilson's Creek in 1861 and participated in the Confederate rump legislatures in Neosho and Cassville later that year. He later served in the Confederate House and Senate. None of these activities disqualified him, as far as Missourians were concerned, from serving in the U.S. Senate from 1879 to 1903.

Missouri life had been disrupted tremendously by the war. Roughly ten times the number of Missourians fought for the Union as for the Confederacy. Thousands of Missourians fled the violence of the war and the guerrillas who supported it. Missouri businesses, including railroads, were disrupted and, in some instances, destroyed. All this notwithstanding, Missourians were quick to forgive those who had wreaked such havoc on their state. Yet another measure of how thoroughly Missourians had gotten over their anger toward the South was the reception they accorded Jefferson Davis, the former president of the Confederacy, when he visited Missouri in September 1875. Davis's trip was aimed ostensibly at promoting agriculture and trade throughout the Mississippi River Valley. His first stop was in the Jefferson County town of De Soto, where, according to the *St. Louis Post-Dispatch*, he was "warmly welcomed." No doubt his warmest reception came in Fulton, the county seat of Callaway County, one of Missouri's largest slave-owning counties during the years leading up to the war. A crowd of from ten to twenty thousand people greeted him in Fulton with "cheers for Jeff Davis repeatedly rising from the assembled." Some in the crowd indicated that they had fought under Davis and for the Confederacy, though the Mississippian tellingly emphasized that he was there "to speak as an American" and that "he did not want to be considered a partisan about anything. . . ." Davis did say that "if ever he removed to a Kingdom it would be the Kingdom of Callaway." When he was finished with his remarks, Davis was treated to a rousing rendition of "Dixie" played by a local band.

While present in central Missouri, Davis was the overnight guest of Missouri Governor Charles H. Hardin in the state's Executive Mansion. A few days later, Davis spoke again to Missourians, this time in Kansas City. Again, he emphasized a message of unity, noting, in particular, "the people who dwell in the [Mississippi River] Valley must be united." He further noted that he came "not to discuss these questions which vex the minds and disturb the harmony which prevails among the people," noting, "If there are any who still entertain a feeling of malice, or cherish bitterness on account of the past, let us withdraw from such."

A final example of how much Missourians were seemingly "over" the bitter feelings associated with the Civil War lies in the way they voted for and supported gubernatorial candidate John Sappington Marmaduke in his 1884 race for governor. A native of Saline County, Missouri, Marmaduke was the son of Meredith Miles Marmaduke, eighth governor of Missouri.

A West Point graduate, class of 1857, the younger Marmaduke defied his Unionist father's advice and joined the secessionist-supporting Missouri State Guard and was commissioned as a colonel by his uncle, Missouri's pro-Confederate governor, Claiborne Fox Jackson.

Ultimately, Colonel Marmaduke resigned his state commission and volunteered for service in the Confederate army, and ended up serving under his Mormon War mentor, Albert Sydney Johnston. Subsequently wounded at the Battle of Shiloh, Marmaduke was promoted to the rank of brigadier general. Despite his strong support for the Confederacy, Marmaduke was chosen by Missourians to be their governor, although his margin of victory was significantly less than that of other Missouri Democrats running on statewide tickets. One newspaper, the *St. Joseph Weekly Gazette*, attributed this outcome to the fact that "it was Marmaduke's service in the Southern Confederacy, and that service alone, which reduced his vote so much below the vote received by all the balance of his associates upon the same ticket. . . ." That judgment notwithstanding, the newspaper proclaimed, "Marmaduke will make so good a Governor that the great masses of the people will be forced to say: If that is your Southern Confederacy, give us some more of it."

There is a suggestion in this last comment that hints at a reason Missourians reconciled relatively easily over their differences within a decade or so after the war. Perhaps it had something to do with the recognition that competent people, regardless of which side they took during the war, needed to work together to promote the best interests of the state, much as Jefferson Davis had argued during his 1875 visit to Missouri. Historian Jeremy Neely has provided an example of this in his book, *The Border between Them: Violence and Reconciliation on the Kansas-Missouri Line* (2007). As Neely points out, after the war, Kansas and Missouri commercial interests overcame their "old partisan rivalries" because they recognized the need to work together to promote railroad construction that promised to serve the interests of the citizens of both states.

But if the lingering war-time hostilities had lessened considerably by the mid-1880s in Missouri, there were still those who nursed the anger and encouraged retribution and rage. Arguably, no one fit this description better than the James brothers, Frank and Jesse. Southern-sympathizing guerrillas during the war, and revenge-seeking outlaws after it, the James boys and their compatriots refused to accept the war's outcome. As the *Kansas City*

Times explained, "They continued the war after the war ended." Jesse James resolved to fight against those who sought to make over the South in the Northern image. And he resolved to seek revenge against all persons who had wreaked havoc on his beloved South and its ways, including the way of slavery. As James's biographer, the talented T. J. Stiles, points out, by the time that Jesse James was shot and killed by a member of his own gang in St. Joseph, Missouri, on April 3, 1882, he had become an anachronism. The nation and the state, "who no longer wished to dwell on their divisions," as Stiles wrote, "had passed James by." In death, James was reborn in the folklore of the nation as a progressive Robin Hood, a social bandit who robbed from the rich so that he could give to the poor. In counter fact, he was a violent, revenge-seeking Confederate sympathizer who could not accept the fact that slavery had ended and that the South had lost not only the war, but also the peace. In that regard, as Stiles has written, "Jesse James was a forerunner of the modern terrorist."

One of the symbols of the future that James seemed to despise intensely was the railroad, and in post–Civil War Missouri it was the railroad that seemed to hold the key to the future for the state and its residents. The building of railroads in Missouri fundamentally changed the lives of Missourians during the generation after the Civil War. Like the steamboats before them, the railroads once again changed people's sense of time and space, where they lived and where and how they worked, even how and where they spent their leisure time.

By the eve of the Civil War, there were only 810 miles of railroad constructed in the entire state. Only the Hannibal & St. Joseph Railroad, connecting those two river cities, crossed the state of Missouri. Begun in 1851 and completed in 1859, the Hannibal & St. Joseph Railroad connected the rich farmlands in northern Missouri to markets in two of Missouri's largest cities and beyond. During the latter half of the Civil War decade, the Missouri General Assembly, controlled by the business-friendly Radical Republicans, incurred unprecedented levels of public debt to promote the building of railroads.

In 1869, the Hannibal Bridge was erected in Kansas City, marking the first time the mighty Missouri River had been spanned anywhere. That bridge, designed by French immigrant engineer Octave Chanute, helped to catapult Kansas City into an era of significant growth, both in terms of population and commercial expansion.

The Pacific Railroad, which advocates had hoped would connect Missouri's two largest cities by means of a Missouri River route, was finally completed in September 1865, five months after the Civil War ended. On September 21, 1865, the first passenger train to cross the state from Kansas City to St. Louis made the trip in fourteen hours, rather than the eighty-plus hours it took by foot or on horseback.

St. Louis and Kansas City were further connected in 1869, with the completion of the North Missouri Railroad. This route arced across the state, connecting the rich farmlands of forty-four counties of northern Missouri and a few counties in southeast Iowa to the emerging urban markets of St. Louis and Kansas City. This connection was greatly enhanced with the bridging of the Missouri River at St. Charles in May 1871.

Two other railroads of the era facilitated population growth and commercial expansion into the Ozarks. The first was the St. Louis, Iron Mountain, and Southern Railway, more commonly known as the Iron Mountain Railway. Originally built to connect St. Louis to the rich iron deposits located in Iron Mountain in southwestern St. Francois County, this line was authorized by legislation passed by the Missouri General Assembly in 1851. The Iron Mountain Railway was completed to Pilot Knob in Iron County in 1858. After a series of financial setbacks and multiple reorganizations, the railroad reached the Missouri-Arkansas state line in November 1872.

Yet another important railroad into the interior of the Ozarks soon after the Civil War was what was known as the Southwest Branch of the Pacific Railroad, which was authorized during the early 1850s to branch off of the main Pacific Railroad east-west route across Missouri. This line aimed to connect the main route to Rolla in Phelps County and Springfield in Greene County. Only eight miles of track had been laid by 1861, with further expansion of the route delayed until after the war. Suspended during the war, work on the line resumed after fighting stopped. By 1866, twelve more miles of track had been laid, this time to Arlington in Phelps County. After multiple financial failures and buyouts, the railroad reached Springfield in 1870 as the South Pacific Railroad. Ultimately, this company was acquired by the St. Louis-San Francisco Railroad (the "Frisco"), which continued to operate in the Missouri Ozarks until 1980.

By 1870, Missouri had 2,000 miles of railroad completed, more than twice the 810 miles it had just a decade earlier. By 1880, that figure nearly doubled again, to 3,965 miles. It seemed as though all Missourians wanted to be on or near a railroad. Communities sought out, solicited, even bribed railroad owners to lay track through or even near their towns, passing large bond issues to foot the bills. Some towns, such as Pilot Grove in Cooper County and Lohman in Cole County, moved to be near railroads. Missourians quickly discovered that they could grow, make, and mine things that people elsewhere in the state and nation wanted, and that those things could be marketed anywhere railroads ran.

But even with the coming of the railroads, a majority of Missourians continued to make their living by farming during the generation after the Civil War, though the presence and promise of the railroads impacted what they grew and how they grew it. Henry Clay Dean, a preacher and political activist during and after the war, urged the expansion of railroads throughout the state in an 1879 speech before the State Board of Agriculture: "We must penetrate every accessible part of the State with railways until everything we have to sell is brought to the door of the market. Our wetlands must be drained and our uplands fertilized, and skilled farmers of other states invited to make their homes among us."

Missouri farmers increasingly became market farmers after the Civil War. Although they had long been used to marketing some of their excess produce to help pay for things they could not grow or make, marketing goods for cash became far more important to them during the years after the war than they were before it. The ongoing effort to attract immigrants to the state, both foreign and domestic, by the railroads and government officials added to the impulse.

Agricultural reformers advocated that farmers focus on commercial farming, maximizing their crop output by turning to "scientific agriculture," the application of scientific methods to farming. To facilitate this effort, the state-supported University of Missouri, urged on by curator and agriculturist Norman J. Colman, established a College of Agriculture in 1870 and in 1882 recruited a well-known agricultural researcher, Jeremiah W. Sanborn, to serve as college dean. Sanborn began holding "institutes" across the state, introducing Missouri farmers to the techniques of scientific farming.

In 1885, Colman, the progressive Missouri farmer, was appointed U.S. Commissioner of Agriculture by President Grover Cleveland. Soon thereafter, Colman partnered with U.S. Representative William Henry Hatch,

Fig. 24: An elderly Norman J. Colman, a leading figure in nineteenth-century agriculture, appears with Governor Herbert Hadley at the Missouri State Fair in October 1910. Credit: State Historical Society of Missouri, Herbert Spencer Hadley Papers, Collection C0006.

yet another Missouri public official who was a former Confederate officer, to persuade Congress to create and fund agricultural experiment stations throughout the country. These stations were to serve as places of scientific agricultural experimentation from which agricultural knowledge could be discovered and disseminated. The Hatch Act, arguably one of the most far-reaching and farsighted efforts of agricultural promotion made during the late nineteenth century, was named for a Georgetown, Kentucky, native who moved to Hannibal to practice law during the mid-1850s, served as a Confederate officer during the war, and engaged in farming in the Hannibal area before being elected to Congress in 1878. Agricultural historian R. Douglas Hurt has called the Hatch Act "one of the most important pieces of legislation passed by Congress because the research conducted at the stations affects every resident in the United States."

Agriculture and agricultural production expanded tremendously in Missouri during the post–Civil War generation. In 1870, Missourians cared for 148,328 farms and had 9,130,615 acres under cultivation. By

1880, those figures had jumped to 215,575 farms and 16,745,031 acres under cultivation.

Dramatic examples of increases in agricultural output and the connected role of railroad expansion occurred all over the state. Wayne County in southeast Missouri had no access to a railroad prior to 1870. But after the small town of Piedmont was made a division point on the Iron Maintain Railway, agricultural production boomed. In 1870, the county had 27,489 acres under cultivation and produced 293,569 bushels of corn. A decade later, 47,234 acres had been brought under cultivation and corn production reached 617,271 bushels. Similar stories of expansion occurred all over the state. Indeed, as a barometer of this growth, the *Kansas City Star* noted in 1893 that "Kansas City received more than five times as much grain in 1892 as in 1888 and more than fifteen times as much as in 1875."

Ironically, the growth in the number of acres under cultivation and the increased productivity of the soil did not bring the universal prosperity for farmers that many had predicted and expected. Even though Missouri agriculturists increased the acreage they cultivated from slightly over nine million acres in 1870 to nearly seventeen million in 1880, the value of the products they produced actually declined from $103,035,759 in 1870 to $95,912,666 in 1880. What was happening, and why? Who or what was to blame for the farmers' relative decline in prosperity?

Many farmers and their supporters blamed outside forces which they claimed victimized them: the railroads that charged them too much for shipping their goods to urban markets; the banks that charged them too much interest when they had to borrow money; the wholesalers who purchased their products before marking up their prices to consumers. Farmers in Missouri and elsewhere tried to organize to help their common cause. In 1870, a former U.S. Bureau of Agriculture employee who had recently moved to Missouri, Oliver Hudson Kelley, organized the first Missouri chapter of the Patrons of Husbandry, more commonly referred to as the "Grange." This organization sought to improve farmers' social and economic lives. Although the Grange spread widely throughout Missouri, and other agricultural states, it never achieved the success its promoters envisioned.

In truth, much of the problem lay with the farmers themselves. Their efforts at expanding production were so successful that their overproduction drove the prices of agricultural products down. In addition, national markets for agricultural goods created by the railroads forced Missouri farmers to compete with agricultural producers from all over the country. As unit prices paid farmers declined, the only solution they could see was to produce still more, hoping that the increased volume of sales would make up for the decline in unit price. Often, they were able to do this only by borrowing money—for seeds, tools and supplies, and late in the century farm machinery—from bankers who charged them high interest rates. It was a vicious circle that led many farmers to greater indebtedness and a growing feeling that they were being taken advantage of by people and forces over which they had no control. As historian Floyd Shoemaker wrote, "The farmer's discontent was heightened when he saw how fortunes were being made in other enterprises."

While the number of farms and farmers increased significantly in Missouri during the second half of the nineteenth century, towns and cities grew even more quickly as labor-saving implements and devices displaced farm hands, causing many laborers to leave rural areas and head to cities in search of work. Colman's *Rural World*, a newspaper published twice monthly in St. Louis "for the benefit of the farmer," noted in 1879 that "with the improved implements and machines we now have, a farmer with one hired man can carry on farming on a larger scale than he could a generation ago with half a dozen hired men." The State Bureau of Labor Statistics noted in its 1885 report that the "expansion of labor-saving machinery on the farm has forced the laborer to seek other employment."

That "other employment" was most likely to be found in one of the many burgeoning towns and cities in Missouri, most of them along railroad lines. Examples of this phenomenon abound, but the case of Helena, a town in northwest Missouri's Andrew County, illustrates the point. In 1878, two local farmers in the area heard that a narrow-gauge railroad between St. Joseph and Albany might run right through their farms. Eager to seize on any economic prospects that might accompany the railroad, the farmers plotted a town site on their lands. The railroad was completed through the aborning town in 1879. By the time the census was taken the next year, the town had thirty-one residents, including a "Grain Dealer," a saloon, a drugstore, a feed mill, and a hotel. The establishment of these businesses attracted more merchants, mechanics, carpenters, and black-smiths. By decade's end, the town had three hundred residents and scores of job opportunities for non-farmers.

Fig. 25: Rural free delivery of mail was introduced into Missouri in 1896. Gustav Fisher, shown in this undated image, was the first mail carrier on the Hermann route. Credit: State Historical Society of Missouri, Edward J. Kemper Collection, Collection No. C4388.

This scenario played out over and over again throughout Missouri during the decades following the Civil War. Sedalia, in Pettis County, grew dramatically because of its location at the intersection of multiple railroads. A small town of roughly 300 on the eve of the Civil War, Sedalia grew to 4,560 people in 1870 and 9,561 in 1880. By 1873, Sedalia was connected directly by rail to markets as far south as Denison, Texas, and as far east as Chicago. By 1876 more than 200 resident railroad employees made their homes in Sedalia. By the mid-1880s the town had four banks, five building and loan associations, at least seven hotels, multiple mills and grain elevators, saw mills, brick-making establishments, and a plethora of merchants, butchers, bakers, milliners, and tailors, plus a requisite number of doctors and the ever-present lawyers. Non-farming jobs were readily available, including by late century in Sedalia, the occupation of "Musician," which was how the soon-to-be King of Ragtime, Scott Joplin, described himself to a census taker in 1900. It was the vibrancy, vitality and commercial growth in Sedalia that had attracted Joplin from Texas several years earlier.

Joplin, Missouri, in the southwest corner of the state, enjoyed the most spectacular growth of any outstate Missouri town during the period from 1875 to 1890. Joplin's growth began during the early 1870s, when iron ore was discovered by Eli R. Moffet, a native of California, and John B. Sergeant, a native of Indiana who identified himself in the 1880 federal census as "Manfr. Of Pig Lead." By the late 1870s, Moffet and Sergeant had linked Joplin to Girard, Kansas, by means of the thirty-nine-mile-long Joplin and Girard Railroad. When that line was sold in 1879 to the St. Louis and San Francisco (Frisco) Railroad, Joplin's iron ore could be marketed all over the country. Joplin, which had not existed in 1870, saw its population soar to 7,038 in 1880 and nearly 10,000 by 1890. As a result, a wide array of business and job opportunities emerged in Joplin, giving residents of the city new and lucrative alternatives to agricultural employment.

Missouri's largest city, St. Louis, grew tremendously during the last half of the nineteenth century. Its population reached 351,189 by 1870 and grew by another one hundred thousand over the next two decades, reaching 451,770 in 1890. The completion of the James B. Eads Bridge across the Mississippi River into Illinois in 1874 represented both a literal and figurative connecting link to eastern cities and markets. The value of manufactured goods produced in St. Louis jumped from an estimated $27 million in 1870 to $114.3 million in 1880, and then doubled again to $228.7 million by 1890. Industrial workers in the city totaled 41,824 in 1880 and 93,610 in 1890. By 1890, St. Louis had become the fourth largest city in the United States, and seemed poised for even further growth and success in the twentieth century.

As spectacular as St. Louis's growth was during this period, Kansas City's was even more dramatic. By 1880, eleven railway lines ran through Kansas City, and displaced farmers and farm laborers from Missouri and Kansas were flocking to the city for jobs in the packing houses and factories that had sprouted up there. Kansas City had 32,000 people in 1870. By 1890, that number had grown to 132,716, making it the twenty-fourth-largest city in the country.

By the 1890s, then, Missouri was increasingly becoming more urban and industrial, although most of its people still lived and worked on farms. In 1891 Missouri Labor Commissioner Willard C. Hall devoted a significant portion of his agency's annual report to the legislature to a description and analysis of manufacturing in the state. He identified manufacturing establishments in 86 of Missouri's 114 counties and the City of St. Louis. This represented 1,849 establishments employing 63,399 workers, 52,434 of whom were males. In providing these figures, Hall was also documenting the changing face of labor in industrializing Missouri.

The growing urbanization of life in Missouri during the late nineteenth century spawned many changes in how residents of the state lived. Cities became increasingly crowded, noisy, and dirty, leading urban residents to seek recreation, temporary relief, and rest from their urban, manufacturing lives. To meet this change, cities began to develop parks, urban spaces with trees and meadows where city dwellers could enjoy a semblance of bucolic ruralness even in the heart of a large metropolitan area. Fittingly, Missouri's largest city, St. Louis, led the way in what historians refer to as the park movement.

St. Louis began to create Forest Park on the outskirts of St. Louis during the latter years of the Civil War. It took more than a decade before the park was completed and open to city residents. When the day finally came, an estimated crowd of some 50,000 people gathered for the park's dedication on June 24, 1876. The park's 1,375-acre space was a heavily wooded tract, significantly larger than the 843-acre Central Park completed in New York City in the same year. Kansas City's Swope Park, named for philanthropist Thomas H. Swope, who donated the 1,769 acres that formed the park, was opened in 1896. Forest Park and Swope Park have for more than a century allowed urban residents the opportunity to commune with nature in ways that would have otherwise been impossible, although for much of the late nineteenth and early twentieth century, at least, those parks were racially segregated. Kansas City Blacks, for example, were confined to a limited area of Swope Park known as "Watermelon Hill."

As urban life became more congested and as negative aspects of urban living—crime, noise, filth, and in some neighborhoods, overcrowding—became more intense, urban elites who could afford it turned to the Missouri Ozarks for recreational hunting and fishing and other outdoor escapes, often employing the growing network of Missouri railroads that could take them deep into the hill country.

Historian Lynn Morrow has pointed out, for example, that by the late nineteenth century, "Rail excursions on the St. Louis and San Francisco Railway (Frisco) . . . made the village of Arlington in Phelps County a gateway to the Ozark outdoors. These beginnings of outdoor recreation . . . brought corporate leaders into a dialogue with small-town businessmen and especially with skilled Ozarks guides." The result, according to Morrow, was that "By the early twentieth century, a few thousand St. Louisans had walked the streets of a bustling Arlington, relaxing a remote distance from smoky, smelly, and industrialized St. Louis." Later, the extension of the St. Louis and Colorado Railway (later reincorporated as the Chicago-Rock Island) to Kansas City, according to Morrow, "attracted another urban market to the Gasconade River." Other areas of the Missouri Ozarks soon lent themselves to urban tourists as well.

Life in Missouri was changing rapidly and dramatically as the nineteenth century drew to a close. The railroads had arguably been a greater

Fig. 26: This postcard image of the Frisco's *Texan* shows the train along the Little Piney River, near the resort community of Arlington early in the twentieth century. Credit: State Historical Society of Missouri, John F. Bradbury Papers, Collection No. RA1652.

Fig. 27: Postcard for the Clubhouse at Boiling Springs in Arlington, Missouri. Credit: State Historical Society of Missouri, John F. Bradbury Papers, Collection No. RA1652.

agent of that change than any other single force. But the changes that occurred in post–Civil War Missouri paled in comparison to those destined to be wrought in the twentieth century by the new form of transportation known as the automobile, and by the Great War that accelerated Missouri's transformation to an urban state. For Missourians, as, indeed, for all Americans, change had barely begun.

SUGGESTED READINGS

Two of William E. Parrish's books offer an excellent window into life in Missouri during the first generation after the Civil War. His *Missouri under Radical Rule, 1865–1870* (1965) and *A History of Missouri, 1860–1875* (1973), both published by the University of Missouri Press, are must reads for understanding Missouri's Reconstruction experience. Also useful is Aaron Astor, *Rebels on the Border: Civil War, Emancipation and the Reconstruction of Kentucky and Missouri* (2012), published by Louisiana State University Press.

Gary R. Kremer's *James Milton Turner and the Promise of America: The Public Life of a Post–Civil War Black Leader* (1991) offers an account of the life of Missouri's preeminent postwar Black leader, as well as insights into the lives of African Americans generally in Missouri during the latter half of the nineteenth century. Kremer's *Race and Meaning: The African American Experience in Missouri* (2014) contains a number of essays on post–Civil War Black life in Missouri, including multiple essays on the history of the state's historically-Black university, Lincoln University. Both books are University of Missouri Press publications.

The topic of the memory of the Civil War and efforts at reconciliation after the war are the subjects of two important works: Jeremy Neely, *The Border between Them: Violence and Reconciliation on the Kansas-Missouri Line* (2007); and Amy Laurel Fluker, *Commonwealth of Compromise: Civil War Commemoration in Missouri* (2020), both published by the University of Missouri Press. Also useful is Berenice Morrison Fuller's memoir, *Missouri Plantation Life* (1937), published by the Missouri Historical Society.

Missouri's most famous outlaw, Jesse James, is the subject of William Settle's *Jesse James Was His Name: Or, Fact and Fiction Concerning the Careers of the Notorious James Brothers of Missouri* (1966) published by the University of Missouri Press. It should be supplemented by the more recent book by T. J. Stiles, *Jesse James, Last Rebel of the Civil War* (2002), published by Alfred A. Knopf.

The post–Civil War economic recovery of Missouri, the expansion of railroads in the state, and the growth of Missouri towns and cities is covered in Lawrence O. Christensen and Gary R. Kremer, *A History of Missouri, 1875–1919* (1997) published by the University of Missouri Press.

The growth of St. Louis during this era is the subject of Adam Arenson, *The Great Heart of the Republic: St. Louis and the Cultural Civil War* (2011, 2015), published by Harvard University Press and reprinted by the University of Missouri Press. Thomas M. Spencer, *The St. Louis Veiled Prophet Celebration: Power on Parade, 1877–1995* (2000), published by the University of Missouri Press, details labor conflict in the city during the late nineteenth century. James Neal Primm's classic work, *Lion of the Valley, St. Louis, Missouri* (1981), Pruett Publishing Company, remains useful.

Kansas City's growth is documented in Charles N. Glaab, *Kansas City and the Railroads: Community Policy in the Growth of a Regional Metropolis* (1962), published by the State Historical Society of Wisconsin. A. Theodore Brown and Lyle W. Dorsett, *K.C.: A History of Kansas City, Missouri* (1978), Pruett Publishing Co., is also strong on the growth of Kansas City in the post–Civil War period.

The Sedalia story is told in Michael Cassity, *Defending a Way of Life: An American Community in the Nineteenth Century* (1989), published by State University of New York Press. Also insightful is Susan Curtis, *Dancing to a Black Man's Tune: A Life of Scott Joplin* (1994), published by the University of Missouri Press.

The city of Joplin's phenomenal growth during the latter part of the nineteen century is documented in a number of works, including G. K. Renner, *Joplin: From Mining Town to Urban Center: An Illustrated History* (1985), published by Windsor Publications, and Jarod Roll, *Poor Man's Fortune: White Working-Class Conservatism in American Metal Mining, 1850–1950* (2020), published by the University of North Carolina Press. H. Roger Grant showed the desire to attract railroads in "Courting the Great Western Railway: An Episode of Town Rivalry," *Missouri Historical Review* 76 (July 1982): 405–20. Also useful, although dated, is Edwin L. Lopata, *Local Aid to Railroads in Missouri* (1937), Parnassus Press.

Lynn Morrow has written extensively about the "discovery" of the Ozarks by urban elites during the late nineteenth and early twentieth centuries. Among his important works on this subject are his essay "Before Bass Pro: St. Louis Sporting Clubs on the Gasconade River," in *The Ozarks in Missouri History: Discoveries in an American Region* (2013), edited by Morrow and published by the University of Missouri Press, and a co-authored work (with Linda Myers-Phinney), *Shepherd of the Hills Country: Tourism Transforms the Ozarks, 1880s–1930s* (1999), published by University of Arkansas Press.

Chapter Six

Missouri in the New Century
Urbanizing Missouri, 1900–1930

"This is no time for slackers, copperheads, or soft pedalists. If
there are any such among us, it is our duty to drive them out and
brand them as traitors."

Governor Frederick Gardner, April 5, 1917

MISSOURIANS LOOKED FORWARD to the twentieth century with anticipation
and optimism. They had every reason to believe that the new century would
bring them good fortune and great prosperity.

By 1900, Missouri's population had reached 3,108,000 people, making
it the fifth largest state in the nation. And as the nineteenth century drew to
a close, the entire country's attention, indeed, the world's attention, turned
to St. Louis, the nation's fourth largest city, and Missouri as the country
prepared to celebrate the centennial of the 1803 Louisiana Purchase. In
April 1899, the Missouri General Assembly authorized the sale of $5 mil-
lion in bonds by the City of St. Louis to support planning for the Louisiana
Purchase Exposition, more commonly known as the St. Louis World's Fair.

Optimism abounded in turn-of-the century Missouri. The Reverend E.
C. McVey, a Methodist preacher from Chillicothe, captured this sentiment
in a sermon titled "The Outlook for the Twentieth Century." In that sermon, McVey expressed the belief that "the 20th century will witness a vast
change for the better in the financial condition of the masses," adding "this
class of people will not be so numerous, nor so destitute in the [new] century as they are today." He also expressed the belief that "the 20th century
will witness a vast change for the better in our social conditions," and that
"the greatest achievement of the 20th century will be the [C]hristianization
of the world." McVey also predicted "the doom of the saloon" before 1910.
There is every reason to believe that Rev. McVey might have agreed with
his more well-known contemporary cleric, the Boston Unitarian, Edward

Everett Hale, who was quoted in the *St. Louis Post-Dispatch* on December 31, 1899, as predicting: "By the end of the twentieth century war will be relegated to the past, as plate armor and chivalry are today."

Neither Americans generally, nor Missourians specifically, had any way of knowing that the worst war the world had ever faced lay in wait only a decade and a half hence. Nor, could they have known that the worst economic crisis in the country's history would come soon thereafter, only to be followed by an even more destructive war, the fallout from which would shape the remainder of the century.

But in the first few years of the twentieth century, Americans and Missourians looked to St. Louis for a glimpse of what they thought the future might hold. Preparation for the elaborately planned world's fair took longer than the fair itself. In addition to the $5 million in St. Louis City money designated for the fair, an equal amount was raised in private donations for the celebration, along with an additional $5 million in federal funds authorized by Congress.

The fairgrounds encompassed some twelve hundred acres on the modern-day sites of the city's Forest Park and the campus of Washington University. The fair's layout was designed by the famed German-born city planner and landscape architect, George E. Kessler. Previously, Kessler had gained fame as the landscape architect of Kansas City and the visionary behind what came to be called the City Beautiful Movement. The city's parks and boulevard system, designed by Kessler, became identifying characteristics of Kansas City.

By the time Kessler took over the planning for the World's Fair, he had become a much-in-demand architect throughout the country. Although the intended opening for the fair was 1903, it was delayed until January 1, 1904, to allow for greater participation by more states and foreign countries. Ultimately, approximately fifty foreign countries staged exhibits, along with forty-three of the then-forty-five U.S. states. Nearly twenty million people visited the roughly fifteen hundred fair buildings, walked the seventy-five or so miles of roads and walkways, and purchased food, drinks, and trinkets from the more than fifty concessionaires who set up shop along "The Pike," a mile-long span that highlighted fair amusements and activities.

The fair showcased new technology and inventions, presented as harbingers of new ways of doing things in twentieth-century America. The Palace

Fig. 28: The Pike, St. Louis World's Fair. Credit: State Historical Society of Missouri, Louisiana Purchase Exposition Snapshots, Collection No. P0093-062.

of Electricity featured a "wireless telephone" machine, also called a "radio-phone." Invented by Alexander Graham Bell, this instrument turned sound waves into light waves and transmitted them to a receiver that turned them back into sound waves, an early version of the radio and the forerunner of the mobile phone. Among the many attractions of the fair was the giant Ferris wheel, which rose 164 feet above the fairgrounds and seemed, as one observer noted, to "plow the clouds." And then there was, for the first time, the forever-after favorite, the ice cream cone.

1904 also marked the year of the election of arguably Missouri's most famous early 20th century reform governor, the St. Louisan Joseph Folk. In many ways, Governor Folk, a Democrat nicknamed "Holy Joe" because of his moralism and strict adherence to the Baptist faith, embodied many of the most visible characteristics of the so-called "Progressive Era," a term used by historians to describe an impulse in favor of social and political reform that characterized much of the country from the 1890s through World War I. Progressives tended to advocate moral reform issues such as prohibition, as well as political reform, such as advocacy of the female franchise and the use of the initiative, referendum, and recall.

In Folk's case, his reform impulse was to oppose and seek to eradicate all forms of civic graft and corruption which he and others deemed to be especially prevalent in the City of St. Louis. Folk saw it as no accident that St. Louis was the only city in the country that warranted two chapters in Lincoln Steffens's muckraking book *The Shame of the Cites* (1904). At center stage of Folk's 1904 campaign was what he called the "Missouri Idea," that citizenship in a democracy required a "civic obligation to enforce the performance of every public trust; bribery is treason, and the givers and takers of bribes are traitors of peace; laws are made to be enforced, not to be ignored, that officials should no more embezzle public power entrusted to them than public money in their custody." Although Republicans won all major state offices besides governor in 1904, and gained control of the state legislature, the Democrat Folk won the governorship by more than thirty thousand votes.

Arguably one of the most interesting trends of the early decades of the twentieth century was the emergence of the automobile as a means of personal transportation, which marked a stepping away from horse-drawn carriages and public means of transportation such as railroads and street-cars. Automobiles played to Americans' keen sense of individualism and self-reliance, providing an efficient means of moving quickly from one place to another. They aided the development of suburbs by facilitating the separation of people from their places of employment, thereby allowing for the creation of "private spaces" where individuals could escape to their personal lives while returning, via their automobiles, to their public lives of work, education, worship, and even recreation.

Early on, the cost of an automobile was so great that only the wealthy could afford to own and drive one. In 1893, the *St. Louis Post-Dispatch* reported that Dr. I. Griswold Comstock, a St. Louis physician, had purchased the first "Auto-Mobile" vehicle in St. Louis at a cost of $3,000, the equivalent of more than $85,000 in purchasing power in 2020, a price far out of reach of the average Missourian.

But not long after the turn of the century, car manufacturing operations began to spring up in St. Louis, and automobiles became increasingly affordable. One of the first such businesses was the St. Louis Automobile Manufacturing, Storage and Repair Company, established late in 1901. By the next year the Automobile Club of St. Louis had formed, and a year later the car club had 70 members—and complaints were already being aired about the poor condition of roads and streets, especially outside the downtown St. Louis area.

By the latter part of the first decade of the twentieth century there were multiple automobile manufacturers in St. Louis. Indeed, in August 1909, the "Made-in-St. Louis Committee of the Missouri Manufacturers' Association" hosted a parade of "Made in St. Louis Autos." Seven automobile manufacturers had entries in the parade: Victor Automobile Company; Moon Motor Car Company; St. Louis Car Company; Dorris Motor Company; Eureka Motor Vehicle Company; Cook Motor Vehicle Company; and A. B. C. Motor Vehicle Company.

This parade was deemed so successful that it was followed by a much larger one a few months later. This time all automobile owners in the city were invited to participate; the invitation revealed just how thoroughly automobile ownership had become a symbol of status by 1908: "You may not have realized it, but the automobile parade will go further to impress strangers in the city with the wealth, progressiveness and culture of St. Louis than any of the other big events, because an automobile represents a man's investment for his pleasure. Your civic pride should therefore dictate to you your duty to have your car in the parade." This was a classic example of the "conspicuous consumption" described by eminent economist and sociologist Thorstein Veblen in his book *Theory of the Leisure Class*, published in 1899, slightly more than a decade before he came to teach at the University of Missouri.

The more automobiles that were purchased, and the more miles that their owners drove them, the more the latter clamored for better streets and roads. By 1910, the Automobile Club of St. Louis had worked out an arrangement with St. Louis County government to oil one hundred miles of roads in the county, with the two entities sharing equally the cost of oiling. The process of oiling, it was argued, would result in "all dust [being] laid and the roads pack[ed] down as hard as a paved street." At the time, nobody seemed to be overly concerned about the possible health risks of pouring crude oil on the dirt roads, even if the smell of it could not have been pleasant.

By 1911, there were over sixteen thousand motor vehicles in Missouri. Governor Herbert S. Hadley appointed a committee to study the best proposed routes for cross-state highways connecting Missouri's two metropolitan centers, St. Louis and Kansas City. To promote this idea, Hadley embarked on a much-publicized "Highway Tour" of the state. Although the governor's effort at creating a cross-state highway failed for lack of funding, his travels and advocacy drew much-needed attention to the state's woefully inadequate roads.

By 1913, on the eve of the First World War, St. Louis had emerged as a major manufacturer of automobiles, competing with Cleveland for third place as a leading car maker, behind first-place Detroit and second-place Indianapolis. The leading manufacturer in St. Louis was the Moon Motor Car Co., which had quadrupled its output over the previous four years.

By 1913, also, Missouri's new governor, Elliot Major, led a campaign to improve Missouri's roads through voluntary activity. In July of that year, Major issued a proclamation setting aside two days in August for volunteers in every Missouri county to come together as a "good roads army" to work on the state's roads "to pull Missouri out of the mud." When the time for work arrived, an estimated two hundred thousand people across the state, including the shovel-toting governor, joined in the work. Among those "volunteering" were some Missouri State Penitentiary convicts, each of whose sentences the governor promised to reduce by fifteen days in return for their road work.

August 1914 witnessed a second "good road days," observed in ninety of Missouri's 114 counties, with one hundred thousand men at work. As before, much of the work consisted of grading, cleaning up roadsides, and filling in holes and washed out places. "Wars alarms," as a newspaper referenced, may have diminished the turnout, although the St. Joseph *News Press/Gazette* insisted, "the peace-loving Missourians are now worrying only about roads."

Missourians faced a somewhat awkward circumstance when war did break out in Europe in 1914. Hundreds of thousands of Missourians were only a generation or two removed from one or the other warring countries. President Woodrow Wilson initially urged all Americans to remain neutral in the conflict; that sentiment suited most Missourians just fine. The *Bethany* [Missouri] *Democrat* reprinted Wilson's address proclaiming American neutrality and endorsed the policy, stating: "Every man who really loves America will act and speak in the true spirit of neutrality, which is, the spirit of impartiality and fairness and of friendliness to all concerned."

Alas, neutrality was not to be. Between 1914 and early 1917, relations between the United States and the Central Powers, especially Germany,

Fig. 29: Cars stuck on a muddy road, evidencing Missouri's need for road improvement, 1910s. Credit: State Historical Society of Missouri, Leonard D. and Marie H. Rehkop Collection of Algert T. Peterson Photographs, Collection No. C3888.

Fig. 30: Governor Elliot Major (*left*) and Governor George Hodges of Kansas work together on a road between Jefferson City and Columbia, August 21, 1913. Credit: Missouri State Archives. Collection No. MS 253.

deteriorated dramatically. As the United States moved closer to declaring war in early 1917, it was a U.S. Senator from Missouri who led the opposition to the United States' entry into the war. Senator William J. Stone, a native of Kentucky born in 1848, had by that time a long and distinguished career in politics. An 1867 graduate of the University of Missouri, Stone entered politics in 1870 as the city attorney for Columbia. He moved to Nevada, Missouri, a few years later and was elected the Vernon County prosecuting attorney in 1874. In 1884, Stone was elected to the U.S. House of Representatives and served in that position until 1891. The next year, he was elected Missouri's governor, and served in that position until 1897. Five years later, he was elected to the U.S. Senate and retained his Senate seat until he suffered a stroke and died on April 14, 1917.

Stone chaired the powerful Senate Foreign Relations Committee as the United States marched to war during the early crucial months of 1917. When President Wilson broke relations with Germany on February 3, 1917, Senator Stone was among the few in the nation who opposed the action.

Only the *Kansas City Journal*, among major Missouri newspapers, sided with Stone. Even the release of the infamously incriminating Zimmerman Telegram on February 28, 1917, failed to move Stone to support President Wilson's position, a stance that caused numerous Missouri newspapers to label Stone as traitorous and cowardly. When Wilson asked Congress for a formal declaration of war against Germany on April 2, 1917, Stone could not bring himself to support his old friend. Instead he joined five other U.S. Senators in voting against the war declaration, although once the war declaration was passed, he threw his support behind it and urged all Missouri residents to do likewise.

Missourians did indeed follow Senator Stone's lead, closing ranks behind President Wilson and the war effort. Speaking to a large "loyalty" crowd assembled in the St. Louis Coliseum on the evening of April 5, 1917, Missouri Governor Frederick Gardner proclaimed his support of the war: "This is no time for slackers, copperheads, or soft pedalists. If there are any such among us, it is our duty to drive them out and brand them as traitors."

No one wanted to be branded a traitor, including the roughly eighty thousand Missourians who had been born in Germany and the two hundred eighty thousand or so who had German-born parents. Many of these first- and second-generation German Americans went out of their way to "prove" their loyalty to the United States, even though it was sometimes difficult for many of them to turn their backs on a country they had once considered their homeland.

Congress's declaration of war produced an outpouring of patriotism in Missouri and the nation. Parades and other demonstrations of support for the war effort occurred all over the state. In Boonville, a city of three thousand people, a crowd estimated at five thousand turned out for a war rally. In southwest Missouri's Mount Vernon, the *Lawrence Chieftain* called for "unadulterated loyalty to the Stars and Stripes . . . by every person in the United States," adding, "No patience should be shown toward any person who is lukewarm in his allegiance to this government. . . ." Parades occurred all over the state, from Kennett to Kirksville and Edina and from Maryville to Joplin, and places in between.

Still, there were tensions between old-stock Americans who traced their ancestry to countries that were among the Allied Powers and those who had connections to the Central Powers, particularly Germany. Historian Petra

DeWitt has documented these tensions in a central Missouri county with heavy concentrations of German Americans: Gasconade County, located along the Missouri River, about eighty miles west of St. Louis.

Although Gasconade County residents, including those in the very German town of Hermann, did not hold any pro-war rallies in the wake of the war declaration, they expressed their patriotism in many ways, including the flying of American flags, the purchase of American Liberty Bonds, the planting of victory gardens, and enlistment in the army to become part of the American Expeditionary Force.

Still, in the eyes of their non-German fellow Missourians, the Gasconade County residents of German heritage were suspect. The residents' efforts at displaying their patriotism notwithstanding, Gasconade was deemed as "one of the worst counties in the state" by the Missouri Council of Defense, according to historian DeWitt. There were many reasons for this. First, relatively few county residents volunteered for military service, although none seemed to defy the draft. According to DeWitt, "Only nine [county residents] enlisted in the army and marines, and six volunteered for the navy." Roughly two thirds of the county's prospective draftees claimed exemption from the draft, either due to dependent relatives, physical ailments, or other reasons. That said, this percentage of exemption requests was roughly the same throughout the country.

Another reason Gasconade County's citizens were suspect was their tepid response to calls to support the war financially. Statewide, 3.8 percent of Missouri residents purchased bonds as part of multiple "Liberty Loan" campaigns. In Gasconade County, less than half that percentage of the county's residents participated, leading the Missouri Council of Defense to refer to them as "slackers."

Yet another criticism of the residents of heavily German Gasconade County stemmed from the fact that the German language continued to be used in the local public schools. Instruction in German persisted in spite of the fact that the State Superintendent of Schools, Uel Lamkin, a California, Missouri-born descendant of early nineteenth-century Kentuckians who migrated to the Show-Me State, called upon schools in the state to stop using the "enemy's tongue" in public school classrooms. Indeed, according to a May 23, 1918, report in the Jefferson City *Daily Capital News*, Gasconade County was one of only three Missouri counties, out of a total of 114, that refused to abandon the use and teaching of German in public schools.

There were also isolated if anecdotal instances of Gasconade County German Americans' less than ardent support of the war effort. Edward A. Ahrens, a Gasconade County minister, preached a sermon in October 1917 in which he allegedly proclaimed that he would not "pray for the victory of the United States in this war," an action that resulted in his being indicted for violating the Espionage Act, a federal law passed on June 15, 1917, aimed at those who interfered with military operations or recruitment of soldiers into the armed services in support of the war. Although indicted, Ahrens apparently escaped prosecution by fleeing the state and taking up permanent residence in Iowa. Another county resident of German descent, August Heidbreder, was arrested in June 1917 for allegedly threatening President Woodrow Wilson's life, a crime that resulted in Heidbreder being fined $100 by an Eastern U.S. District Court judge.

Arguably, the most intense conflict over community loyalty that occurred in Gasconade County during World War I happened in the small town of Potsdam in the northwestern portion of the county during the summer of 1918. The problem began when the Richland Township school board denied use of the Potsdam School building to the local Farm Bureau. Gasconade County Farm Bureau club chairman, A. F. Wulff, attributed this decision to the school board's opposition to the U.S. war effort. The tension further increased when the school board refused to host a gathering for National War Savings Day on June 28, 1918. Soon thereafter, the county superintendent of schools ordered the school board to open the Potsdam school "for all patriotic meetings or for any purpose that might aid the war effort."

The school board re-opened the school to public meetings, but by this time news of the controversy had reached St. Louis, and city newspapers there began lambasting Potsdam and its citizens for being pro-German. Soon thereafter, and driven by this negative publicity, a group of men from neighboring Osage County descended on the Potsdam Post Office and nailed an American flag to its porch. Meanwhile, a Potsdam couple, Dr. Howard Workman and his wife Lottie, began a petition drive to change the name of the post office (and thereby the town) from the German-sounding and Germany-connected "Potsdam," to the more acceptable "Pershing," in honor of the famous Missouri-born U.S. General and commander of the American Expeditionary Force. The United States Post Office made the name change official in October 1918, although tension over the change persisted: some community members were tired of the adverse publicity and wanted to demonstrate their loyalty, while others resented being forced to turn their backs on their patrimony and also resented the federal government intervening in what they thought was a local matter.

War conditions demanded, among other things, a need to produce food for the American allies in Europe, whose countries were unable to produce sufficient food for themselves. Even before the U.S. entered the war, American farmers, Missouri farmers among them, had been called upon to increase their food production and citizens of the state and nation had been asked to reduce their consumption of goods needed for the war effort.

The desire for increased agricultural production spurred interest in and support for scientific agriculture. Enrollment in the University of Missouri's College of Agriculture grew dramatically and university outreach to farmers throughout the state, made possible by the 1914 Smith-Lever Act, became an effective and efficient way to teach farmers how to harness the lessons of science to increase their efficiency and productivity.

In 1915, the Missouri State Farm Bureau Federation formed, with offices in each county, to assist extension efforts. Two years later, hundreds of local farm clubs in the state organized the Missouri Farmer's Association (MFA). William Hirth, publisher of the organization's official magazine, the *Missouri Farmer*, was chosen as the organization's president, a position he continued to hold for many years.

Within days of the passage of the Declaration of War, U.S. Secretary of War, Newton D. Baker, called for each state to organize Councils of Defense to coordinate its war effort. In Missouri, Governor Frederick Gardner appointed the dean of the University of Missouri's College of Agriculture, Dr. Frederick B. Mumford, to chair this group. Gardner emphasized that "the burden of war will be placed on the shoulders of the farmers," and his wife, Missouri's First Lady, Jeannette Gardner, took guests at the Governor's Mansion out behind the official residence in Jefferson City, "and with hoe in hand, demonstrated how the first family planned to feed itself by cultivating a garden." The *Lawrence Chieftain* ennobled the work of agriculturalists by proclaiming, "Do you know that the young man on the farm, who uses his full energies to raise a big crop of food is doing just as much for his country as the town boy who takes his gun and goes to the front?"

Governor Gardner tried to get everyone in the state involved in the war effort, including the state's African Americans. When he approached Black leaders about how best to do that, they responded that they wanted their own statewide organization that they could control. They proposed the idea of a Missouri Negro Industrial Commission, composed of and run by African Americans, which would allow Black citizens to demonstrate their commitment to the war effort.

Gardner created the Missouri Negro Industrial Commission on February 12, 1918, appointing sixteen commissioners and charging them to "have a voice in their own upliftment and to discover, ferret out, survey and recommend remedies for their own betterment." The commission's first goal was to organize African Americans in the state, especially farmers, behind the war effort, encourage them to sell war bonds, and teach them to practice better agricultural methods, increase acreage under cultivation and crop production, and conserve food and materials. The first commissioners were, like the governor, all Democrats, and they were unsalaried. The commission was chaired by Nathaniel C. Bruce, a Virginia native and a graduate of Tuskegee Institute in Alabama, where he studied under the famed Missouri-born scientist, George Washington Carver. Bruce came to Missouri early in the twentieth century to serve as principal of a Black high school in St. Joseph. In 1907 he established an agricultural school for African Americans near the town of Dalton in Chariton County. The Dalton Vocational School, sometimes referred to as "the Tuskegee of the Midwest," served students from multiple counties in the region over the course of more than half a century.

Under Bruce's leadership, commission members held more than forty meetings across the state, "urging and stimulating our race's old time loyalty, fidelity and hearty, persistent labor." By the end of 1918, the commission had sold over six hundred thousand dollars' worth of war bonds, while also dramatically increasing agricultural production among Black farmers.

One of the most dramatic "Loyalty Demonstrations" held in the state during the war occurred in St. Louis in June 1918, when thousands of African Americans gathered at the Coliseum for a parade and rally in support of the war. Festus J. Wade, a local bank president and one of the few whites in attendance, noted that "In all my experience in St. Louis I never have seen a more inspiring demonstration of patriotism than this."

According to a *Post-Dispatch* report of the event, "one of the Negro speakers demanded to know if the negroes who fight to make the world safe for democracy will find America safe for them when they return." These remarks were met with great cheering and affirmation.

Just as African Americans contributed to the war effort, so too did the women of Missouri. To recruit women for the labor force in the wake of wartime demands on men, Governor Gardner asked women to register for service. On July 28, 1917, more than 118,000 Missouri women signed up to take intensive courses in stenography, accounting, bookkeeping, telegraphy, filing, salesmanship, and office machine use. Thousands more signed up later. Ultimately, women assumed men's positions when the war created labor shortages. They also served by the thousands in county chapters of the American Red Cross, raising funds for the national chapter through ice cream socials and bake sales, and sewing and knitting for American soldiers.

Although war's end brought relief and even exhilaration, Americans faced a new and especially lethal challenge in the fall of 1918, just as the conflict was drawing to a close: the dreaded Spanish Influenza that would result in a worldwide pandemic that, before the disease ceased to spread, ended up killing more people than had died in the war.

The epidemic appears to have begun in the spring of 1918 among American soldiers stationed at Fort Riley, Kansas. It then traveled to Europe with American soldiers and quickly spread around the world. Before it had run its course, the Spanish flu infected half a billion people, or more than one-quarter of the world's population. Estimates of the number of people who died from the Spanish flu worldwide vary greatly, with some running as high as one hundred million people.

Not surprisingly, in Missouri the Spanish influenza took its greatest toll in the state's urban areas, where the heaviest concentration of people lived. Influenza cases began being reported in Kansas City during the last week of September 1918. By the end of that month, five cases had been reported there. Within a week, the *Kansas City Star* was referring to the city as being in the throes of an epidemic. By that time, there were twenty-four influenza-related deaths and fifty-six new cases of the disease, and the city's General Hospital was full and turning away new patients.

Initially, health care providers tried to downplay the seriousness of the outbreak. Dr. E. H. Bullock, superintendent of the hospital, minimized the threat to the general population. Nine days into the epidemic, according to historian Susan Debra Sykes Berry, "no effective steps had been taken. . . . The schools remained open, the street cars were crowded and dirty, crowds were not limited, and thus far city government had done nothing."

Over the next several weeks, and even months, Kansas City officials tried with varying degrees of success to control crowds and stem the spread of the disease. Ultimately, an estimated 2,300 people died of influenza in Kansas City over the course of the last several months of 1918 and early 1919. The mortality rate (718 deaths per 250,000 population) from influenza in Kansas City made that city one of the hardest hit in the nation, with a mortality rate greater than New York, Chicago, Cleveland, Detroit, or even St. Louis. The latter city had a much lower mortality rate, only 536 per 250,000.

The key to St. Louis's lower death rate seems to have been the aggressiveness with which that city sought to prevent the spread of the disease. Within days of the discovery of influenza in St. Louis in the fall of 1918, local officials moved to ban social gatherings of all types. In early October, Dr. Max C. Starkloff, St. Louis City Health Commissioner, ordered the closing of schools, churches, theaters, saloons, dance halls, and sporting events. Still, deaths occurred. One of the victims was Congressman Jacob Meeker, a native of Indiana who died only nine days after his fortieth birthday. Congressman Meeker, who represented Missouri's Tenth District, was thought to have contracted influenza on a trip to Jefferson Barracks for the Red Cross less than a week before his death. A former pastor of the Compton Hill Congregational Church in St. Louis, Meeker was a divorced father of four who married his stenographer on his death bed, seven hours before he died.

In early November 1918, Dr. Starkloff issued even stricter rules, closing down department stores, general merchandise stores, even factories "and every other business place which is not, in Dr. Starkloff's opinion, essential to the absolute needs of the people." As was the case with his previous month's restrictions, Dr. Starkloff was attacked by scores of businessmen and others who stood to lose tens of thousands of dollars because of the forced closures. These protests notwithstanding, Dr. Starkloff stood firm, supported fully by St. Louis Mayor Henry Kiel and the city police force.

The quarantine was lifted on November 18, when the flu seemed to abate, but reinstated in early December when influenza returned with a vengeance. On December 6, 1918, the *Post-Dispatch* reported an astonishing 937 "new influenza cases" and thirty deaths from the disease on the previous day. Four days later, there were sixty influenza deaths. By Christmas that year, cases declined sharply; soon after the holiday, the quarantine was lifted. When it was all over, by spring of 1919, more than thirty-one thousand St. Louisans had been infected and 1,703 city residents had died. Dr. Max Starkloff continued to live in St. Louis until his death at the age of eighty-three on January 15, 1942. In his obituary, he was remembered as a valiant physician: "Over the protests of merchants who vowed their business would be ruined by it, he imposed a strict quarantine on the city, savings [sic] thousands of lives by the action."

The flu struck in less crowded areas in outstate Missouri as well. In Cape Girardeau, Mayor Harold H. Haas proclaimed a citywide quarantine to extend from December 6, 1918, through December 15, 1918. The quarantine prohibited any public gatherings, including attendance in theaters, lodges, churches, schools, and conventions. Pool halls and bowling alleys were directed to close at 6:00 p.m. and "all stores, saloons, confectionaries, lunchrooms, restaurants, and all other places of business must adhere strictly to the rule forbidding needless loitering in their respective places of business." By December 20, Haas was able to report "Only 22 new cases of influenza . . . in the city yesterday, a drop of more than 50 percent" from the previous day.

In the small southwest Missouri town of Ash Grove, the nurse service department of the Red Cross reported "the influenza epidemic still serious." The November 19, 1918, issue of the *Springfield News Leader* noted, "There are 21 patients in the emergency hospital [in Ash Grove]," which was the Presbyterian Church auditorium and basement. Springfield, too, converted a church (South Street Christian) into a hospital after seventeen influenza-caused deaths occurred on October 10, 1918. The Columbia *Evening Missourian* reported 259 patients in multiple makeshift hospitals on October 17, 1918. By December 17, state prison officials reported three hundred to three hundred fifty cases of influenza "at present" in the Missouri State Penitentiary and a total of fifteen deaths, although they noted tersely: "situation very much improved." No part of the state escaped the influenza; Missourians' lives were turned upside down in a way not again experienced for more than a century when the Coronavirus pandemic struck the state in 2020.

World War I changed Missouri and the nation in a multitude of ways. One way was that it accelerated the movement to grant women the right to vote, which Missouri lawmakers had been denying women for more than half a century. In 1875 Missouri women tried to get the Constitutional Convention held that year to include the female franchise in the state's new constitution. The only time the issue came up in the convention proceedings, however, was when convention delegate Albert Todd of St. Louis proposed giving women the right to vote as "a remedy against . . . negro voters precipitated upon us." Todd was still angry over the ratification of the Fifteenth Amendment, which enfranchised African American men five years earlier, in 1870.

Throughout the late nineteenth century, various women's organizations in Missouri had advocated for women's right to vote. Clara Cleghorn Hoffman of Kansas City, president of the state's branch of the national Women's Christian Temperance Union, advocated for women's right to vote, as did a number of local women's clubs throughout the state, such as the Wednesday Club of St. Louis, the Runcie Club of St. Joseph, the Kansas City Athenaeum, the Tuesday Club of Jefferson City, along with various local chapters of the National Association of Colored Women in the state. In 1911 a new suffrage organization, the Missouri Equal Suffrage Association (MESA), organized in St. Louis. Affiliate suffrage clubs formed in Warrensburg and Kansas City. In 1913, members of the MESA began circulating petitions aimed at putting the ballot in the hands of women. Subsequently, these women submitted their petitions to state legislators and called for a November 1914 vote on a provision to grant women the franchise, a request upon which the legislators failed to act.

Undaunted, in 1916 women mounted an effective and dramatic effort at advocating for their right to vote with the formation of the "Golden Lane" at the Democratic National Convention, held in St. Louis that year. Suffragists by the thousands from all over the country lined the street leading to the convention headquarters at the old City Art Museum at Nineteenth and Locust. Although the convention passed a lukewarm endorsement of women's right to vote, this time momentum was on the side of the suffragists.

World War I provided the impetus needed to pass the suffrage amendment. First, it became glaringly apparent to male lawmakers that it was inconsistent to be fighting a war "to make the world safe for democracy" while simultaneously denying the vote, the fruit of democracy, to half of the nation's citizens. Second, women's valiant efforts to support the war through their work for the Red Cross, food conservation, and other volunteer efforts left many men embarrassed at continuing to deny women the right to vote.

Fig. 31: Governor Frederick Gardner signs federal suffrage amendment, July 3, 1919. Credit: State Historical Society of Missouri, Carl Deeg photograph, Women of the Mansion Photograph Collection, 1834-1933, Collection No. P0536.

The women's suffrage amendment to the U.S. Constitution was finally passed on June 4, 1919, supported by the Speaker of the House, Missourian Champ Clark. On July 3, 1919, Missouri became the eleventh state to ratify the Nineteenth Amendment, which declared that the "right of citizens of the United States to vote shall not be denied or abridged by the United States or by any State on account of sex." When Tennessee ratified the amendment on August 18, 1920, the requisite three-fourths of the states in the Union had endorsed the amendment. At that point, Missouri women, like their sisters throughout the country, had at long last prevailed—they finally had the right to vote, in large part through the efforts of activist women in women's clubs and other volunteer organizations across the nation.

Another change that resulted from World War I was the passage of another amendment to the U.S. Constitution, one that many clubwomen, as well as their male supporters, had been advocating for since before the turn of the twentieth century, the outlawing in the United States of the manufacture, sale, and transportation of alcohol. This issue had long divided Missourians. During the 1880s Missouri passed a "local option" law that gave counties and local governmental entities the authority to decide whether they wanted to be "wet" or "dry." "By 1917," according to historian Richard Kirkendall, "ninety-six of Missouri's one hundred fourteen counties were totally or partially dry, while St. Louis, Kansas City, St. Joseph, Springfield, Joplin, and several smaller communities remained wet." Religion and ethnicity were critical factors in determining whether a community decided to be wet or dry. Those counties with a prevalence of Missourians with German, Austrian, Italian, or Irish ancestry, many of whom were also Catholic, Episcopalian, Lutheran, and Jewish, tended to be wet. By contrast, counties whose populations were composed predominantly of "old stock" Americans with roots in the Upland South, especially Baptists and Methodists, tended to be dry. This chasm was graphically illustrated in the Central Missouri counties of Cole and Callaway, separated only by the Missouri River. Callaway County, with its heavy concentration of residents with ancestral roots in Virginia, Kentucky, and Tennessee, and its large population of evangelical Christians, was dry. Cole County, with its large number of German immigrants and their descendants, many of whom were Catholic or Lutheran, was wet. A tavern at the south end of a Missouri River bridge, connecting the two counties, became a watering hole for thirsty travelers during the early twentieth century. Dubbed by locals "The Last Chance, First Chance Saloon," the bar captured the sentiment of division between the wet and dry communities.

Prohibition for all of Missouri came in the wake of the ratification of the Eighteenth Amendment to the U.S. Constitution. Originally passed by Congress on December 18, 1917, it took more than a year for the required number of states to ratify it. That happened on January 19, 1919. The Missouri legislature ratified the amendment one day later, when it no

Fig. 32: Temperance Rally, New Franklin, ca. 1910. Credit: State Historical Society of Missouri, Lilburn A. Kingsbury Collection, Collection No. C3724.

longer mattered, on January 20. Subsequently, the federal Volstead Act was passed to implement the Eighteenth Amendment.

The Eighteenth Amendment and the Volstead Act had multiple, dramatic effects on the lives of Missourians. First, it ruined or nearly ruined the businesses of the many people in the state engaged in the brewing, liquor, and wine trades in Missouri. Brewers, distillers, and winemakers tried to adjust, with varying degrees of success. Second, the amendment and the Volstead Act created a booming black market for the sale and consumption of alcohol, leading directly to the rise of organized crime in the state, especially in the metropolitan areas of Kansas City and St. Louis. Kansas City gained a reputation as a "wide open" town of lawlessness during the Prohibition decade of the 1920s, giving rise to such crime figures as John Lazia, a notorious Kansas City mobster, who operated out of the city's "Little Italy" section and worked closely with city boss Tom Pendergast, who described him as "one of my chief lieutenants." According to historian Donald B. Oster, Lazia had "connections with both the underworld and the police department" and "could sometimes provide a bridge between the

two." Lazia was gunned down by gang rivals on July 10, 1934, at the age
of thirty-eight. Prohibition spawned numerous gangs in St. Louis as well,
including Egan's Rats, the Hogan Gang, the Pillow Gang, the Cuckoos,
and the Green Ones, the latter of which was, as one historian has written,
"distinctly Sicilian." The Green Ones dominated bootlegging in St. Louis
by the early 1920s, led by boss Vito Giannola and his "enforcer," Alphonse
Palazzolo. Palazzolo was killed by rival gang members on September 9,
1927. His boss, Giannola, was likewise murdered a few months later, on
December 28, 1927.

World War I brought with it many demographic changes in the state
and nation as well. For one thing, it created enormous labor shortages at
precisely a time when more workers were needed. When fighting broke out
in Europe in 1914, European immigration, averaging approximately one
million people a year, virtually stopped. With Europe torn apart by the war,
the United States became the workshop and principal agricultural producer
for the world.

With an increased demand for laborers, and a diminished labor supply
from the traditional white, male labor force, employers increasingly looked
to African American migrants from the South and from rural Missouri to
fill their labor needs. This movement of African Americans into northern
and midwestern cities that began in about 1915 and continued for more
than five decades became known as the "Great Migration."

African Americans were attracted to Kansas City to work in the meatpacking industry and as janitors in factories and other businesses. Many of
them settled in the West Bottoms, near the packing houses and factories.
But some rural Blacks wanted to escape the congested urban environment,
and they managed to find an alternative lifestyle available in a community that emerged just west of the Blue River and south of Raytown Road,
near the eastern city limits of Kansas City, and roughly two miles from
downtown. On October 29, 1915, a white man, J. W. Couch, and his
wife, Laura, platted what came to be known as "Couch's 1st Addition."
Recognizing a potential market when they saw one, the Couches began
building small houses in this new subdivision and selling them exclusively
to African Americans.

What attracted Blacks to this area? Most important, the houses there
were more affordable than those in the downtown area. What's more,
in "Couch's," an African American could buy land and a house on an

installment plan, with small weekly payments. Thus, Couch's 1st Addition was a place where Blacks could become landowners, something that had been extremely important to African Americans ever since emancipation. The 1920 federal census revealed that 96 of the 108 households in the community at the time were occupied by residents who lived in houses they owned, an astonishing eight-nine percent. To be sure, these were not elaborate or extravagant houses, most of them two-room, frame, shotgun structures built on wooden piers sunk into the ground. They lacked bathrooms, indoor plumbing, and central heat. At least some of the houses had dirt floors. In a late-life interview with this author, one community resident, Gertrude Gillum, recalled "some [women] would sweep designs in the floor and they did not want you to mess up their floors."

Another reason so many African American migrants from the South and from rural Missouri chose to live in Couch's was because it evoked a landscape and lifestyle already familiar to them. Although within the city limits of Kansas City, the area remained quite rural. Southern and rural Black arrivals quickly discovered that they could replicate their semi-subsistent lifestyle, by planting large gardens, raising chickens, butchering hogs, and milking cows. Neighborhood families established large vegetable gardens in which they raised a variety of produce, including mustard and collard greens, tomatoes, sweet potatoes, green beans, asparagus, and corn. Residents also raised fruit such as peaches, pears, blackberries, strawberries, and raspberries. October brought a community "hog kill," when residents participated in communal butchering.

To augment their diet of homegrown meat, fruit, and vegetables, residents fished in the Blue River and hunted squirrels and rabbits in the nearby woods. Although the neighborhood was rural, it was within walking distance of the 31st Street streetcar stop. Both men and women left the neighborhood by streetcar to look for or report to work. Some men found work in construction. Others found employment at one of Kansas City's meatpacking plants, particularly those of the Swift, Armour, and Wilson corporations. Still others found jobs as elevator operators, cooks, or janitors in downtown hotels or office buildings. Women who worked outside the home most often did so as maids, laundresses, cooks, and seamstresses.

The women who were left behind cared for their and their neighbors' children and did so without any modern conveniences, including indoor

Fig. 33: Henry Kirklin, a self-proclaimed "Market Gardener" in Columbia, was an active commercial agriculturalist from the early 1880s through at least the first three decades of the twentieth century. Credit: State Historical Society of Missouri, Boone County, Missouri, Black Archives Collection. Collection No. C4057.

plumbing, electricity, or natural gas. It was a hard life, but one aided by the overwhelming presence of two-parent households and a sense of community buttressed by strong institutions, including well-attended churches, lodges, and the Dunbar School, which provided elementary education to all the neighborhood children.

A similar circumstance emerged at roughly the same time across the state, just beyond the western limits of the City of St. Louis. As was the case with Kansas City, many Southern and rural Missouri Blacks abandoned their rural homes and headed for St. Louis in the hope of obtaining good-paying jobs that were emerging because of the war. Ultimately, this "Great Migration" strained the ability of St. Louis's racially segregated neighborhoods to provide suitable housing for African Americans. In 1916, St. Louis passed a segregation ordinance aimed at keeping African Americans from spilling over into white-owned residential areas. Although this ordinance was soon declared unconstitutional, it exacerbated racial tensions and revealed a white public attitude in favor of residential segregation. Black competition for jobs and living space spilled over into violence in the infamous East St. Louis, Illinois, Race Riot during the summer of 1917. At least forty

African Americans were killed during this riot, perhaps many more. Many African Americas fled across the Mississippi River into St. Louis to escape the violence.

Not surprisingly, as was the case in Kansas City, white entrepreneurs in St. Louis saw an opportunity to make money. The white owners of the Olive Street Terrace Company began to sell lots exclusively to Blacks in and near a community known as Kinloch. As was the case in Couch's, African Americans were attracted to Kinloch because the place offered them the opportunity not only to become landowners, but also to continue their rural, semi-subsistence lifestyle.

Among the early migrants to Kinloch was the family of Sylvester Smith. The Smith family moved from Mississippi to St. Louis in 1914 and lived in East St. Louis at the time of the riot. In a late-life interview, Smith recalled how, as a young child, he and his family crossed the Mississippi River over a bridge, on foot, and found safety in a cornfield near Kinloch. Eventually, the family bought property in Kinloch and Sylvester, his parents and thirteen siblings, made that community their home, all living in a four-room house.

One consequence of the growing concentration of African Americans in cities during the 1920s and beyond was the renewed interest in Black culture and Black consciousness, in large part due to continuing overt discrimination against Blacks. African American writers of the day, such as W. E. B. DuBois, James Weldon Johnson, Claude McKay, Jean Toomer, Countee Cullen, Langston Hughes, and Zora Neale Hurston, wrote of both oppression and racial pride. Hughes, a native of Joplin, Missouri, became one of the most prolific and famous of this cohort. His books *The Weary Blues* and *Fine Clothes to the Jew* assured him lasting literary recognition.

This movement, which was centered in New York City and came to be known as the Harlem Renaissance, extended all the way to Missouri, in this case primarily in the form of a musical revolution. As ragtime music pioneered by Scott Joplin (of Sedalia) gave way to jazz, Black Missourians helped lead the way. Jazz first came to the state, according to historian Richard Kirkendall, on riverboats bound from New Orleans to St. Louis. Soon African Americans in St. Louis developed their own jazz groups, such as the Missourians, featuring nationally famous Cab Calloway. The Missourians were considered one of the best jazz bands from the South when they traveled to New York City and performed in the legendary Savoy Ballroom.

Arguably, Missouri's most famous jazz musician of the Roaring Twenties was Will "Count" Basie, who arrived in Kansas City as a penniless piano player in the mid-1920s. Basie played with Walter Page's Blue Devils until Page dissolved the band; thereafter Basie joined Benjamin "Bennie" Moten, another Kansas City jazz great. Once on his own, Basie described his own style of music as follows: "I don't dig the two-beat jive the New Orleans cats play because my boys and I got to have four heavy beats to a bar and no cheating." When Moten died in 1928, the Count took the band to new heights, carrying it to national and even international acclaim. Among the jazz artists that Basie influenced was the inimitable saxophonist Charlie "Bird" Parker.

Another African American whose childhood roots were in Missouri attained international fame only after leaving what she perceived as a racist and oppressive society in the 1920s United States. St. Louis native Josephine Baker's first show business break came in 1924 when she won a part in the New York musical "Chocolate Dandies," in which she received recognition for her comedic role as a member of the chorus line. In 1925 Baker left the United States to tour with Caroline Dudley's Revue Negro in Europe, where she became an overnight sensation and was celebrated as the toast of Paris. By the late 1920s she was headlining at the Folies Bergère and other European jazz clubs and drawing huge audiences and rave reviews.

For its part, the riverport city of St. Louis emerged as a rich center of urban blues from the 1920s to the 1940s. Mary Johnston and Alice Moore were among the famous women who sang in the classic blues style during the late 1920s. A number of innovative blues pianists also performed in local riverfront saloons, brothels, and gambling houses in the St. Louis and East St. Louis red-light districts, including Lee Green, Roosevelt Sykes, Walter Davis, and Peetie Wheatstraw, who billed himself as "The Devil's Son-in-Law." Henry "Mule" Townsend, one of the greatest blues musicians of all time, came to St. Louis from Mississippi in the teens. The son of blues musician Allen Townsend, "Mule" was taught to play the guitar by local artist Dudlow Joe, and by the late 1920s had launched a career that saw him recording music over the course of nine consecutive decades prior to his death in 2006.

Yet another instance of the emergence of Black culture in post–World War I urban Missouri was the origins and flourishing of the National Association of Colored Professional Baseball Clubs and its Negro National League. The league, formed in 1920 because major league baseball would not allow Black players to participate in the majors, was originally composed of eight teams, including the Kansas City Monarchs and the St. Louis Giants.

Although the post–World War I era in Missouri history witnessed a flowering of Black culture, it is important to remember that this remained a period of overt racial discrimination, segregation, and even racial violence in the state. No doubt the most egregious example of this reality was the persistence of lynching of Blacks. Between 1900 and 1931, mobs in the state lynched at least seventeen Black men. On April 29, 1923, for example, a mob in Columbia lynched James T. Scott, a thirty-five-year-old Black janitor employed by the University of Missouri. Scott was charged with assaulting the teenage daughter of an MU professor and was taken by force from the city jail by a white mob. None of Scott's murderers was ever brought to justice.

The Roaring Twenties came to a decisive halt in late 1929, in the wake of the October 29 stock market crash. Lives began to change as the bottom dropped out of the national and worldwide economies. Hardly anyone in the state or the nation was prepared for the hard times that would characterize the next decade and a half.

SUGGESTED READINGS

Lawrence O. Christensen and Gary R. Kremer, *A History of Missouri, 1875 to 1919* (1997); and Richard S. Kirkendall, *A History of Missouri, 1919 to 1953* (1986), both published by the University of Missouri Press, offer a good starting point for understanding this period of Missouri history.

The 1904 Louisiana Purchase Exposition, or St. Louis World's Fair as it is popularly known, has been the subject of much writing, including Dorothy Daniels Birk, *The World Came to St. Louis: A Visit to the 1904 World's Fair* (1979), published by Bethany Press; Stuart Seely Sprague, "Meet Me in St. Louis on the Ten-Million Dollar Pike," *Bulletin of the Missouri Historical Society* 32 (October 1975): 26–32. Harper Barnes, *Standing on a Volcano: The Life and Times of David Rowland Francis* (2001), published by the

Missouri in the New Century 181

Missouri Historical Society Press, provides extensive coverage of the former governor and future diplomat, who also served as president of the Louisiana Purchase Exposition.

The role of landscape architect and city planner George Kessler, who served as planner for the St. Louis World's Fair, and also for the city beautiful movement in Kansas City and St. Louis, is told in Edward C. Rafferty, "Orderly City, Orderly Lives: The City Beautiful Movement in St. Louis," *Gateway Heritage* 11 (Spring 1991): 40–65; and William H. Wilson, *The City Beautiful Movement in Kansas City* (1964), published by the University of Missouri Press.

The story of early automobile travel in St. Louis and Missouri is told in *Four Wheels, No Brakes: A History of the Early Development of the Automobile in St. Louis* (1930), published by the St. Louis Society of Automobile Pioneers. Also helpful is Floyd C. Shoemaker, "Modern Highway Development in Missouri," in *Missouri and Missourians: Land of Contrasts and People of Achievements* (1943), vol. 2, 510–13. Also helpful is David C. Austin and Thomas J. Gubbels, "A History of the Missouri State Highway Department," a study completed in 2008 for the Missouri Department of Transportation. An online version of this study may be accessed by searching "Thomas Gubbels, 'A History of the Missouri State Highway Department.'" Newspapers covered the emergence of automobiles in the state extensively, and especially the early efforts to improve Missouri's roads and highways, including the "Lift Missouri Out of the Mud" campaign. Scores of Missouri newspapers may be accessed through Newspapers.com.

Missouri during the era of World War I has been the subject of many works. John C. Crighton, *Missouri and the World War, 1914–1917: A Study in Public Opinion* (1947) remains useful. It was published by the University of Missouri Press. Historian Christopher Gibbs argues that Missouri resistance to involvement in World War I was more widespread than this book suggests. His *The Great Silent Majority: Missouri's Resistance to World War I* (1988), published by the University of Missouri Press, deserves consideration. Especially useful to this study has been Petra DeWitt's *Degrees of Allegiance: Harassment and Loyalty in Missouri's German-American Community during World War I* (2012), published by Ohio University Press. Also helpful has been David W. Detjen, *The Germans in Missouri, 1900–1918: Prohibition, Neutrality, and Assimilation* (1985), published by the

University of Missouri Press. G. K. Renner's essay, "Prohibition Comes to Missouri, 1910–1919," *Missouri Historical Review* 62 (July 1968): 363–97, is helpful as well.

There is considerable literature on the struggle for the female franchise in Missouri. Two books offer a good starting point: Virginia Laas, ed., *Bridging Two Eras: The Autobiography of Emily Newell Blair, 1877–1951* (1999), published by the University of Missouri Press, and Margot McMillen, *The Golden Lane: How Missouri Women Gained the Vote and Changed History* (2011), published by the History Press.

The story of the Spanish Influenza is told in Kevin C. McShane, "The 1918 Kansas City Influenza Epidemic," *Missouri Historical Review* 63 (October 1968): 55–70; and Robert Wilson, "St. Louis and the 1918 Influenza: The Impact of Nonpharmaceutical Interventions," *Missouri Historical Review* 105 (January 2011): 94–108. Newspapers of the period also followed closely developments associated with the Spanish Influenza.

Black baseball is the subject of Janet Bruce, *The Kansas City Monarchs: Champions of Black Baseball* (1985), published by the University Press of Kansas; and Buck O'Neil, with Steve Wulf and David Conrads, *I Was Right on Time: My Journey From the Negro Leagues to the Majors* (1996), published by Simon & Schuster.

Chapter Seven

Missouri in Crisis
The Great Depression and World War II

**"Don't you think it about time that we poor devils, both white
and black, that are being evicted and thrown out on the mercies
of the world more and more get together for protection of
ourselves and our families?**

The Reverend Owen Whitfield, October 20, 1938

MISSOURI'S RANKING AMONG the most populous states in the Union declined
steadily during the first three decades of the twentieth century. When the
century began in 1900, Missouri was the fifth largest state in the Union. By
1910, it had dropped two spots, to seventh. By 1920, it stood at ninth, and
by 1930, it had fallen to tenth. Despite the state's persistent efforts to attract
outsiders as residents, Missouri seemed to be an increasingly less attractive
destination to immigrants than other places, especially the Sun Belt states
of California, Arizona, and Florida. Indeed, historian Richard Kirkendall
has noted, "The only outsiders who were finding the state attractive in substantial numbers were blacks moving out of the South [and out of rural
Missouri]." By April 1930, a total of nearly sixty-nine million Americans
lived in "urban conditions," or 56.2 percent of the nation's population. In
Missouri, 1,859,119 people lived in urban areas, defined as cities and other
incorporated places containing 2,500 or more residents, with 1,770,248
Missourians living in rural places. Thus, for the first time in its history,
Missouri was more urban than rural, with 51.2 percent of its population living in urban areas, a direct consequence of the attraction of cities as places to
achieve the American dream during World War I and beyond. Most of these
new urbanites were migrants from rural areas of the state who were leaving
their farms because it was increasingly difficult to make a living there.

The Great Depression that spread across an entire decade of the American
experience in the 1930s is widely thought of as having begun in the wake

of the October 1929 Stock Market Crash. In reality, the Depression had begun for American farmers, Missourians among them, nearly a decade earlier.

The roots of the Depression can be seen in the national response to World War I, which ended with an Armistice on November 11, 1918. Simply put, Americans, including Missourians, were shocked and chagrined by the carnage of the war. Many thought that the worldwide conflict had been a natural consequence of "foreign entanglements," something with which Americans had long been uncomfortable. And if it was indeed the case that too much involvement with foreign powers had brought the United States into the conflict, perhaps, the same Americans argued, peace could be maintained by avoiding interaction with other countries going forward. An example of this position, which became known as Isolationism, was evidenced in a St. Louis gathering of the American Legion in May 1919, the first-ever stateside meeting of that organization. The American Legion, which had originated in Paris, France, just two months earlier, took the spirit of isolation even further, blaming foreign immigrants for labor unrest and social conflict in postwar America. They promoted the notion of "100 percent Americanism," which was also the slogan of the 1920s Ku Klux Klan, and urged lawmakers to deport immigrants who, they charged, were not ready to be assimilated into American life. This anti-immigrant sentiment, a reoccurring phenomenon throughout state and national history, would surface prominently again nearly a century later during the "America First" campaign of President Donald J. Trump.

Thus, America during the 1920s became an isolationist country that turned inward, away from the international community and increasingly toward its own people and own businesses. For a while, this worked just fine, because of the pent-up demand for manufactured and consumer goods that Americans had been forced to do without during the war years. Eventually, however, American markets were saturated and the American sentiment for foregoing trade with non-American markets led other countries to retaliate in like manner, by refusing to buy American-made goods.

Nowhere was this process more clear than in the area of agricultural production. Missouri farmers had responded positively to the call to dramatically increase their productivity as part of the war effort. And, as mentioned, during the World War I years and the 1920s, Missouri and other states witnessed the maturation of the emerging scientific agriculture movement, with an increased emphasis on the use of commercial fertilizers, the hybridization of crops (especially corn), and the rotation of crops. The need for increased production also contributed to advances in mechanization. Tractors, which greatly facilitated agricultural production, began to make their appearance in Missouri during the early 1920s, and over the course of the decade the price of tractors fell dramatically, putting them within reach of a growing number of the state's farmers. By the time the Great Depression hit Missouri, agricultural overproduction had driven farm prices so low that farmers struggled to survive.

This phenomenon of decreasing markets was evident in every sector of the state's economy. Manufacturing in the state declined dramatically because of greater supply than demand, with both wholesale and retail sales dropping significantly. During the first four years of the Depression, retail sales in Missouri dropped by approximately fifty percent. As a result, the state's unemployment rate rose to nearly sixteen percent in 1930 and more than doubled to thirty-eight percent two years later. St. Louis unemployment rose to thirty percent by 1932. Mining in the Tri-State area of southwest Missouri also suffered. As historian Richard Kirkendall has noted, "By 1932, thousands of unemployed and partially employed people lived in a huge 'Hooverville' [of impermanent, makeshift shelters] on the west bank of the Mississippi [River in St. Louis]." High rates of unemployment, the decline in wholesale and retail sales, the failure of hundreds of banks in the state, all resulted in a huge reduction in tax revenues, which led, among other things, to the elimination of two hundred faculty and staff positions at the University of Missouri and to a reduction in salaries for those employees who remained.

The man who faced the challenge of leading Missourians through the early years of the Great Depression was Republican Governor Henry S. Caulfield, a native of St. Louis. A lawyer by training, Caulfield served in Congress and as a judge, among other public positions, before being elected governor in the national Republican landslide of 1928 that saw Herbert Hoover rise to the presidency. As historian Franklin Mitchell has written, "Caulfield follow[ed] the lead of President Herbert Hoover, [and] rejected a still larger role for the state and federal government in combating the Great Depression." Like Hoover, Caulfield believed government should stay out

Fig. 34: Governor Lloyd Stark presents first unemployment compensation check received by any Missourian to unemployed construction worker, Robert Skibicki of Jefferson City, 1939. Credit: State Historical Society of Missouri, Ruth Rust Studio Photographs, 1922-1946, Collection No. P0860.

of business affairs and that relief, if it was needed, should be provided by private religious and charitable organizations.

Caulfield's successor, the Democrat Guy B. Park, a native of Platte City who was elected in the Franklin D. Roosevelt wave election of 1932, was only slightly more inclined than his predecessor to advocate for government intervention in the economy. When he did, it was primarily for federal, rather than state, intervention. Park looked primarily to President Franklin D. Roosevelt and the federal government for Great Depression relief. As historian Charles T. Jones Jr., has written, "Following Roosevelt's inauguration in March [1933], Park and the General Assembly moved to bring Missouri in line with the federal programs and agencies created to overcome the depression."

An early challenge in 1933 was that the state of Missouri had insufficient funds with which to operate. Early in the year, State Auditor Forrest Smith, a Ray County native and future Missouri governor, struggling to adjust to the dramatic reductions in state revenue, reported that "[State government] Department heads at present have to buy many of their supplies from their own money, and supply houses have been unable to collect for some deliveries."

By mid-September 1933, halfway through FDR's first year in office, Governor Park and the state legislature faced a seemingly insoluble problem: state revenue was roughly $4 million less than anticipated. The state of Missouri had only about $15,000 in its general revenue fund, clearly not enough to meet the monthly state payroll of $300,000. In addition, state officials were notified that Missouri needed to come up with an additional $250,000; failure to raise this money, federal relief director Harry Hopkins warned, would jeopardize Missouri's eligibility to receive much-needed federal relief money.

On September 15, 1933, a banker from Jefferson City, Howard Cook, president of the Central Missouri Trust Company, met with the State Board of Fund Commissioners to propose a solution to the state's dilemma. The board was composed of four statewide elected officials, all Democrats: Governor Park; State Treasurer Richard R. Nacy; State Auditor Smith; and Attorney General Roy McKittrick.

Howard Cook was no stranger either to the banking business or to Missouri politics. Born in Mexico, Missouri, in 1889, he moved to Jefferson

City with his family in 1901, after his father, Sam B. Cook, was elected secretary of state in the 1900 election. Secretary of State Cook lost his bid for reelection in 1904. In 1905 he became president of the Central Missouri Trust Company, a financial institution that had been established in the capital city in 1902. Regarded as a bank with strong ties to the Democratic Party in Missouri, the Central Missouri Trust Company's first president was former Democratic state treasurer and governor of Missouri, Lon V. Stephens.

Except for a two-year stint in the U.S. Army during World War I, Howard Cook had worked at the Central Missouri Trust Company since 1915. He assumed the bank presidency after his father's death in 1931. Like his father, Howard Cook was a state Democratic Party activist and was especially close to Governor Guy Park and State Treasurer Richard Nacy. Indeed, following his one term as state treasurer in 1937, Nacy went to work for the bank (and would eventually become its president, in 1955).

The solution to the state's financial difficulty arrived at by Governor Park, State Treasurer Nacy, Cook, and the members of the fund commission was as simple as it was bold. Mr. Cook agreed to make available to the state of Missouri up to $1 million to allow it to meet the state payroll for two months and so that the state could meet its obligation to the federal government, thereby remaining eligible to receive sorely needed federal relief funds. The state legislature would be called into special session and pass bills allowing the bank to be repaid as money became available in the general revenue fund of the state treasury. The Central Missouri Trust Company would charge no interest on the advance of money made to the state, but neither would the bank pay the state any interest on funds it held for the state. This was no small consideration, given the fact that the trust company had several millions of dollars of state money under its control, much of it in the form of bond proceeds that could not be placed in general revenue. This arrangement continued for years and secured the Central Missouri Trust Company's role as a major player in Missouri politics and banking for at least a generation.

The Great Depression took its toll on countless Missourians from all walks of life. Stories of suffering, loss, and resilience abound from those years and reveal a strength of character that twenty-first-century Missourians may have difficulty understanding. As the child of two Depression-era parents, my own upbringing was filled with these kinds of stories. None had

Fig. 35: This 1938 cartoon by famed editorial cartoonist Daniel R. Fitzpatrick drew attention to the widespread impact of the Great Depression on all Americans, Missourians included. Credit: State Historical Society of Missouri.

a greater influence on me than those told to me by my mother, Gertrude Hausmann Broker Kremer. Born in 1922, Gertrude was a middle child of seven born to a German immigrant father and a St. Louis-born mother who tried to eke out a living on a rocky, hilly farm in Osage County during the Depression. By 1934, when Gertrude was twelve, the family's fortunes hit rock bottom, this as Gertrude's mother, Leona, died at the age of thirty-nine of an embolism. She left behind her forty-nine-year-old widowed husband

and six children, ages three to seventeen. A seventh child, Rudolf, had died at the age of three, in 1930.

Gertrude's family was so poor when her mother died that the family could not afford to pay the mortician's sixty-five-dollar fee for the funeral and burial. This was a reduced rate that did not include embalming, which resulted in Leona's body beginning to decompose before burial, and the Catholic priest who presided over the funeral not allowing the casket to be brought into the church interior, a slight that pained Gertrude for the remainder of her life. The Hausmann neighbors took up a collection to help pay for the deceased woman's funeral, but their pennies, nickels, and dimes totaled only twelve dollars—they, too, were financially strapped. To make up the difference, twelve-year-old Gertrude and her fourteen-year-old sister cut dozens of loads of cordwood with a crosscut saw and hauled load after load by team and wagon to the undertaker to pay for their mother's funeral.

The next year, Gertrude graduated from elementary school—like many Depression-era children in rural Missouri, she never had a chance to go to high school—an event that was about as formal an occasion as there was in life in the northern Ozarks in 1935. Although the ceremony called for "dressing up," the best Gertrude could do, with the help of her older sisters, was to fashion a dress from feed sacks. Worst of all, she had no shoes to wear, except a hand-me-down pair of men's work shoes—brogans—that fit her all too well. Her classmates laughed at her attire.

Soon after her graduation, Gertrude was sent by her father to work as a domestic servant for a middle-aged widow, a family acquaintance, who lived in the St. Louis suburb of Maplewood. The widow shared her home with her adult daughter, her daughter's husband, and an infant grand-daughter. This sort of multi-generational shared living was a common way Missourians adapted to the challenges imposed by the Depression. Gertrude, now a teenager, took care of the entire household, which included cooking, cleaning, and doing laundry for a family of four, plus caring for the baby. She was paid $198 for fifty-two weeks of work per year. Assuming that she worked "only" forty hours per week, she earned less than ten cents per hour, although it is likely she worked much more. Arguably, the biggest perquisite of this job was that she received "free" room and board, thus diminishing the number of people her father had to care for, and providing her with far more residential comforts than were available to most, if not all, her friends and relatives back in Osage County.

For Gertrude, and for countless others who grew up in Depression-era Missouri, life was both hard and harsh. The harshness was added to by some of the most challenging weather Missourians had ever experienced, especially during the summers of the mid-1930s. The problems associated with the Great Depression—high rates of unemployment and low prices for agricultural products—were exacerbated by the droughts and heat waves of 1934 and 1936.

As early as May 1934, Dean Frederick B. Mumford of the University of Missouri's College of Agriculture was warning that "Continued drought in Missouri will result in great damage to wheat, oats and pastures." By September that year, the *Marshfield Mail* claimed that the state's residents faced "the most devastating drought of Missouri's recorded history." G. L. Davis, Emergency Agricultural agent for Franklin County, estimated that the drought cost Missouri farmers $218 million, with the largest loss, $96 million, resulting from the loss in corn production. Additionally, newspapers from across the state regularly reported on starving and thirsty livestock, parched pastures, and brown fields and crops.

In St. Louis, temperatures in 1934 reached at least 100 degrees for twenty-nine days and killed 420 people. The high temperature that summer in St. Louis was 111 degrees. The heat was even worse in 1936. The temperature reached at least 100 degrees on eighteen separate days in St. Louis in 1936, with 322 people dying from the heat by July 30 that year. All told, the summer of 1936 witnessed thirty-seven days in triple digits—the worst heat wave in St. Louis history. Thousands of city residents flocked to city parks to sleep on blankets on the grass. In a late-life interview with this author during the late 1990s, Kansas City resident Irene Whitley Marcus recalled that during the hot months of the Depression years, she and her teen-age sisters often slept in a Kansas City park and their grandfather would stop by on his way to work in the morning and wake them. Rainfall in St. Louis through July and August amounted to a paltry 1.5 inches, roughly one-fourth the normal precipitation.

And then there were floods. A 1935 flood in the Missouri River basin occurred in the spring of that year. In early June the Missouri River broke through dikes east of Hermann and flooded more than 80,000 acres of farmland, blocking highways and causing more than $1 million in crop damage. More than two hundred families were forced to leave their homes in Cedar City, across the river from Jefferson City. U.S. Highway 40 opposite St. Charles was inundated, and in Howard County, river bottoms were covered with flood waters. All told, some 700,000 acres of Missouri land was flooded, destroying crops and the hopes of Missouri farmers.

Fig. 36: Swamp Timber Country. View of several buildings, including J. B. (John) Hale General Merchandise Store, next to a plank road, ca. 1908. Dunklin County. Credit: State Historical Society of Missouri, Merritt F. Miller Collection, 1906-1927, Collection No. C3921.

Another devastating flood occurred in the Mississippi River valley two years later, despite the U.S. Army Corps of Engineers' efforts to rebuild levees and engage in other flood control measures.

The number of refugees in the wake of the 1937 flood proved overwhelming. Author David Welky noted, "They came from every race and social class, although poor whites and African Americans tended to live closer to the river and suffered disproportionately." Three thousand refugees from the flood sought shelter in the Mississippi County seat of Charleston, with another twenty-five hundred doing so in the Dunklin County town of Kennett. Unfortunately, the racial bias that plagued the state and nation then and now followed refugees into the camps. Historian John Fisher noted, "camps were segregated and charges of discrimination in the distribution of supplies and conscripted work surfaced."

Two years later, the Missouri Bootheel, the southeastern tip of the state comprising all of New Madrid, Dunklin, and Pemiscot counties, as well as parts of several other counties, again became the focal point of a crisis, with what came to be known as the "Sharecroppers' Protest of 1939." The roots of this event lay decades earlier, in the late nineteenth century, with the efforts that began during the 1890s of reclaiming the "Swampeast" lowlands for agricultural purposes. For more than a generation, large lumber companies, such as the Gideon-Anderson Lumber and Mercantile Company and the Himmelberger-Harrison Lumber Company, employed hardscrabble workers from Kentucky and Tennessee to harvest the timber of the Mississippi River basin. As the land was being cleared, people such as Otto Kochtitzky, a native of South Bend, Indiana, and a self-taught engineer, worked to drain the swamps and convert the rich alluvial soil of the basin into arable land. The most ambitious of these draining projects was the creation of the Little River Drainage District. As the land was drained, and as the boll weevil began to take its toll on cotton farming in the South, the so-called "cotton culture" moved north, to the Missouri Bootheel. With it came thousands of African Americans who hoped to make a living off the land as farm laborers and sharecroppers.

President Roosevelt's New Deal programs helped many Missouri farmers. The Agricultural Adjustment ACT (AAA) that went into effect on May 12, 1933, helped to increase prices of agricultural products by reducing supplies. The federal government purchased livestock for slaughter from farmers while also paying them subsidies to reduce the amount of land they had under cultivation. As a consequence, as historian Richard Kirkendall has pointed out, "by 1937 [farm prices] were 80 percent higher than they had been in 1932."

But New Deal agricultural programs benefitted the owners of the land rather than those who worked it. The federal programs that paid landowners not to produce crops (to keep the prices of agricultural products from dropping further) had reduced the owners' need for full-time farm laborers, including the Bootheel sharecroppers who planted, weeded, and picked the cotton there. Not only did the landowners not share their subsidy payments with the croppers, but in 1938 they began a mass eviction of croppers from the tenant houses they occupied on planters' land, hoping to hire the tenants back as day laborers as needed, without providing them with housing.

That greedy and cruel action was devastating to the sharecroppers, many of whom found themselves being evicted from their homes late in 1938, even as winter approached. In response, a local African American preacher, Owen Whitfield, organized a protest.

A native of Mississippi, Whitfield was among the thousands of African American sharecroppers who migrated to the Missouri Bootheel during the 1920s as the Southern cotton culture moved into that region. The 1930 federal census listed him as being thirty-five years old that year, living in Mississippi County, with his wife, Zella, and the couple's seven children, ranging in age from five to fifteen.

The method of protest chosen by Whitfield was a mass demonstration at the intersection of two major highways in the Bootheel. As he told a newspaper reporter in late 1938, "Don't you think it about time that we poor devils, both white and black, that are being evicted and thrown out on the mercies of the world more and more get together for protection of ourselves and our families?" On the morning of January 9, 1939, Whitfield arranged for more than one thousand demonstrators, sharecroppers and their families, to camp along the highways near the intersection of U.S. Highways 60 and 61. A majority of the demonstrators were African American, although there were some white sharecroppers among the group. According to historian John Fisher, "Those moving to the roadside had little other than a few blankets and strips of canvas to protect them from the January cold."

The protest was enormously successful in drawing attention to the sharecroppers' plight. Newspaper reporters from all over the country descended on the Bootheel to gather material for stories about the southeast Missouri sharecroppers. Within days, stories about the protest appeared in newspapers from Vermont to Oregon, and from Texas to Wisconsin. Among the people captivated by the plight of the sharecroppers was First Lady Eleanor Roosevelt. She, in turn, wrote about them in her widely read, syndicated newspaper column, "My Day," on January 31, 1939. State and local officials were embarrassed by the protest, as well as by the stories that emerged about the poor treatment of the sharecroppers. Many southeast Missouri landowners were both embarrassed and angry. They refused to believe, however, that a Negro could have planned such an elaborate protest. Many

Fig. 37: View of sharecroppers with Highway 61 behind them, January 1939. Credit: State Historical Society of Missouri, Arthur Witman Photographic Prints Collection, 1936–1956, Collection No. S0836.

blamed an eccentric white planter named Thad Snow for the protest. But, as historian Leon Ogilvie has written, "they were wrong . . . the leader was Whitfield."

Less than a week after the demonstration began, state and local authorities devised a scheme they hoped would end it. Declaring the protesters to be hazards to public health and safety, they physically removed them and their meager possessions from the roadsides, loading them into trucks and carrying them to temporary camps far from the highway. The camps were no more healthful than the roadsides.

Meanwhile, Whitfield kept up the pressure, albeit from a distance. Because of threats on his life, Whitfield retreated to St. Louis, where he continued to raise money and supplies for the protesters, as well as direct their activities from afar. By the end of 1939, however, Whitfield had gained a concession from landowners to stop evicting tenants. Likewise, he succeeded in increasing the Farm Security Administration's presence and activities in the Bootheel. The FSA, a New Deal agency created in 1937 to address the problems associated with rural poverty, established programs in the region to help sharecroppers, including building group labor camps and cooperatives for sharecroppers and day laborers. Although the gains from the sharecroppers' protest were not as transformational as Whitfield and others had hoped, the protest did improve the croppers' lives. Still the region continued to be characterized as a place of "rich land and poor people." And the Black-led demonstration, as historian John Fisher has noted, "also foreshadowed the widespread peaceful protests for racial equality and voting rights led by Martin Luther King, Jr., and others that were to come in the 1960s."

The Civilian Conservation Corps (CCC) was one of the most popular and successful of the New Deal programs. Established on April 5, 1933, the CCC was created to give young men between the ages of eighteen and twenty-five(later amended to include those seventeen to twenty-eight years old) manual labor jobs related to conservation and natural resource development of publicly owned lands. To be eligible to participate, the young men had to be unmarried, unemployed, and from a family in need. Participants admitted to the CCC earned a wage of $30 per month, $25 of which was sent directly home to their families by the program's administrators. While active in the CCC, the young men received shelter, clothing, and food, thus further relieving their families of having to provide those necessities for them.

The CCC was run by the U.S. Army and the federal Soil Erosion Service. According to historian Richard Kirkendall, "By 1937, CCC had thirty-seven camps in Missouri and over fourteen thousand enrollees. . . ." Military discipline was imposed on the enrollees, many of whom completed elementary and secondary school requirements while living in the camps. In 1935, the CCC established camps at Delta, Hayti, and New Madrid, in the Missouri Bootheel, where workers labored on the seemingly endless task of clearing brush, digging and maintaining drainage ditches, and building bridges and fences.

Historian James Denny has pointed out the critical role that the CCC played in developing Missouri state parks, established in 1917, especially in the Ozarks. According to Denny, "the first CCC camps [in Missouri] were established in three Ozarks state parks: Sam A. Baker, Meramec, and

Roaring River. Within a year, four thousand men would be employed on 40,000 acres of Missouri park lands."

The New Deal Rural Electrification Administration (REA)also greatly improved the lives of rural Missourians. The bill that created it was signed into law by President Roosevelt on May 11, 1935. The goal of this new federal agency was "to initiate, formulate, administer and supervise a program of approved projects with respect to the generation, transmission and distribution of electric energy in rural areas."

Prior to the establishment of the REA, electrical service was rare in rural America. The cost of providing electricity to homes in rural areas exceeded what the commercial utility companies could afford. As a consequence, rural housewives cooked on wood stoves, did laundry on washboards, and ironed with clumsy and inefficient flatirons. Their husbands worked during daylight hours in barns and workshops without the aid of electric lights, motors, or tools. Household lighting was provided entirely by kerosene lamps. Only rarely were farmers able to afford Delco, Genco, or Fairbanks Morse generators, usually fueled by gasoline, kerosene, or diesel fuel, and even those who could afford them bemoaned their inefficiency and unreliability.

The REA promised to change all that by making loans and technical advice available to groups that would organize "to build their own electric utilities." A preliminary meeting of central Missouri farmers interested in bringing electrical service to their communities was held in late December 1938 in the Osage County Courthouse in Linn and orchestrated largely by University of Missouri county extension agents. One of the first challenges was getting enough farmers to sign up for the service to meet the minimum requirement of at least three customers per mile of line for every one hundred miles. In addition, each subscriber to the service would have to pay a $5 initial membership fee and agree to pay for a minimum of forty-kilowatt hours (at a rate of three dollars and fifty cents) each month. These were no small requirements, especially with the Great Depression being nearly a decade old. Finally, on February 22, 1939, twelve central Missouri men signed incorporation papers to create Three Rivers Electric Cooperative. The first contract for building power lines was awarded in early 1940, and in April of that year the first pole was set by the cooperative. The pole-setting ceremony was a festive occasion, one that included a prayer of thanksgiving and the reading of a petition by the Reverend Alphonse Nicolas, pastor of Our Lady Help of Christians Parish in Frankenstein, and one of the original incorporators. The Reverend Nicolas christened the pole by crashing a kerosene lamp against it, while proclaiming, "Let there be light!" Many more poles were set in the weeks and months that followed. Ultimately, rural electrification changed the lives of countless Americans, rural Missourians among them.

The spirit of isolationism combined with the economic struggles during the decade of the 1930s caused many in the state and nation to turn a blind eye to events in Europe and Asia, where totalitarian governments bent on a militaristic expansion moved the world ever closer to another world war. Most Missourians remained isolationist during the 1930s, convinced that Americans should focus their energies on solving the very real problems here at home, rather than interjecting themselves into the affairs of foreign countries halfway around the world. They tended to agree with their United States senator, Bennett Clark, who was in the forefront of the mid-1930s effort aimed at keeping the United States neutral in the European and Asian hostilities that were building. As historian Richard Kirkendall has noted, "The alarming march of events abroad in 1938—the Japanese move into China, the prolonged civil war in Spain, and Hitler's takeover of Austria and the Sudetenland—challenged the hold of isolationism and pacifism on the Missouri mind."

Missouri Democratic Governor Lloyd C. Stark, a native of Louisiana, Missouri, was a 1908 graduate of the U.S. Naval Academy and a World War I Army veteran who had participated in the Meuse-Argonne offensive of 1918. Elected as governor in 1937, he became a leading advocate for U.S. military preparedness. In that regard, he had the strong support of Missouri's other U.S. senator, Harry S. Truman from Independence. Like Stark, Truman's world view had been shaped by his military service in World War I. Truman believed firmly in the prospect of peace through strength. Both Stark and Truman would be strong supporters of President Franklin D. Roosevelt's efforts to prepare Americans for their entry into the second world war, a prospect that by 1940 began to look inevitable.

In truth, it was not, as many people contend, the New Deal programs of the Roosevelt administration, helpful though they were, that pulled Americans or Missourians out of the Great Depression. It was the preparation for America's entry into World War II that accomplished that feat. Nearly a year before the bombing of Pearl Harbor, for example, workers began construction of the St. Louis Ordnance Plant at 4300 Goodfellow

Boulevard, on the city's northwest edge. Construction of the facility employed some seventeen thousand workers on the $110 million construction project. The plant began producing ordnance in little more than a week after the Japanese attack on Pearl Harbor. At its peak, in 1943, the St. Louis Ordnance Plant employed some thirty-five thousand people, with women making up half its work force. Over the course of the war, more than eighty-six thousand people would find jobs at what was commonly referred to as the "Cartridge Plant." The plant was also a flashpoint for racial conflict. In June 1942, three hundred African Americans marched in protest of the plant's segregated production lines. Full racial integration of the plant occurred in December 1944. McDonnell Aircraft Corporation, founded in 1938 at St. Louis's Lambert Field, gained its first contracts in 1940, and within a year was employing more than five thousand workers, more than half of them women. The Pratt and Whitney Aircraft Corporation in Kansas City employed more than twenty thousand workers at its wartime peak, many of them women. In Springfield, the Reynolds Manufacturing Company and the Producers Produce Company devoted themselves to war work, the latter company using a labor force that was more than seventy-five percent female. Throughout the state, workers who had been unable to find employment during the Great Depression went to work, and a disproportionate percentage of the work force was female.

The building of Fort Leonard Wood near the Pulaski County town of Waynesville during the early 1940s illustrates the point of how the monumental effort at war preparedness led to jobs for Missourians. The origin of Fort Leonard Wood lay in the growing fear of Adolf Hitler and his Nazi war machine during the late 1930s. American isolationism during the 1920s and 1930s had led to the relative decline of the U.S. Army as an effective fighting force, with some analysts ranking it as low as eighteenth in the world in 1940. With the fall of France to the Germans in 1940, U.S. governmental officials, including new Army Chief of Staff George C. Marshall, moved to enlarge the nation's armed services and greatly expand military training.

President Franklin D. Roosevelt signed the Burke-Wadsworth Act, also known as the Selective Service and Training Act, which established a national draft in September 1940. A push began for creating new and better training facilities for the anticipated 1.4 million draftees who would soon be entering the Army.

The next month, the War Department decided to build a new base for the Seventh Corps Area Training Center just south of Waynesville, in the south-central Missouri Ozarks. The camp was to be built to accommodate thirty-five thousand men at a projected cost of $35 million.

The War Department began to move as quickly as possible to acquire the sixty-five thousand acres of land needed to build the base. Twelve thousand acres of the Mark Twain National Forest were immediately available, thanks to the recent creation of the national forest area on September 11, 1939. The remainder of the land needed had to be acquired from the roughly two hundred landowners in the area. In all, the project required the relocation of approximately three hundred local families and the evacuation of a half dozen or more communities. Some of those forced to move protested the government's intrusion. Others saw leaving their homes as a patriotic duty that they were obligated to perform.

The responsibility of building the base fell to the Army Corps of Engineers. Their first challenge, after securing the land, was clearing it, a process begun during the winter of 1940. Groundbreaking began on December 3, followed shortly thereafter by the arrival of would-be workers into the area. With the negative effects of the Great Depression still holding sway, men in search of work came from a one-hundred-mile radius. As Fort Leonard Wood historian, Paul W. Bass, put it, "One week after the groundbreaking . . . a steady stream of workers began arriving in the area overnight. Over 7,000 vehicles a day inched along the two-lane Route 66. In early fall, 1940, Waynesville had a population of about 462. Within a few months, its population increased ten-fold to over 4,000."

By early spring 1941, the project employed nearly thirty-one thousand workers with a weekly payroll of more than $1.3 million, said by historian Bass to be "the largest single payroll in the United States." The building of Fort Leonard Wood understandably spawned a real estate and civilian housing boom, as well as the emergence of all sorts of service industry businesses, long before any soldiers were stationed there. By the time that soldiers did begin to arrive at Fort Leonard Wood, in May 1941, Pulaski County had been forever changed.

Change came even more quickly after the Japanese bombed Pearl Harbor and the United States declared war against Japan and Germany in December 1941. One of the many challenges faced by Army officials was providing recreational opportunities for the tens of thousands of GI's stationed at Fort Leonard Wood. The National USO (United Service Organization, Inc.) arranged for events on base throughout the war years and established USO centers in Waynesville, Rolla, and Lebanon. A local resort on the Gasconade River known as Pippin Place became a popular gathering place for officers.

One of the dramatic consequences of the presence of the fort in the Ozarks was the introduction of a great deal of cultural diversity into a region of the state that previously had been characterized by its homogeneity. Soldiers who had emigrated to the United States from countries all over the world found themselves confronted with the challenge of facing locals who harbored hostility to outsiders. Although some Pulaski County residents welcomed the exposure to new people and cultures, others resisted what they saw as a threat to their way of life. African American soldiers had an especially difficult time, given the racial segregation of the Army itself, as well as the segregation of the community in which the fort was located. African American soldiers often sought their recreation in Jefferson City, an hour's drive from the fort, where an African American USO welcomed them. Occasionally, Fort Leonard Wood commanders tried to arrange special events on base for Black soldiers. Such was the case on November 21, 1942, when African American poet, playwright, and novelist Langston Hughes was brought in to entertain the "colored troops." In 1942, also, a Black officers' club was established on the base.

Even though it had occurred thousands of miles away, the Japanese attack on Pearl Harbor frightened Missourians. No one felt safe. Soldiers from St. Louis's Jefferson Barracks began patrolling bridges, railways, and major roads. An ammunition plant at Weldon Spring was heavily guarded.

A practice blackout was held in St. Louis on Sunday, December 14, 1941, one week after the Pearl Harbor bombing. Blackouts began first with neighborhoods, then sections of the city, and, finally, the whole city itself. They were carried out under the direction of city Civil Defense Coordinator Harry D. McBride. Volunteers traveled around the city, making certain all residents and businesses complied with the order. Private planes soared above the city, trying to make certain that no lights that could serve as beacons for enemy aircraft were visible from the sky. Meanwhile, an effort was launched to recruit thirty-two thousand Missourians for a statewide air defense system that would allow the army to intercept enemy aircraft in the event of an attack.

In St. Louis, Henry S. Caulfield, director of public welfare, and a former Missouri governor, directed the city's medical division staff to prepare for treating casualties. First aid posts were set up throughout the City of St. Louis and the county, and hospitals in the area were surveyed as to their ability to serve as field hospitals and were stockpiled with medical and surgical supplies.

Pearl Harbor also touched off a mass enlistment of Missourians who wanted to serve in the armed forces to defend their country and seek revenge on the Japanese. In St. Louis, more than four hundred would-be sailors showed up at the downtown Navy recruiting office on December 8, 1941, the morning after the Pearl Harbor bombing. Another three hundred fifty men showed up at the Army recruiting office.

In Missouri's capital city, sirens whistled the lights out at 10:00 p.m. on Monday night, December 14. Traffic stopped, and an eerie silence prevailed for twenty minutes. One hundred thousand volunteers statewide staffed battle stations and prepared for an attack that never came. Many of the would-be volunteers were too young to serve, others among them too old. Still others were not physically fit enough, many having suffered from malnutrition and inadequate health care during the lean 1930s. On December 19, the *St. Louis Post-Dispatch* reported that since the Pearl Harbor bombing, 402 applications for service had been received; 152 (38 percent) of those applying had been accepted. In the small southeast Missouri town of Poplar Bluff, within eleven days after Pearl Harbor, 144 men had applied for enlistment in the Navy and Naval Reserve. Because of citizen interest, the recruiting station remained open twenty-four hours a day, seven days a week. In Chillicothe, eight "boys" applied to enlist in the Navy within forty-eight hours of the Pearl Harbor attack. By Christmas Day in 1941, forty-three St. Joseph area youths had tentatively been accepted for service in the Navy and Marine Corps.

The war required sacrifice on the part of everyone, something that a generation of Missourians hardened by the shortages and deprivations of the Great Depression found tolerable. As the one-year anniversary of the Pearl Harbor attack neared, gas rationing was imposed by the federal government. The first day of gas rationing in St. Louis, November 1, 1942, saw a dramatic decrease in the number of cars on the streets. St. Louis police captain Fred H. Gabbe, head of the police department traffic division, estimated that rationing reduced the number of cars on St. Louis streets by half. Automobile owners were required to register their vehicles and get gas ration books. The books entitled car owners to purchase four gallons of gasoline a week. Fuel rationing was also aimed at addressing a desperate rubber shortage as the United States began to experiment with and then start to produce synthetic rubber, the consequence of Japanese control of the primary rubber producing nations of Malaya and Dutch East Indies. Car registration also required car owners to report the number of tires they owned—five per car being the maximum allowed. Tire rationing had begun early in 1942. Gas rationing was perceived to be a particularly difficult challenge in rural Missouri, where mass transit was unavailable, and where farmers, for example, often had to travel great distances to access public services or market their produce.

In the Stoddard County town of Dexter, and presumably elsewhere, the impending imposition of gas rationing led to a run on filling stations just prior to the effective date. At least some St. Louis County residents decided to move to the city, where they could access public transit.

By September 1942, farm machinery, too, was being rationed. "Certificates of War Necessity" could be obtained by farmers. Likewise, there was food rationing, aimed at diverting food from civilian to military consumers. Meat, especially beef, was rationed, as were dairy products, canned and dried fruits and vegetables, canned fish, and poultry.

World War II brought both opportunities as well as challenges to the state's African American population. The war opened new job possibilities in St. Louis and Kansas City and accelerated the urbanization of the state's Blacks, a phenomenon that had already been transpiring for decades. It also provided Blacks with an opportunity to demonstrate, once again, their importance in American society. Finally, it provided all Americans, Black and white, an opportunity to see clearly what could happen when racism, such as that espoused by Adolf Hitler, was allowed to be carried out to its logical extreme on a federal or state level.

A lynching of a Black man in Sikeston (Scott County) in 1942, this at a time when other Black men were fighting and dying as American soldiers in the European and Pacific theaters of war, seemed particularly disturbing and paradoxical to many Americans. The disgraceful incident unfolded after Sikeston police arrested Cleo Wright, a twenty-six-year-old Black mill worker and ex-convict, shortly after 1:30 a.m. on January 12, 1942. He was accused of attacking a local white woman in her home. Wright allegedly resisted arrest and pulled a knife on policemen, after which officers responded by shooting him four times and severely beating him with a flashlight. Near death, Wright was bandaged and sutured at the local hospital, which provided only emergency treatment to Black patients, and then transferred to the local jail. At 11:30 a.m. that same day, a Scott County mob stormed the jail, overpowered the state troopers on guard, and removed the prisoner. The mob tied Wright to the back of a car, dragged him through the streets of Sunset Addition, Sikeston's Black district, and finally set the battered corpse on fire, a clear warning to other African Americans that they, too, could be killed if they angered local whites. Wright's death certificate noted that he was the victim of "violence by persons unknown," even though the murder was perpetrated by a mob in a small town, where everyone knew everyone else.

Wright's brutal murder dramatically linked American racism to the barbarities perpetrated by America's enemies in the horrific war, the totalitarian regimes of Nazi Germany, Fascist Italy, and Japan. While Black soldiers were fighting and dying in a second world war waged for democracy in Europe and the Pacific, the brutal lynching reinforced the notion that African Americans remained second-class citizens on the home front. As one Black newspaper editor bitterly commented, "Remember Pearl Harbor . . . and Sikeston, Missouri."

The public outrage over Wright's murder prompted the U.S. Department of Justice to conduct a federal investigation of the lynching, but its efforts proved futile. On July 30, 1942, a federal grand jury refused to return any indictments against the Sikeston mob, despite what appeared to be a strong legal case. It concluded that the members of the lynch mob had denied Wright due process, but had committed no federal offense since Wright was either dying or already dead. Nevertheless, the U.S. government's prosecution of Wright's lynchers set a precedent for federal intervention into civil rights cases, and the federal government would urgently renew its investigation of such cases in postwar America in its attempt to protect African Americans' civil rights.

The end of the war in Europe came with the unconditional surrender of Germany on the morning of May 7, 1945. Newspapers all over the state carried headlines, such as "War in Europe Over!" (Macon), "War in Europe Ends—VE Declaration Today," (St. Joseph), "German Surrender Ratified," (Joplin), "War Ends in Europe," (Moberly).

All that remained was for the Japanese to surrender and bring an end to the war in the Pacific Theater as well. As it turned out, the unconditional surrender of the Japanese came in the wake of a decision by President Harry S. Truman, the Missouri-born former U.S. senator who was serving as FDR's vice-president when the latter died in April. It was Truman who ordered the dropping of atomic bombs on the Japanese cities of Hiroshima (August 6, 1945) and Nagasaki (August 9, 1945). Within less than a week after the dropping of the "A-bombs," the Japanese surrendered unconditionally. Unofficial reports of the surrender reached St. Louis about 2:30 in the morning on August 14, 1945. People poured into the streets of the city to celebrate. Henry Ruggeri scrambled to open his tavern on the south side. Churches opened their doors, and, as a *St. Louis Post-Dispatch* reporter noted, "young women kissed any guy in uniform." Stationed in Guam, Navy Pharmacy Mate, 1st Class, Norman L. Dickey wrote to his mother back in Cabool, "Everyone here has had their fingers crossed, hoping for the latest and best news. We hadn't much heart for writing, until we heard the final word of surrender. Naturally, everyone is very happy about it, but it is a sort of an unexplainable quiet joy . . . ."

In Missouri's capital city, Mayor Jesse N. Owens urged all stores to close and churches were asked to open their doors. Residents began to look forward to an end to rationing, and a local newspaper carried an article proclaiming, "Hey Gals, You May Get Nylons by New Year's." The formal end to the war came on the deck of the battleship *USS Missouri* on September 2, 1945, when representatives of the Japanese government signed the official surrender documents.

The war took a heavy toll on Missourians, including my own family. My mother, Gertrude Hausmann, married her childhood sweetheart, Army Air Corpsman Theodore R. Broker, on December 6, 1943, while Ted was home on military leave. The couple spent a brief honeymoon together before Ted returned to service and was shipped to the South Pacific theater of war. My mother never saw him again. On December 5, 1944, one day short of the couple's one-year wedding anniversary, Ted died when the B-24 "Liberator Bomber" on which he served as a tail gunner crashed. He never met the baby girl, my sister, who had been conceived during the couple's all-too-short honeymoon. Such were the ways of war, and the heartbreaking sacrifices that everyday people, Missourians among them, were called upon to make. More than four hundred fifty thousand Missourians served in the armed forces during World War II, roughly three hundred thousand of them as draftees. With war's end, suddenly tens of thousands of Missourians, as well as the loved ones they had left behind, looked forward to getting back to the lives they had known in their home state before the war. For good or bad, however, their lives would never be the same.

SUGGESTED READINGS

Anyone interested in this period of Missouri history should begin by reading Richard S. Kirkendall's *A History of Missouri, 1919–1953* (1986), published by the University of Missouri Press. Also helpful is Walter A. Schroeder and Howard W. Marshall, *The WPA Guide to 1930s Missouri* (1986), published by the University Press of Kansas. J. Christopher Schnell, Richard J. Collings, and David W. Dillard, "The Political Impact of the Depression on Missouri, 1929–1940," *Missouri Historical Review* 85 (January 1991): 131–57, focuses on the state's political response to the Great Depression.

The stories of the Central Missouri Trust Company's bailout of Missouri state government during the early depression, of Gertrude A. Hausmann, and of the rural electrification movement are told in Gary R. Kremer, *Heartland History: Essays on the Cultural Heritage of the Central Missouri Region* in 3 vols. (2000–2004), G. Bradley Publishing and City of Jefferson. For a good history of the 1937 Flood, see David Welky, *The Thousand-Year Flood: The Ohio-Mississippi Disaster of 1937* (2011), published by the University of Chicago Press.

The story of the reclamation of "swampeast" Missouri as well as the Sharecroppers' Protest of 1939 is told in John C. Fisher, *Southeast Missouri from Swampland to Farmland: The Transformation of the Lowlands* (2017), published by McFarland & Company, Inc., Publishers. Additional works to be consulted on the sharecroppers' protest include Louis C. Cantor, *A Prologue to the Protest Movement: The Missouri Sharecropper Roadside Demonstration of 1939* (1969), published by Duke University Press; and Jarod Roll, *Spirit of Rebellion: Labor and Religion in the New Cotton South* (2010), published by the University of Illinois Press. Also useful is Bonnie Stepenoff, *Thad Snow: A Life of Social Reform in the Missouri Bootheel* (2003), published by the University of Missouri Press.

Senator Harry S. Truman's emergence as a supporter of American involvement in World War II is the subject of Mark Steven Wilburn, "Keeping the Powder Dry: Senator Harry S. Truman and Democratic Interventionism,

1935–1941," *Missouri Historical Review* 84 (April 1990): 311–37. The Fort Leonard Wood story, and its impact on the region of the Missouri Ozarks where it was built, is told by Paul W. Bass, *The History of Fort Leonard Wood* (2016), published by Acclaim Press.

The story of the struggle for social and racial justice in St. Louis during the era of the Great Depression and World War II is told in a number of works, including Keona K. Ervin, *Gateway to Equality: Black Women and the Struggle for Economic Justice in St. Louis* (2017), published by University Press of Kentucky; and Priscilla A. Dowden-White, *Groping Toward Democracy: African American Social Welfare Reform in St. Louis, 1910–1949* (2011), published by the University of Missouri Press. Also helpful is James W. Endersby and William T. Horner, *Lloyd Gaines and the Fight to End Segregation* (2016), published by the University of Missouri Press.

The story of the Cleo Wright lynching is told by Dominic J. Capeci Jr., *The Lynching of Cleo Wright* (1998), published by University Press of Kentucky.

.

Chapter Eight

Hope and Change in Post–World War II Missouri, 1945–1969

"I feel sort of helpless about it. . . . I don't like to believe war is ahead, but if there's anything history teaches us, it's that war is inevitable.

Dr. Edwin F. Gildea, October 12, 1962

FOR A TIME after World War II, it seemed as though anything was possible. A country that could defeat the Axis powers could accomplish almost anything. No problem seemed too big to take on, no challenge too great. There was a pervasive optimism throughout the state and nation, and a widespread feeling that government, especially the federal government, could bring about an almost utopian society.

By the time that World War II came to an end, Americans, Missourians among them, were tired of doing without and making do. They had endured a decade and a half of economic insecurity, food and consumer goods shortages, and deprivation of consumer conveniences. Many had delayed marriage, starting a family, and purchasing big-ticket items, such as automobiles and houses. Their pent-up desire to be consumers of goods and services would drive the national economy to a level never experienced.

One of the first challenges facing the more than sixteen million Americans who had served their country in the armed services was the transition back into civilian life. Hundreds of thousands of those World War II soldiers were Missourians.

Arguably, one of the most important actions taken by the federal government to help returning soldiers was the Servicemen's Readjustment Act of 1944, more commonly referred to simply as the "GI Bill." There were many challenges facing the returning servicemen. None was more urgent than the housing shortage. A provision of the GI Bill provided a government guarantee of 50 percent of a loan to a qualifying veteran, up to $2,000, to assist with buying or building a house, repairing or altering a house already owned by a veteran, or paying off debts or back taxes incurred while the former soldier was in the service.

To be sure, the flood of servicemen and women returning from the war created a heightened demand for new housing. In January 1946 the St. Louis *Globe-Democrat* reported, "St. Louis faces the problem of finding living quarters for 6000 more families in the next three months, during which an estimated 40,000 more servicemen will return to the city."

The *Kansas City Star* framed the problem this way: "Kansas City faces the hard fact that our own servicemen are shut out of their city. They went away to fight the battles of the people back home and now the home folks have filled up all the living space. No self-respecting community can take such a situation lying down." In Kansas City, the city board of zoning adjustment dealt with the housing shortage by, among other things, granting "many permits for persons to live in remodeled garages and other such buildings." "In many cases," the local newspaper reported, "persons converted garages into living quarters without obtaining permits."

There were many consequences of the housing shortage, the most obvious of which was that, thanks to the guaranteed loans available to veterans, there was a tremendous postwar boom in the building industry and in building-associated businesses. The demand for building supplies drove an increase in manufacturing of construction-related goods and competition for workers who could produce those goods. Similarly, an increased demand for construction workers put them in high demand, elevating their wages and facilitating their ability to unionize. The result was a sort of golden age for workers who could be relatively easily trained to build houses, or build the things needed to build houses.

Another feature of the GI Bill that had a tremendous impact on Missourians was a provision that offered assistance for returning servicemen who wanted to attend college. Speaking on the Drury College campus in Springfield on March 15, 1946, U.S. Army General Omar D. Bradley, a native of Moberly, Missouri, who had recently been appointed to head the U.S. Veterans Administration, touted a college education as "a gateway to opportunity," saying it was the thing desired "more than anything else" by returning service men and women.

According to University of Missouri President Frederick A. Middlebush, enrollment at the university had risen to 6,600 students just before the war. By the fall of 1945, however, the number of students had dwindled to below 2,000. Law school enrollment dropped from an annual average of 160 to 17 during wartime. By the fall of 1946, however, enrollment had climbed to 10,600, with roughly seventy percent of the increase made up of students on the GI Bill. Dr. Thomas Brady, university vice president, said the university would "continue our ban on girls from other states" so as to ensure the school's ability to "accept Missouri students and all male veterans."

The dramatic increase in enrollment created challenges and headaches for university administrators and hardships for students. The university brought in surplus barracks from Fort Leonard Wood, as well as Quonset huts and government-owned trailers. By fall 1946 there were three trailer camps on or near the MU campus providing student housing for veterans and their families in cramped spaces. "G.I. Village" was home to two hundred sixty-five trailers and another one hundred fifty trailers were located at "Fairway Village," formerly the university golf course.

Rothwell Gymnasium was home to 174 veterans, with a similar number housed in a university maintenance shop. Unlike prewar students, many of those on the GI Bill were married, forcing the university to provide for the students' families as well. Many of the temporary housing units were inadequately heated, prompting a group of about one hundred students to march on Jesse Hall, the main administration building, in January 1947 to protest the conditions under which they lived. One of the student protesters commented that Jesse Hall was chosen as the demonstration site, in part, "because it was warm there."

Clearly, housing all the many new students was a challenging problem, as was feeding them. An emergency cafeteria was set up in Crowder Hall, the "chow line" for which was often more than a block long. The university had no choice but to seek immediate assistance from the legislature for funds to build more classrooms as well as dormitories with cafeterias.

Other higher education institutions, including the state's community and junior colleges, faced similar growing pains after the war. Moberly Junior College enrollment grew by more than forty percent during the first year after the war, while Joplin Junior College reported the largest enrollment in the school's eight-year history in October 1946.

Fig. 38: A small cluster of student housing trailers for University of Missouri students on Sixth Street, Columbia, ca. 1946. Credit: State Historical Society of Missouri, University of Missouri Photograph Collection, 1848-1995, Collection No. P0088.

The GI Bill changed the entire college experience by opening the opportunity for a college education to working-class Missourians, persons who a generation earlier, might have either stayed on the farm or entered the labor force right out of high school. Suddenly, college was no longer only for the rich and privileged.

It was also no longer only for unmarried eighteen- to twenty-year-olds. GI Bill students tended to be older than traditional students and, arguably, more serious and purposeful. They tended to view college less as a place to party and more as a place to prepare for a good-paying job, even launch a career. GI Bill students changed campus traditions. Restricting campus contests such as the selection of a homecoming queen to unmarried students was abandoned. So, too, was upper-class harassment and hazing of freshmen. After all, what sophomore, junior, or even senior wanted to risk a fight with a battle-hardened veteran in order to make a "frosh" wear a beanie and pay homage to him?

Another profound impact that World War II had was the change in the role and status of American women. The war forced many women to fend for themselves in ways that were uncommon, even unknown, during the decade or so prior to the war. Because of the shortage of men available to work during the fighting, women were recruited and left the house (many finding themselves working outside the home and for wages for the first times in their lives) to work in jobs previously thought of as "men's work." Newspaper want ads during the war sought out women workers for all sorts of factory work, from assemblers, to machinists, to welders: "Cupples Co. needs women 18–40; Factory Work; Essential; Steady." "Women—18–45. For General Factory Labor in Essential Activity. No Previous Experience Required." "Factory Workers—Girls. Women. White. Age 18 to 40. Essential War Work; No Experience Necessary. American Stove Company. 2001 S. Kingshighway."

There were other consequences of the war. One was the dramatic increase in the number of babies born in the immediate postwar period. Many individuals, Missourians among them, had postponed marriage and having children during the difficult Depression years. And the forced separations of many couples associated with the draft and mandatory military service further delayed marriage and starting a family through the mid-1940s.

War's end, however, and the return of millions of GI's, and the emergence of a strong postwar economy, driven by consumer spending, led to a dramatic increase in the number of babies being born during the decade and more following World War II. This "baby boom," in turn, wrought changes in the state and the nation that few could have imagined in 1945.

According to a 1954 report produced by the Kiplinger Washington Letter, the main reason for the baby boom was prosperity: "Young folks see relatively clear economic sailing, so go in for families." By the fall of 1952, as the baby boom children were reaching school age, the Missouri Department of Education announced that it expected twenty thousand more children enrolled in the state's public schools than had been enrolled the previous year. School districts all over the state scrambled to adjust to the large influx of new school children. As the superintendent of schools in St. Joseph, Missouri, noted, the school district there was unprepared: "[O]ur buildings and offerings were geared to a pre-1945 birth rate." He acknowledged that St. Joseph would need thirty-eight to forty additional school rooms to accommodate the boomers through the eighth grade, to say nothing of high school. Maryville's Eugene Field School anticipated "a record 528 students" in the fall of 1955. School districts all over the state sought to pass new bond issues and tax levies that would allow them to build new schools and hire more teachers. And the boomers kept coming! In 1945, sixty-seven thousand babies were born in Missouri. By 1954, that number jumped to ninety-four thousand.

Another postwar challenge was a growing uneasiness with the racial status quo. World War II brought great opportunity for millions of African Americans, including those in Missouri. The war opened new job possibilities for African Americans in St. Louis and Kansas City, thereby increasing the urbanization of the state's population. It also drew attention to the incongruity of African Americans fighting and dying to defeat the racism of German dictator Adolf Hitler and his Axis allies, while still being subjected to racial discrimination and repression in their homeland.

Black leaders such as W. E. B. DuBois and A. Philip Randolph urged African Americans to engage in a "Double-V" campaign, calling for victory both abroad and at home. Coming out of the war, a growing number of African Americans challenged the racial status quo. The war and their war experiences led many Blacks to believe that their long struggle for equality was nearly over.

Several immediate postwar occurrences encouraged this optimism. One was the legal challenge to what were known as "restrictive covenants" that emerged in St. Louis immediately after the war. Restrictive covenants were provisions written into legal land documents that prohibited the sale of property to anyone not of the "Caucasian Race." This practice was common throughout Missouri, especially in towns and cities. J. D. and Ethel Shelley, a Black couple who had left Starkville, Mississippi, for St. Louis just before the war began to try to build a better life for themselves and their six children, purchased a house at 4600 Labadie Street in St. Louis. Two days after the family moved into the house, in October 1945, two white neighbors, Louis and Fern Kraemer, sued to evict the Shelleys, citing a restrictive covenant attached to the house's deed. The restriction, dating to 1911, barred any owners of the property from transferring property ownership to "persons of the Negro and Mongolian race."

The Kraemers argued in court that they would "suffer irreparable injury and irremediable damage to their property" if the Shelleys were permitted to retain title to their property. The Kraemers were supported in their efforts by a group calling itself the Marcus Avenue Improvement Association.

While a local court refused to evict the Shelleys, the Missouri Supreme Court overturned their ruling in December 1946 and called for the enforcement of the covenant, even though it acknowledged the inadequacy of acceptable and affordable housing for African Americans in St. Louis. Emil Koob, president of the Marcus Avenue Improvement Association, rightly noted that the court's decision would mean that other restrictive covenants in the city would remain in effect.

Instead, the Shelleys' attorney, George L. Vaughn, appealed the decision to the U.S. Supreme Court. Vaughn, a native of Columbus, Kentucky, was a graduate of the Walden University Law School in Tennessee, and had moved to St. Louis during the World War I era. He helped establish the city's Citizen Liberty League and was active in the St. Louis Civil Rights struggle until his death in 1949.

The U.S. Supreme Court heard the *Shelley v. Kraemer* case and in May 1948 ruled that the restrictive covenant was unenforceable and that the Shelleys had the right to live in their home. The May 4, 1948, edition of *The St. Louis Star and Times* quoted Mrs. Shelley, who worked as a maid at the Welsh Baby Carriage Co., as saying, "All we wanted was a decent place to rear the children." Mr. Shelley worked as a laborer at the George L. Cousins Contracting Co.

Another occurrence in 1948 that lifted the hopes of African Americans for a more just and equitable society was U.S. President Harry S. Truman's directive, issued on July 26, 1948, ordering the racial integration of the nation's armed forces. The policy mandated "that there shall be equality of treatment and opportunity for all persons in the armed services without regard to race, color, religion or national origin."

Still, there were struggles along the way. Change was hard, halting, and at times violently resisted. June 21, 1949, marked the first day that the public swimming pools in St. Louis opened to Blacks and whites. Violence occurred at the Fairgrounds Park Pool almost immediately after the pool opened at 2:00 p.m. that day. Angry whites protested the presence of African Americans at the pool, and fights broke out between them and the badly outnumbered Blacks. Gangs of white youths roamed the park, some armed with sticks and clubs, randomly attacking and beating African Americans. A Black man and a white youth were stabbed, and at least ten other persons were injured. It took some four hundred policemen to restore order. Mayor Joseph M. Darst ordered Director of Public Welfare John J. O'Toole to re-instate the policy of racial segregation at the city's pools, a circumstance that prevailed for the next year. On June 22, 1950, attorney George W. Draper II and Rose Taylor, secretary for the local chapter of the NAACP, sued the city after both were refused access to Fairgrounds Park Swimming Pool. Their suit asked for the city pools to be reopened to African Americans. They also asked for $10,000 in compensatory damages and $25,000 in punitive damages. One month later, U.S. District Judge Rubey M. Hulen ordered the City of St. Louis to admit Negroes to all open-air swimming pools under their control, although he declined to award any monetary damages. His order went into effect at 6:00 a.m. on Wednesday, July 19, 1950. Fifty years later, Attorney Draper's son, George W. Draper III, served as the Chief Justice of the Missouri Supreme Court.

Another victory for civil rights supporters during the postwar era came in 1950 in a court challenge to the University of Missouri's policy of refusing to admit African American students to the school. Gus Ridgel, a Poplar Bluff student, sought admission to the graduate school at Columbia, and Elmer Bell Jr. and George E. Horne, both from St. Louis, sought admission to the university's Rolla School of Mines. All were denied admission be-cause of their race. On June 27, 1950, Cole County Circuit Judge Sam C. Blair held that all Missouri state-supported institutions of higher learning must admit Negroes if they were qualified students and if the courses they sought were not offered by Lincoln University, Missouri's historically-Black university.

In the fall of 1950, nine African American students enrolled at Mizzou, Ridgel among them, ending the more-than-a-century-old practice of not admitting African Americans. Access to elementary and secondary educa-tion without regard to race in Missouri had to await the famous *Brown v. Board of Education* decision, handed down by the U.S. Supreme Court in May 1954. The next month, the Missouri Commission on Education asked the state attorney general what effect the *Brown* case would have on the state's racially segregated schools. He responded that the state's school seg-regation laws were null and void. Integration, as the U.S. Supreme Court ordered the next year, must proceed, "with all deliberate speed."

The Supreme Court's mandate notwithstanding, the integration of Missouri's public elementary and secondary schools did not always go smoothly. Integration of public schools in St. Louis and Kansas City, where ninety percent of the state's Black school-aged children lived, got off to a slow start. A major problem with implementing the *Brown* decision in Missouri's two largest cities was that Blacks were segregated into all-Black neighborhoods. Integration of a school district meant little if the district itself was virtually all-Black. Consequently, even though most Missouri school districts were legally desegregated by the 1960s, a majority of Black students were still attending all-Black schools.

One way to address this form of segregation was to bus students from one district into another, but difficulties often multiplied when school districts began busing students to try to achieve racial integration. The process that occurred in St. Louis illustrates the problem. During the 1961-1962 school year, the city's school board decided to bus pupils from predominantly or all-Black schools. The twenty schools receiving the bused students were all-white, and ninety-five percent of the bused pupils were Black. The students were bused as entire classes, meaning that even with busing, the students tended to remain in segregated classroom settings.

A decade later, during the early 1970s, a group of north side Black parents sued the St. Louis City Board of Education, alleging that the city's school system remained racially segregated and in violation of the U.S. Constitution. After nearly a decade of legal machinations, the plaintiffs won their case, with a federal judge ordering the state of Missouri to fund an effort that included busing to desegregate the city's public schools. In 1986 court-ordered desegregation plans were extended to Kansas City. By 1990 the state of Missouri reached the billion-dollar mark in payments to St. Louis and Kansas City school districts for court-ordered desegregation. Missouri Attorney General Jay Nixon sought for years to end mandatory busing to achieve desegregation in St. Louis and Kansas City, finally succeeding in 1999 in making the efforts at desegregation voluntary instead of mandatory.

If there was a dominant fear in the state and nation during the generation after World War II, it was the fear of international communism. Although the Soviet Union had been a critical American ally in the fight against the Axis Powers during World War II, Americans' fear of the Soviets' international ambitions took hold even before the war had ended. Arguably, that fear was most forcefully articulated by none other than Winston Churchill, the former (and future) prime minister of the United Kingdom. On March

5, 1946, in response to a personal invitation from President Harry Truman, Churchill delivered a momentous speech at Westminster College in Fulton, Missouri. It was in that speech, formally titled "Sinews of Peace," that Churchill warned against the expansionist policies of the Soviet Union, proclaiming that "an iron curtain" had "descended across the [European] continent," behind which the "Soviet Sphere" was emerging in a diabolical plot aimed at world domination through a totalitarian state.

Many observers mark what came to be known as Churchill's Iron Curtain Speech as the beginning of the Cold War, a time of mutual mistrust and fear that put both former allied nations at odds, if not into armed conflict against one another. Across the United States, the fear of international communism grew exponentially with the explosion of the Soviets' first atomic weapon on August 29, 1949, followed shortly thereafter by the "fall of China" and the creation of the People's Republic of China by Chinese Communist leader Mao Zedong, on October 1, 1949.

Churchill's Iron Curtain speech, interestingly, was memorialized some forty-four years later by former President Ronald Reagan, also at Westminster College. The date was November 9, 1990, the one-year anniversary of the fall of the Berlin Wall. The occasion was the dedication of the sculpture "Breakthrough," created by Churchill's granddaughter, Edwina Sands. Reagan was less than two years removed from the presidency, and his speech was one that conflicts with the message of President Donald Trump's proposed wall, separating Mexico from the United States in the twenty-first century. In his speech, titled "The Brotherhood of Man," Reagan had this to say about walls separating people: "In dedicating this magnificent sculpture, may we dedicate ourselves to hastening the day when all God's children live in a world without walls."

The early Cold War years produced a suspicion of African American intellectuals throughout the country, some of whom allowed their frustration with persistent postwar racism to praise what they perceived as a more open, egalitarian Soviet society. In some cases, the FBI scrutinized the writings and behavior of African American university faculty members. Such was the case at Lincoln University, Missouri's historically Black university in Jefferson City.

In the fall of 1948, a much-respected Lincoln University history professor, Dr. Lorenzo J. Greene, launched a new scholarly publication called the *Midwest Journal*, described by Greene as "A Magazine of Research and

Creative Writing." In the second issue of the journal's first volume, published in the summer of 1949, Greene included a controversial essay, titled "Role of Students in China's Struggle," by Shu-yi Yang. In the essay, Yang identified the Soviet Union as a source of hope "for the peasant countries in Asia." He went on to document the positive role he claimed students had played in the Chinese Communist Revolution. In the next issue of the journal, published in the fall of 1949, Greene included an essay by the distinguished African American scholar and activist, W. E. B. DuBois, a man who would subsequently become a member of the American Communist Party. DuBois's contribution to the *Midwest Journal* was a short (three-page) essay titled "The Freedom to Learn." In that essay, he encouraged Americans to put aside their fears of communism in favor of studying and understanding it: "If . . . the United States fears the doctrines of Karl Marx and Frederick Engels; if Americans do not believe in the work and thought of Lenin and Stalin; if they regard Communism as not only dangerous but malevolent, then what this nation needs most of all is the free and open curriculum of a school where people may study and read Marx, know what Communism is or proposes to be, and learn actual accomplishments."

Both of these essays were controversial, and Greene's decision to publish them risky, but the decision to do so was consistent with his commitment to use the *Midwest Journal* as a vehicle for the free exchange of ideas, including, perhaps especially, controversial ones.

The Yang and DuBois essays attracted the attention of U.S. Justice Department officials, this after the Jefferson City printer employed by Greene to print the journal became concerned about the "subversive" content he saw in the two issues he printed. He contacted the Kansas City office of the FBI. Subsequently, Greene was visited in his campus office and questioned by FBI agents who continued to monitor his activities, and the journal, in an effort to make certain that he was not personally engaged in subversive activities. In a late-life interview, Greene told me that a few years later he was called into the Lincoln University president's office and told by the president that Missouri legislators had threatened to reduce the university's budget unless the controversial *Midwest Journal* ceased publication. The journal's last issue was published in 1955. For the remainder of his life, Greene regarded the journal as one of his greatest accomplishments, and he resented the legislators who had caused its demise and the Lincoln University administrators who had bowed to the political pressure to end its publication. Contemporaneously, one of Greene's colleagues at Lincoln University, an African American sociologist named Oliver Cromwell Cox, was monitored by the FBI because of what the bureau regarded as his subversive and inflammatory sociological writings, including his most famous book, *Caste, Class and Race*, a critique of capitalism, published in 1948. Such was the fear and repression engendered by the anxiety over the spread of communism in the post–World War II world.

The fear of communism became even more intense in 1950, when Communist North Korea, supported by the Chinese Communists, invaded South Korea, a U.S. ally. Soon, tens of thousands of American soldiers were being sent to South Korea to help repel the invasion. One of these soldiers was my cousin, Virgil A. Kaver, who prior to his military service lived on a Warren County farm near the small town of Dutzow. Virgil was the eldest son of my dad's half-brother. Born in December 1929, he enlisted in the Army in 1948, served two years on active duty, was discharged, and then reactivated in September 1950, after the fighting began in Korea. He was sent to Korea in January 1951, wounded in March, sent to Japan to recuperate, and then sent back to Korea. On May 18, 1951, his unit was overrun by hostile forces. He was wounded again and captured. He was listed as Missing in Action. For weeks his parents did not know if he was dead or alive. On June 8, 1951, he was able to contact them and tell them he was alive and a prisoner of war in China. Over the course of the next two years, he was permitted to contact his parents only intermittently. He was frequently beaten, deprived of food, and forced to engage in hard labor. He was finally released in April 1953, three months before the fighting ended in Korea. In my childhood and adolescence, my cousin was a reminder of the dangers and threat of communism, the barbarity of the "Red Chinese," and a reminder of the need for eternal vigilance against both. I remember as a child reading a letter Virgil wrote to my dad upon his release from internment. He told my dad he wanted to do simple things he had been unable to do in prison. He told my dad he could not wait to go squirrel hunting with him.

Over the course of the war (1950–1953), nearly thirty-seven thousand American soldiers were killed in action in the war, including 944 Missourians. Among the Missourians killed was Robert Bennett, a native of Newburg, Missouri, near Rolla, a veteran of World War II fighting in Europe. In 1945, Bennett met and subsequently married a German woman named Erika Millek who worked at a U.S. Army camp PX in the town of Kaufbeuren. The couple remained in Germany until 1948, when they decided to move to the United States so that their expected child could be born in America.

The couple moved in with Robert's parents in Newburg, while he continued to serve in the Army at nearby Fort Leonard Wood. By 1950, Erika was pregnant again and living with her husband and daughter at his new station in Texas. The new baby girl was born on June 28, 1950. With a three-day pass in hand, Sergeant Bennett moved his wife and daughters back to his parents' home in Newburg, while he prepared for his next assignment. The Korean War had begun on June 25, 1950, three days before his daughter's birth. Sergeant Bennett was sent back to war.

Bennett was among the soldiers who was assigned the task of trying to recapture the South Korean capital of Seoul from the invading Communists. On September 18, 1950, Bennett wrote of the horror of the war to his wife. He told her he had seen more brutality and death in his short stay in Korea than he had seen throughout his entire European tour of duty during World War II. Two days later, Sergeant Bennett was killed.

Meanwhile, Bennett's widow, Erika, was living in Newburg, Missouri. For the remainder of her life, she never forgot the day a soldier came to her front door to tell her that her husband had been killed. The shock lasted for days, refusing to go away. What would she do? What would happen to her and her two young daughters?

The fact that she was not an American citizen complicated an already overwhelming situation. She had little money, and months passed before arrangements could be made for her to collect the monthly government benefit—less than $50 a month—due her as the surviving spouse of an American soldier killed in action. In the meantime, a local grocer granted her a line of credit so that she could purchase food for herself and her daughters. She pondered returning to her hometown so that she could be with her mother, but it was now under Soviet control, and she feared what the future there would hold for her and her children. Ultimately, she decided against returning to Europe and resolved to stay and make the best of her new life in the United States, reasoning that her husband had given his life for this country. She got a job in the PX at Fort Leonard Wood, learned to drive, and made the best of a life forever altered by the Cold War that had turned hot.

One manifestation of Cold War fear in Missouri was an effort to build a hydrogen bomb (H-bomb) factory in the state. After the Soviet Union exploded its first atomic bomb on August 29, 1949, many Americans, including Missouri native and president of the United States Harry S. Truman, felt the need for the United States to develop an even more powerful weapon of war than those deployed on the cities of Hiroshima and Nagasaki—the hydrogen bomb. Although production of the so-called H-bomb was controversial in many quarters, Missouri Congressman Albert Sidney Johnson (A. S. J.) Carnahan (D-8th District), quickly latched on to the idea of building a hydrogen bomb factory in Missouri, in the congressional district he represented.

Carnahan hoped to see the H-bomb factory built amidst the rugged natural beauty of the Irish Wilderness, a 1,258-square mile tract of land spread over Oregon, Shannon, Carter, and Ripley counties. The idea was endorsed by U. Lewis Lindley, chairman of the Irish Wilderness Development Association, who urged Missouri Governor Forrest Smith to support the plan and advocate for it in Washington. Lindley argued that the Irish Wilderness met all requirements for security and seclusion: it was close to power sources; had ample supplies of fresh water and local labor; and good rail connections. Residents of the small Oregon County town of Thayer asked Carnahan and other Congressional leaders to support the plan, largely because of its promise to provide jobs for local residents.

In August 1950, Carnahan led the Missouri congressional delegation to the White House for a meeting with President Truman. Acting as spokesman for the group, Carnahan tried to persuade the president that the Irish Wilderness was the perfect place for an H-bomb factory. Despite this appeal, and Carnahan's personal friendship with Truman, an alternative site outside Missouri was selected. Although at the time many residents of the Ozarks were disappointed by the decision and the loss of what they hoped would be plentiful high-paying jobs, future generations of Missourians who loved the pristine beauty of the Irish Wilderness would be forever grateful that it had not become the location of a hydrogen bomb factory.

Yet another consequence of the Cold War was the development of a new federal highway system, a goal of Truman's successor in the White House, President Dwight David Eisenhower, Supreme Commander of the Allied Forces during World War II. In his role as an army officer in Europe, Eisenhower had been impressed by the German system of national roads throughout the country, and realized that a federal highway system in the United States would be a critical factor in deploying troops throughout the nation in the event that the Cold War turned hotter. In 1954, the president appointed an army general, Lucius Clay, to the chairmanship of a committee to devise a plan to create an interstate highway system. Clay's committee ultimately recommended that the federal government spend $100 billion over the course of ten years to build forty-thousand miles of interstate highways, linking all American cities with a population of more than fifty thousand persons. This plan was incorporated into law in 1956 with the passage of the Federal Highway Act, with Eisenhower proudly signing the law into effect in June 1956.

Eisenhower's push for the creation of an interstate highway system paralleled another profound change that was occurring in the state and nation in the period immediately following World War II. This was the move to the suburbs by inner-city residents, a trend that had begun during the 1920s, as more and more Americans purchased automobiles, their cars providing them with the freedom and flexibility to flee the inner city at the end of the workday and return to their jobs in the city early the next day. The trend had slowed, and even reversed, during the lean and difficult years of the Great Depression and World War II, but war's end reinvigorated the desire to move to the suburbs, where real estate was cheaper, housing was less crowded, schools were newer, and shopping easier. Spurring the postwar suburbanization was "white-flight," a term brought about as racial integration, including busing, expanded. As the 1950s gave way to the 1960s, many white inner-city residents fled the city to escape the prospect of living and working alongside African Americans or sending their children to school with Blacks. Indeed, white flight from St. Louis and Kansas City was one of the defining characteristics of postwar life in Missouri.

With the flight to the suburbs came a growing demand for better and more expansive highways that would facilitate travel between suburb and city. Thus, in the mid-1950s, the Oakland Express Highway, which ran east from Hi Pointe to Vandeventer and Chouteau avenues in St. Louis was built, followed by the Third Street Expressway, which opened in 1955, connecting the riverfront to Gravois Avenue at 12th Street. By the late 1950s, Interstate 70 was nearly complete, connecting the state's two most populous metropolitan centers that lay at Missouri's western and eastern borders.

And across the state, highway and street improvements paid homage to the ever-growing influence of the automobile, including the building of fast-food restaurants to accommodate always-on-the-go Missourians. The first McDonald's restaurant in the state opened on August 30, 1958, in the St. Louis suburb of Crestwood, at 9915 Highway 66, marking the beginning of a fundamental transformation in the way Missourians ate. The restaurant, owned by Bill Wyatt and his partner, Don Kuehl, featured a "walk-up-service stand" with a limited menu of hamburgers, fries, milkshakes, and sodas. The serving staff in McDonalds throughout the country at the time was all-male, a mandate dictated by the franchise founder, Ray Kroc. Within little more than a year, five McDonald's restaurants were operating in the St. Louis area, all of them featuring the well-loved 15-cent hamburgers.

By the summer of 1959, a McDonald's Drive-In had opened in Springfield, at 501 West Sunshine. In March 1959, the first McDonald's Drive-In opened in Jefferson City on what was then called Highway 50 West, modern-day Missouri Boulevard. The owner of the restaurant, Charles Monroe of Jefferson City, boasted to a local newspaper that "36 hamburgers can be prepared in 110 seconds with average serving time less than 20 seconds per order. He said his unit expects to handle around 70,000 burgers and 31,000 shakes a month and as many as 1,700 orders of French fries daily." By 1960, "fast food," first recognized as a term in a Merriam-Webster Dictionary in 1951, was well on its way to becoming a normal way of dining for many Missourians, whose increasingly busy lives left decreasing amounts of time for meal preparation at home.

In the 1960 presidential election, the Democratic Senator John F. Kennedy carried the state of Missouri, garnering 898,897 votes to Vice President Richard M. Nixon's 855,509. Kennedy was only forty-three years old when elected, the first American president to be born in the twentieth century and the first Catholic to hold the office. He exuded charm, optimism, and a deeply held conviction that the twentieth century belonged to America. On January 20, 1961, President Kennedy delivered a stirring and memorable inaugural speech, calling on Americans to "Ask not what your country can do for you—ask what you can do for your country." He also made it clear the lengths to which he would go to combat international communism, proclaiming, "We shall pay any price, bear any burden, meet any hardship, support any friend, oppose any foe to assure the survival and success of liberty."

The most dangerous test of this commitment came less than two years later, in what came to be known as the Cuban Missile Crisis, an event whose memory still evokes anxiety in me nearly six decades later. President Kennedy was informed by U.S. intelligence sources that the Soviet Union was attempting to install nuclear missiles on the island nation of Cuba, which had only recently succumbed to a communist revolution led by Fidel Castro, a place that sits only ninety miles off the coast of Key West, Florida. On Monday evening, October 22, 1962, President Kennedy went on live national television and delivered an eighteen-minute speech in which he announced that American military force would be used to prevent Soviet ships carrying nuclear weapons from reaching Cuba. He also demanded the removal from Cuba of all Soviet missiles currently there. Many, perhaps most, Americans, including Missourians, feared that the United States stood on the brink of nuclear war. Asked by a *St. Louis Globe-Democrat* reporter to respond to the president's speech, Dr. Edwin F. Gildea, professor of psychiatry and head of that department at Washington University School of Medicine, responded: "I feel sort of helpless about it . . . I don't like to believe war is ahead but if there's anything history teaches us, it's that war is inevitable. I see no evidence that we have any techniques that will keep us from having another war, maybe next week, maybe later. . . ."

Nuclear war—and the assured mutual destruction of the world's two superpowers—was averted on that occasion, but its prospect lingered like a gloomy cloud over everyone's head. After the incident, and for a decade thereafter, students in the state's and nation's public schools practiced hiding under their desks when air raid sirens went off, and survivalists built personal bomb shelters in the yards of their suburban homes and stockpiled food and water for the coming nuclear war and its apocalyptic aftermath.

Meanwhile, for all the hope engendered by the legal successes of the late 1940s and early 1950s—the *Shelley v. Kraemer* decision of 1948, the ending of racial segregation of the armed forces by President Truman, the opening of St. Louis City swimming pools to African Americans, the integration of the University of Missouri, and the *Brown v. Board of Education* decision—racial discrimination remained a serious problem in the state and nation.

And the problem was not only real but multifaceted. In 1960, a study by the Missouri Human Rights Commission, a state-funded entity created in 1957 to further the cause of civil and human rights in the state and nation, found that in St. Louis and Kansas City, where a majority of the

Fig. 39: St. Louis Civil Defense duck-and-cover exercise in school, 1952. Credit: State Historical Society of Missouri, Arthur Witman Collection, Collection No. S0717-2770.

state's African Americans lived, "the great mass of Negro workers remains on the lowest level of employment." In St. Louis more than ten percent of all nonwhite males in the labor force were unemployed, compared with 2.8 percent of white males. Blacks were also confined mainly to the lowest paid jobs. An examination of all industries revealed that twenty-two percent of white male laborers were craftsmen, foremen, or kindred workers; only eight percent of the Black males were so employed. While only five percent of whites were employed as common laborers, twenty-one percent of Blacks fell into that category. Only three percent of the Black males in the labor force were classified as professionals, as opposed to eleven percent of white males.

In other parts of the state things were just as bad, if not worse. The Missouri Advisory Committee to the U.S. Commission on Civil Rights reported in 1963 that employment discrimination existed throughout the state. Referring to circumstances in the Audrain County community of

Mexico, the report noted: "The economy of the Negro community is kept at a substandard level as a consequence of Negroes being restricted to menial and low-salaried jobs. Their range of occupations is narrowed down to custodial or janitorial workers. . . ."

Things improved somewhat with the passage of the federal Civil Rights Acts of 1964 and 1965, but discrimination remained a problem, especially for the majority of African Americans. And then came the assassination of Dr. Martin Luther King Jr., in Memphis, Tennessee, on April 4, 1968. In the wake of King's murder, cities across the country erupted in violence.

The most violent of the responses to King's death in Missouri occurred in Kansas City, where a protest emerged in the wake of city officials' refusal to close schools in response to the tragedy. This angered Kansas City's African American students, particularly since schools across the river in Kansas City, Kansas, were closed in commemoration. Back in Kansas City, Missouri, approximately three hundred Black students marched to city hall to demand the closing of the schools. The gathering was dispersed by police, who used tear gas on the unarmed protesters. Later the same day, five all-Black schools were closed temporarily after police again used tear gas, this time against a group of students gathered outside Lincoln High School.

That evening, frustration and anger in the Black community spilled over into violence. Carloads of African Americans reportedly hurled Molotov cocktails at city police officers. Kansas City Mayor Ilus Davis declared a state of emergency and soon announced the first emergency curfew in the city's history. Soon, also, police chief Clarence M. Kelly, a Kansas City native who had served as an FBI special agent for nearly two decades before becoming the top cop in Kansas City in 1961, authorized his force to shoot any fire bombers. The entire nine-hundred-person police force was called out by local officials, along with 1,700 National Guardsmen and 168 Missouri State Highway Patrolmen, ordered to Kansas City by Governor Warren E. Hearnes. On the first day of rioting, three persons were killed, fifty-four injured, and 175 arrested. The next day the situation escalated, as five more Black citizens were killed and at least ten persons were wounded as police and soldiers exchanged gunfire with citizens.

Eager to demonstrate that Missouri law enforcement personnel could handle the situation without federal intervention, Governor Hearnes increased the National Guard force to 2,200 and added dozens of state

Fig. 40: Protesters march on the highway in Kansas City as part of a protest in the wake of the assassination of Martin Luther King. Credit, Ilus Winfield Davis Papers, State Historical Society of Missouri. Collection No. K0375.

troopers from central and eastern Missouri. During the second evening of rioting, sixty more persons were arrested and fifty-seven more were injured, seven by gunfire. The night ended with more than 275 people arrested, bringing the total number of arrests to more than one thousand, and extensive property damage, almost all of it confined to the Black community. Although the violence soon ended, racial tensions remained elevated.

Across the state, St. Louis avoided the violence experienced in Kansas City, largely by bringing a variety of civil rights leaders together to plan a memorial march and service honoring Dr. King. On April 5, 1968, seventy-five St. Louis civil rights leaders gathered at Mid-City Community Congress on Delmar Boulevard to plan a march and memorial service for Palm Sunday, April 7, 1968. The planning meeting included both militants and moderates, many of whom shouted at each other and called each other names. Finally, Attorney Morris Hatchett, president of the St. Louis branch of the NAACP, asserted himself: "We're all black. . . . This battle of name-calling has got to go."

The parade held on April 7 began at the Gateway Arch, with approximately seventy-five hundred people participating. African Americans led the march, with whites joining the procession in the rear. By the time that the march reached its destination of Forest Park, the crowd had swelled to approximately thirty thousand people, including St. Louis mayor Alfonso J. Cervantes. The march extended for eight miles. Arguably, it was the leaders' ability to overcome their differences and to join in a common celebration of Dr. King's life that allowed St. Louis to avoid the violence witnessed in Kansas City.

Some political leaders tried to blame the civil rights movement and protests associated with it on communists. Among those was one of Missouri's most ardent Cold Warriors during the 1960s, a young Congressman from the Texas County town of Licking. Richard Ichord was born in Licking on June 27, 1926. He served in the U.S. Navy from 1944 to 1946 and then attended the University of Missouri in Columbia, graduating in 1949, the year that the Soviet Union successfully exploded its first atomic bomb and the Chinese Communists ousted the Chinese Nationalist Party from power. Like many of his generation, Ichord imbibed a deep and lasting fear of the threat of international communism.

After completing an undergraduate degree at the University of Missouri, Ichord enrolled at the institution's School of Law. He completed law school in 1952, the same year he won a seat in the Missouri House of Representatives. He held that seat for the next eight years. In 1958, his legislative colleagues elected him Missouri's youngest-ever Speaker of the House.

In 1960, Ichord challenged incumbent A. S. J. Carnahan for the Democratic nomination for Missouri's 8th District congressional seat. Although Carnahan was favored to retain his seat, Ichord defeated him. Thus, in January 1961, Ichord began a twenty-year tenure in the U.S. House of Representatives.

Ichord quickly gained prominence in Congress. Like many Americans during the early-to-mid-1960s, he became an increasingly hostile opponent of communism. His principal venue for fighting communism became the House Un-American Activities Committee (HUAC), whose chairmanship he assumed in 1969. In the wake of the urban riots of the late 1960s and the anti-Vietnam War riots of the same period, Ichord and HUAC tried unsuccessfully to connect all protests and civil unrest to communism. Ichord was a strong supporter of the Vietnam War and of American military might, arguing, "Military weakness does not promote peace. It breeds war."

Ichord continued to serve as the chair of HUAC until the committee was dissolved in 1975. By that time both Ichord and the committee had endured much criticism as controversial conspiracy chasers. Four years after the disbanding of HUAC, and in the face of his impending retirement from Congress, Ichord co-authored, with Californian Boyd Upchurch, *Behind Every Bush*. The book provided a platform for Ichord to defend his and the committee's actions against what he regarded as "subversive influences" and "internal threats" against the American status quo.

Although there was no evidence that the turmoil of the 1960s was either driven or inspired by communist organizers or ideology, the protests and disturbances were no less disruptive or disturbing.

There were many instances of conflict between Missouri landowners and the federal government during the generation after World War II. More often than not in these private-land related standoffs, the federal government ended up using its power to deprive Missourians of their land and in some cases their way of life, thereby further exacerbating the centuries-old tension between the state's residents and the federal government.

A case in point was the so-called "urban renewal" movement of the 1950s and 1960s, even if the sentiment behind urban renewal was well-intentioned. Although there had been federal efforts at eliminating blighted urban areas during the interwar years, the post–World War II effort had its roots in President Harry S. Truman's 1949 State of the Union Address, in which he noted that "Five million families are still living in slums and firetraps. Three million families share their homes with others."

The federal Housing Act of 1949, also known as the Taft-Ellender-Wagner Act, sought to use federal money to address conditions in urban slums. In Missouri, it soon became apparent that the focus of urban renewal, so-called pockets of urban blight in need of destruction and repurposing, was land that provided housing and businesses to African Americans in inner cities. An unfortunate consequence of the effort was the destruction of long-standing African American neighborhoods in many parts of the state, resulting not only in the displacement of thousands of individuals, but also the loss of important communities of color such as the Mill Creek Valley neighborhood in St. Louis, the Sharp End in Columbia, and the

Foot in Jefferson City. Decades later, African Americans who had lived, worked and shopped in those neighborhoods, as well as their descendants, grieved over the loss of their way of life and felt anger toward those who had forced these changes.

Similarly, conflict over land occurred in rural Missouri, in the heart of the Missouri Ozarks, during the 1960s. The issue there was the creation of the Ozarks National Scenic Riverways, which would become the nation's first congressionally designated park for the preservation of a wild river system. The project began in 1959, when Missouri Governor James T. Blair Jr., and Missouri's two U.S. senators, Thomas C. Hennings and Stuart Symington, began talking with officials of the National Park Service, the Forest Service, and the Fish and Wildlife Service about a way to preserve

Fig. 41: Mill Creek Valley in St. Louis, 1957. This neighborhood and the people who lived in it were victims of urban renewal. Credit: State Historical Society of Missouri, Arthur Witman Collection, Collection No. S0732-607.

the pristine beauty of three of Missouri's most majestic Ozarks streams: the Current, Jack's Fork, and Eleven Point rivers. Missouri already had two state parks in the Ozarks region: Round Spring State Park near Eminence, in Shannon County, and Alley Spring State Park, also in Shannon County. Subsequently, Missouri Congressmen Thomas B. Curtis and Richard H. Ichord introduced legislation aimed at transferring these rivers into the National Park System.

Again, what had begun as a well-intentioned effort, in this case to protect the natural beauty of these Ozarks streams and to guarantee their preservation for future generations of visitors, Missourians among them, ran afoul of local property owners' desire to control and direct the use of their own property. The locals did not want any outside, bureaucratic officials of the federal government telling them what they could or could not do with their land.

It quickly became apparent that if the federal government wanted to have its way it would have to seize the land through the power of eminent domain, legally wresting control of the land from local owners, and paying them fair market value for the land. Beginning in 1967, local landowners began suing the federal government to maximize the price they would receive for their property. The legal disputes were contentious and emotional, with many landowners being forced to transfer to the federal government land that had been in their families for generations.

As the tumultuous 1960s came to a close, Missourians wondered what the next chapter in their history would be. Many, if not most, had come to embrace the feeling that skepticism and suspicion of the federal government would not soon subside.

SUGGESTED READINGS

Richard Kirkendall's *A History of Missouri, 1919 to 1953* (1986) covers the immediate postwar period of Missouri history. Lawrence H. Larsen, *A History of Missouri, 1953 to 2003* (2004) picks up where Kirkendall's book leaves off. Both books were published by the University of Missouri Press.

The GI Bill and its multiple impacts on Missouri life and institutions of higher education can be traced through major Missouri newspapers of the time, including those published in St. Louis, Kansas City, Springfield, Columbia, Jefferson City, Joplin, and Moberly. These newspapers can be accessed through the Newspapers.com website: (https://www.newspapers .com/).

Biographies of major Missouri post-WWII figures not only deal with the GI Bill and the challenges of postwar life in the state, but also with the emergence of communism as a major issue in the postwar years. David McCullough's biography of the thirty-third U.S. president, *Truman* (1992), is helpful. It was published by Simon & Schuster. Likewise, Alonzo L. Hamby's *Man of the People: A Life of Harry S. Truman* (1995), published by Oxford University Press, is useful. Both books deal with Winston Churchill's Iron Curtain ("The Sinews of Peace") speech and with Truman's role in integrating the armed forces. For more on this latter issue, readers should consult Jon E. Taylor, *Freedom to Serve: Truman, Civil Rights, and Executive Order 9981* (2013), published by Routledge Press.

African American life in postwar Missouri is chronicled in Lorenzo J. Greene, Gary R. Kremer, and Antonio F. Holland, *Missouri's Black Heritage* (1993), published by the University of Missouri Press. The battle for equal access to education for students of all races is told in Monroe Billington, "Public School Integration in Missouri, 1954–1964," *Journal of Negro Education* 35 (1966): 252–66; and Judge Gerald W. Heaney and Dr. Susan Uchitelle, *Unending Struggle: The Long Road to an Equal Education in St. Louis* (2004), published by Reedy Press. Gail Milissa Grant, *At the Elbows of My Elders: One Family's Journey Toward Civil Rights* (2008) documents the efforts by attorney David M. Grant and other family members to advance the cause of civil rights, especially in St. Louis, during the postwar period. It was published by the Missouri History Museum.

White flight from urban centers and urban renewal in Missouri are covered in a number of works. For the St. Louis experience, see Colin Gordon, *Mapping Decline: St. Louis and the Fate of the American City* (2008), published by the University of Pennsylvania Press. Also helpful is Clarence Lang, *Grassroots at the Gateway: Class Politics & Black Freedom Struggle in St. Louis, 1936–1975* (2009), published by the University of Michigan Press.

Mary Kimbrough and Margaret W. Dagen, *Victory Without Violence: The First Ten Years of the St. Louis Committee of Racial Equality (CORE), 1947–1957* (2000) documents CORE's efforts to combat segregation in St. Louis in the postwar period. Kenneth S. Jolly, *Black Liberation in St.*

Louis, Missouri, 1964–1970 (2006), published by Routledge, documents the civil rights movement in St. Louis during the late 1960s.

The Kansas City story is told by Sherry Lamb Schirmer, *A City Divided: The Racial Landscape of Kansas City, 1900–1960* (2002), published by the University of Missouri Press. See, also, Kevin Gotham, *Race, Real Estate and Uneven Development: The Kansas City Experience, 1900–2000* (2002), published by State University of New York Press. Also helpful is Charles E. Coulter, *Take Up the Black Man's Burden: Kansas City's African American Communities, 1865–1939* (2006), published by University of Missouri Press. Thomas Frank's *What's the Matter with Kansas? How Conservatives Won the Heart of America* (2005) focuses particular attention on the white flight from Kansas City into suburban Kansas in the wake of the racial integration of neighborhoods during the second half of the twentieth century. More recently, G. S. Griffin, *Racism in Kansas City: A Short History* (2015), published by Chandler Lake Books, takes up the same issue.

The Federal Bureau of Investigation's interest in Lorenzo J. Greene and the *Midwest Journal* is discussed in Pero Gaglo Dagbovie, *The Early Black History Movement, Carter G. Woodson, and Lorenzo Johnston Greene* (2007), University of Illinois Press. There are a number of works on the life and work of Oliver Cromwell Cox. Christopher A. McAuley, *The Mind of Oliver C. Cox: The African American Intellectual Heritage* (2004), published by University of Notre Dame Press is especially useful.

The 1968 civil unrest in Kansas City in the wake of the assassination of Martin Luther King Jr., is told in Joel Rhodes, "It Finally Happened Here: The 1968 Riot in Kansas City, Missouri," *Missouri Historical Review* 91 (April 1997): 295–315. Also helpful is David Kerrigan Fly, "An Episcopal Priest's Reflections on the Kansas City Riot of 1968," *Missouri Historical Review* 100 (January 2006): 103–12.

Chapter Nine

Suburban Growth and Rural Decline,
Missouri in the Late Twentieth Century, 1970–2000

"In the last decade, politics has gone from the age of 'Camelot,'
when all things were possible, to the age of 'Watergate,' when all
things are suspect.

Congressman William L. Hungate, July 9, 1975

MISSOURIANS BEGAN THE decade of the 1970s much as they had concluded
the 1960s, with racial and civil unrest in the state's major cities, division
over the efficacy and morality of the Vietnam War, debate over the proper
role of women in a modern society, worry about the economy, and an overall concern about crime.

The federal census of 1970 revealed that Missouri's population had grown
by 357,586 persons over the course of the previous decade, a rate of more
than eight percent. According to contemporary accounts, "Virtually all of
[this growth] . . . occurred in metropolitan areas—and within the metropolitan areas . . . the increase was heavily concentrated in the suburbs."
Moreover, census figures suggest that the growth in population between
1960 and 1970 "was due entirely to natural increase" rather than migration
into the state.

Much of this natural increase reflected the coming of age of the baby
boomers, who were getting married and starting families of their own. They
were also abandoning the inner cities for the suburbs, a trend that had, as
mentioned, begun with their parents' generation. The population of the
City of St. Louis declined from 750,026 in 1960 to 608,078 in 1970. This
exodus from the inner city was made almost entirely by whites who objected to the growing urban trend toward racial integration. As neighborhoods,
schools, parks, and shopping centers became more racially diverse, and,
many argued, more crime-ridden, and as African Americans were elected
to urban public offices, a growing number of whites fled to the suburbs,

leaving behind African Americans and a disproportionate number of poor people who could not afford to move. While St. Louis City's population declined, St. Louis County's population grew from 703,502 in 1960 to 947,231 in 1970. The St. Louis suburb of Hazelwood more than doubled in size during that same period. Creve Coeur grew from 5,122 people in 1960 to 8,967 in 1970, an increase of 75.1 percent. Florissant's population increased by forty percent during the same period.

Similarly, the population of Kansas City grew only slightly, from 475,538 to 485,518, while surrounding suburbs grew dramatically. Lee's Summit and Raytown nearly doubled in population, while Blue Springs and Grandview nearly tripled. Independence rose sixty percent, to 110,700 people. Many white Kansas City residents crossed State Line Road into Johnson County, Kansas.

Rural counties in Missouri held their own at best during the decade; many decreased in population, continuing a trend in rural decline that had begun during World War I. The rural counties of southeast Missouri were especially hard hit. Pemiscot County lost more than one-third of its population between 1960 and 1970, while neighboring counties of Mississippi, New Madrid, and Dunklin counties also suffered sharp declines. In all, sixty-two counties and the City of St. Louis lost population over the decade.

Whether one lived in a city, the suburbs, or in rural Missouri, there was much to be unsettled about, perhaps foremost was the ongoing disillusionment with the seemingly endless war in Vietnam. My own frustration with the war was exacerbated by the fact that one of my high school classmates and closest friends, Army PFC Paul A. Hasenbeck of Freeburg, Missouri, had been Missing in Action in Vietnam since April 21, 1967, when he and his squad disappeared while returning from a combat patrol near Chu Lai, Quang Ngai Province, South Vietnam. The fate of Paul and his comrades has never been determined.

Although he was elected to the presidency at least in part because he pledged to end the war in Vietnam, Richard Nixon had failed to fulfill that pledge after a year in office. In a televised address on April 30, 1970, Nixon announced that American forces in Vietnam would be carrying out bombing missions in neighboring Cambodia, an action aimed at weakening the supply chain of North Vietnamese forces. Many Americans interpreted Nixon's action as expanding the war, rather than ending it. Antiwar protests erupted in many parts of the United States, including most famously on the campus of Kent State University in Ohio. During that protest, four Kent State students were killed by gunfire from Ohio National Guardsmen sent to campus to control protesters.

Publicity surrounding what became known as the "Kent State Massacre" led to widespread student protests throughout the country, including in Missouri. In Columbia, at the University of Missouri, an estimated crowd of two thousand students gathered on Rollins Field (now Stankowski Field) to protest the Cambodian bombings and the Kent State killings. The protest included burning President Nixon in effigy. Speaking to the assembled protesters, student leader Karl Kampschroeder proclaimed, "it is time to turn this country around and tell it that it is wrong." Protests on the University of Missouri-Columbia campus continued for days and included a march on the home of Chancellor John Schwada, who denied students' request to cancel classes on the campus.

In St. Louis, hundreds of students protested on the campuses of the University of Missouri-St. Louis, Webster University, St. Louis University, and Washington University. Protests turned violent at "Wash U" when arsonists set fire to the Air Force Reserve Officer Training Corps (ROTC) building. By this time, ROTC buildings on college campuses had become lightning rods for antiwar protests and demonstrations against the military.

President Nixon faced other challenges that also directly impacted Missourians. One was the dramatic increase in oil and fuel prices that grew out of the 1973 Arab-Israeli War. In 1973, members of the Organization of Arab Petroleum Exporting Countries (OPEC) placed an embargo on the export of Arab oil going to a list of countries they perceived as being on the side of Israel in the war, which, of course, included the United States. The Arab Oil Embargo hit the United States hard, largely because Americans had grown increasingly dependent on foreign oil. Within a short time, gas prices in the United States began to rise precipitously, the price of crude oil jumping from $2.90 a barrel before the embargo to $11.65 a barrel in January 1974. Not only did Americans bear the brunt of sky-high prices for gas and fuel oil, but they faced gas shortages that frayed the nerves of all Americans, including Missourians. Gas shortages meant long lines at gas pumps, limits on the number of gallons one could purchase, reductions in travel by private automobile, vacations cancelled, lost revenue for tourist destination points such as the Lake of the Ozarks, a reduction in the sale of gas-guzzling cars and lost state revenue in the attendant fuel and sales taxes, and more.

No doubt the oil embargo played a significant role in nurturing an anti-Arab, anti-Muslim frame of mind that peaked in the United States at decade's end with the Iranian-hostage crisis, a harrowing and nationally embarrassing event that began on November 4, 1979, when Iranian students demanding the overthrow of the U.S.-backed Shah of Iran, attacked the American embassy in Tehran and held those they found inside the building—fifty-two American diplomats and citizens—captive for 444 days. The incident became especially poignant for Missourians when they learned that a suburban St. Louis man, Marine Sergeant Rodney "Rocky" Sickmann, was among the captives. Sickmann had been part of the security detail assigned to guard the embassy.

My own experience with anti-Iranian hostility occurred during the winter of 1979–1980, on a snowy day when I took my kids to a Jefferson City park for a sleigh ride. The quiet of the nearly deserted park was broken by the screaming of a group of teenaged boys who were walking nearby, demanding that the "camel jockey" get the hell out of their park. I looked around to discern the victim of their wrath, only to discover that it was I, sporting a dark beard and dark hair, mostly covered by a stocking cap. My physical appearance, accentuated by a swarthy complexion and a prominent aquiline nose, prompted the group of young men to conclude that I was an Iranian interloper who had invaded their public space. Until the young men discovered that I was as American as they were, I was made to feel the same intense irrational hatred that has characterized so much anti-foreign hostility in America, then and now.

Faith in government, especially at the federal level, suffered increasingly during the 1970s. There were many reasons for this, including the feeling on the part of many citizens that their government had deceived them about the course of the war in Vietnam, a reality documented in 1971 with the publication of the "Pentagon Papers" by the *New York Times*. Arguably, disillusionment peaked for many people with the events and circumstances surrounding the Watergate break-in and cover-up, and the eventual resignation of President Richard M. Nixon. Perhaps it was Missouri congressman William L. Hungate, a member of the House Judiciary Committee that had undertaken the impeachment proceedings against the president, who best

expressed the attitude among his fellow Missourians when, in announcing his decision not to seek reelection to Congress in 1975, he expressed
regret that in the course of his tenure politics had gone "from the age of
Camelot [under John F. Kennedy] where all things were possible, to the age
of Watergate, when all things were suspect."

The 1972 gubernatorial election in Missouri brought a change in both
style and substance to Missouri politics with the election of Christopher
S. "Kit" Bond to the state's highest office. Kit Bond was only thirty-three
years old when he was elected, making him the youngest governor in state
history. He was the first Republican elected to the office in twenty-eight
years. A sixth-generation Missourian, Bond grew up in Mexico, Missouri,
where his father served as a vice president of A. P. Green Companies, a
fireclay manufacturer and major Missouri employer for many years. Allen
Percival (A. P.) Green was Bond's maternal grandfather.

Bond received an elite education, attending high school at the Deerfield
[Massachusetts] Academy and earning an A.B. degree from Princeton
University. In 1963 he earned a law degree from the University of Virginia
School of Law. He served several years as a law clerk to the Chief Judge of
the United States Court of Appeals for the Fifth Circuit in Atlanta before
going to work for a Washington, D.C., law firm.

Bond moved back to Missouri in 1967, intent on a career in politics.
In 1968 he ran for Congress in Missouri's 9th congressional district, being
only narrowly defeated by incumbent William Hungate. After this defeat,
Bond went to work as an assistant attorney general for newly elected
Missouri Attorney General John C. Danforth. Danforth was only thirty-
two years old when he became the first Missouri Republican to be elected
to a statewide office in forty years. Like Bond, Danforth was educated in
elite American schools, in his case, Princeton and Yale.

Kit Bond was elected state auditor in 1970, before running for governor
in 1972. In his gubernatorial campaign, Bond promised fresh ideas and a
new direction for state government. He campaigned heavily against the
status quo, promising to undo the "spoils system" he identified with his
predecessor, Democratic Governor Warren E. Hearnes. Years later, many
then-young Missouri Republicans remembered Danforth and Bond as
"reformers" who attracted young, idealistic people who credited the two
leaders with inspiring their own interest in Missouri politics. Reflecting
back on that time in 2019, from the perspective of nearly half a century,

former Missouri Republican Congressman Tom Coleman noted, ". . . the Missouri Republican Party became THE reform party in the state. With no successes state wide in 40 years, the party was an obvious choice for young people to join who didn't want to play ball with the special interests or the vestiges of the Pendergast political machine."

Bond was widely regarded as a moderate. Evidence of his moderation could be found in the position he took on many issues, including what became one of the most controversial topics of the decade: the ratification of the Equal Rights Amendment (ERA) to the United States Constitution.

Passage and ratification of the ERA was a major goal of the Women's Movement of the 1960s and 1970s. First written by Alice Paul and Crystal Eastman in the 1920s, the ERA consisted of fifty-two words that proposed to guarantee that equal rights could not be denied any citizen "on account of sex." The proposed amendment was first introduced to the U.S. Congress in 1923 and failed to pass. It surfaced again in Congress in 1971, and it passed both houses in 1972. After President Nixon signed the legislation, it was submitted to state legislatures for ratification.

Initially, it looked as though the ratification of the amendment would proceed quickly and easily. Many states ratified the ERA during the first year after Congress's action, including Missouri's neighbor and perennial rival, Kansas.

Missouri Governor Christopher S. Bond endorsed the ratification of the ERA, and Missouri House of Representatives member, Democrat DeVerne Calloway, led efforts to hold hearings on gender discrimination in the state. State Representative Sue Shear introduced ratification legislation in the House, but the bill failed to pass. In the Senate, the Judiciary Committee killed the ratification effort by refusing to send it on for a vote by the full Senate.

Arguably, and ironically, the person who did more than anyone to kill the passage of the Equal Rights Amendment in the Missouri legislature was a woman. And not just any woman, but an urban Democrat who also happened to be the first woman elected to the Missouri senate.

Her name was Mary Gant. The daughter of a Kansas City electrician and union organizer, Gant was born in the heart of the Great Depression and experienced difficulty as a young mother of three who was abandoned by her husband. She survived that experience through hard work, guile, and resilience, and she thought the ERA was unnecessary and that it bordered on giving women preferential treatment. She also thought the issue of gender discrimination could be better addressed at the state level. Instead of the ERA, Gant proposed new state legislation, telling a Jefferson City reporter in 1973: "A better equal pay for equal work law will do more for the women of Missouri than ratification of the Equal Rights Amendment." Gant added, "I feel it's a woman's own fault if she doesn't make it in her job."

Gant's comments and stand on the ERA played into the hands of the leaders of the Stop ERA movement, including national spokesperson Phyllis Schlafly and Missouri anti-ERA leader Anna McGraw of Webster Groves. Schlafly, a native of St. Louis with degrees from Washington University and Radcliffe College, was a conservative activist who emerged as a national figure opposed to feminism, gay rights, and abortion. Her self-published book, *A Choice, Not an Echo*, appeared in 1964 in support of Barry Goldwater's presidential candidacy and laid the foundation for her "family values" advocacy for the next half century. Senator Gant's position on the ERA also provided cover for male legislative opponents of the ERA, who could simply say they opposed the measure because Senator Gant did.

Closely allied to the fight over the Equal Rights Amendment was the conflict over abortion, which concerned and divided Missourians perhaps like no other issue. Rising in the early 1970s, the argument over a woman's right to choose vaulted into public consciousness and conversation on January 22, 1973, when the U.S. Supreme Court rendered its long-awaited decision in *Roe v. Wade*. This case originated in Texas in mid-1969 when a twenty-one-year-old Texas woman, pregnant with her third child, sought an abortion. At the time, Texas law allowed for the termination of a pregnancy only in cases of rape or incest, and then only "for the purpose of saving the life of the mother."

Attorneys for the plaintiff ("Jane Roe" was the woman's pseudonym used for the legal proceedings) challenged the Texas law in the U.S. District Court for the Northern District of Texas. On June 17, 1970, a three-judge panel of that court declared the Texas law unconstitutional, finding that it violated the right to privacy found in the Ninth Amendment to the U.S. Constitution. This decision laid the groundwork for an appeal to the U.S. Supreme Court. Oral arguments in the Supreme Court case were heard on December 13, 1971. The case was reargued on October 11, 1972, after the retirement and replacement of two high court justices.

The *Roe v. Wade* decision, rendered on January 22, 1973, was decided by a 7-2 majority in favor of the Texas woman's right to an abortion. Writing for the majority, Justice Harry Blackmun argued that a woman's right to an abortion stemmed from her right to privacy found in the Fourteenth Amendment to the U.S. Constitution, and that a state's authority to restrict that right was narrow and limited and placed a burden on the state to show a "compelling state interest" in restricting said right. Justice Blackmun argued that during the first trimester of pregnancy, decisions about whether or not to terminate a pregnancy should be left up to a pregnant woman and her doctor. During the second trimester, the state's "compelling interest," according to the opinion, was in the health and well-being of the mother. Only in the final trimester did the state's interest extend to the life of the unborn child.

Roe v. Wade touched off a firestorm of conflict between those who argued that life began at conception and that the "compelling interest" of the state should be in protecting the fetus or unborn child, and those on the other side of the issue who argued that a woman had a right to control her own body and therefore to choose for herself whether to terminate a pregnancy.

The legal fight over abortion predated the 1973 *Roe v. Wade* decision. In 1971, Missouri State Representative DeVerne L. Calloway introduced legislation aimed at legalizing abortion in Missouri. At the time, Missouri law, which dated to 1835, allowed for an abortion to be carried out only if it was deemed necessary to save the life of the pregnant woman. The fact that her proposed bill was co-sponsored by two other urban Democrats identified the effort as a Democratic initiative. From the beginning, the leading opposition to legalizing abortion came from the Missouri Catholic Conference and its lobbyist Louis DeFeo.

Calloway saw her advocacy for abortion rights as an extension of her nearly life-long struggle on behalf of equal rights for all. A native of Memphis, Tennessee, Calloway got her start as a human rights advocate as a Red Cross worker in China and India during World War II. She protested the segregation of Black soldiers in Red Cross facilities. After the war, she moved to Chicago and became involved with the Congress of Racial Equality (CORE). During the early 1950s, she and her labor-activist husband, Ernest Calloway, moved to St. Louis, where, among other things, they published a newspaper, *Citizen Crusader*, later renamed *New Citizen*, that focused on Black political and civil rights in St. Louis.

In 1962, DeVerne Calloway was elected to the Missouri General Assembly, making her the first African American woman to serve in the Missouri legislature. As a legislator, Calloway fought for any number of causes, including increased aid to public education, services and assistance for dependent children and the poor, and prison reform.

Abortions for reasons other than the health of the mother became legal in Missouri in 1973, after the U.S. District Court in Kansas City ruled that Missouri's restrictive law was unconstitutional. By 1976, the number of abortions obtained by Missouri women had doubled over the number obtained in 1972. According to Garland Land, director of the Missouri Center for Health Statistics, more than fourteen thousand legal abortions were performed in Missouri in 1976, the means by which one in six pregnancies in the state was terminated. More than one-third of all abortions reported in 1976 were performed on teenage girls, ninety-three percent of whom were unmarried. Another one-third of abortions were attributed to women between the ages of twenty and twenty-four, three-fourths of whom were also single. More than 3,750 married women sought abortions as well, leading Land to conclude that there could be "a growing tendency among married couples to use abortion to control family size."

Rightly or not, the issue of abortion rights quickly became identified with the Equal Rights Amendment, although there were many advocates of the latter who were opposed to the former. Illustrative of the point was a 1977 editorial written by the Reverend Edward J. O'Donnell in the Catholic publication, *St. Louis Review*. O'Donnell maintained that "advocates of ERA . . . consistently equate women's rights with the right to abortion." O'Donnell further argued that "women's liberation groups" pushed passage of the ERA "because they believe it will solidify the legal "right to abortion established by the 1973 Supreme Court decision."

During his 1980 campaign for reelection to the Missouri Senate, James W. Murphy, a Republican from St. Louis, said of women's rights advocates, "They feel ERA and abortion are connected. If ERA would pass, you would never be able to stop taxpayer funds from being used to pay for abortions."

In 2000, as discussions about resurrecting the ERA occurred in the Missouri legislature, Douglas Johnson, legislative director for the National Right to Life Committee, wrote an op-ed piece for the *St. Louis Post-Dispatch*. Titled "Saying the Equal Rights Amendment would not affect abortion is wrong," this essay argued, "[there is] substantial and concrete evidence that

the specific ERA language could have a sweeping pro-abortion impact."
Indeed, as late as 2019, a senior Republican Missouri senator made the
following comment in a Senate hearing on the renewed effort to ratify the
ERA: "What would Jesus do on abortion? The majority of this is about
abortion. I know what Jesus would do in this realm." There was no doubt
in his mind that the ratification of the ERA would strengthen the effort by
pro-choice forces.

Another "right-to-life" issue surfaced in Missouri during the decade of
the 1980s. In 1983, twenty-five-year-old Nancy Cruzan had an automobile
accident in Jasper County, just south of Carthage. Although responding law
enforcement officers concluded immediately that the accident had killed
Cruzan, she was still legally alive. Left in what was described as "a persistent
vegetative state," Cruzan was placed under the state's care at the Missouri
Rehabilitation Center in Mount Vernon.

By 1988, five years after the accident and with Cruzan's condition having
shown no signs of improvement, her family made the painful decision to
ask the Rehabilitation Center staff to stop feeding and hydrating Cruzan
through tubes, knowing that these actions would result in her death. The
staff of the state-operated facility could not, however, honor the family's request without a court order. Thus began a legal case that would impact the
entire country's attitude toward an individual's right to die, and the right of
family members to decide for incapacitated loved ones the degree to which
life-saving medical technology could or should be used to prolong life.

The legal case began with a lawsuit filed by a lawyer, acting on behalf
of Cruzan's parents as her guardians, against the state of Missouri and the
Rehabilitation Center. The case was filed in Jasper County Circuit Court
in October 1987. After a trial that was closely followed by national news
organizations, Judge Charles Teel issued a judgment on July 27, 1988. In
his decision, Teel ruled that Cruzan's parents had the right to withhold
nutrition and hydration from Nancy, thus allowing her to die.

The Teel decision came amid a national debate over the right to die, one
that, ironically, existed only because of medical science's ability to prolong
life beyond previously long-accepted norms of viability. The Cruzan court
decision was heard not long after Karen Ann Quinlan's right-to-die case was
heard by the New Jersey Supreme Court in 1987.

Like the Quinlan case, the Nancy Cruzan case ended up in a supreme
court, in this case, the state of Missouri's highest court. Oral arguments

in the case were heard in late September 1988. Obviously tortured by the case, and deeply divided over it, the justices of the Missouri Supreme Court ruled 4-3 that no one, not even Cruzan's parents/guardians, had the right to refuse treatment for her. Still determined to do what they thought was the right thing for their daughter, Cruzan's parents appealed the decision to the U.S. Supreme Court. On June 25, 1990, that court rendered its verdict in the first "right-to-die" case ever heard by the nation's highest court. It upheld the Missouri Court's earlier judgment by a 5-4 vote, noting that removal from life support required "clear and convincing evidence" that such an action was consistent with the patient's intentions. A major consequence of this case was the creation of advance health directives, in which individuals prepared papers, typically as part of their "living wills," to make known their intentions should they ever be involuntarily put on life support and therefore unable to speak for themselves. Within one month of the U.S. Supreme Court's ruling, the national Society for the Right to Die noted that it had received approximately three hundred thousand requests for information about advance directives. Nancy Cruzan died on December 26, 1996. Sadly, tragedy continued to plague the Cruzan family; six years after his daughter's death, Nancy Cruzan's father took his own life.

Distrust of government, and even hostility toward it, coalesced into two powerful movements during the late 1970s and early 1980s. Both movements had dramatic, long-lasting impacts on the role and size of Missouri government. The first was part of a taxpayer revolt, begun as California's fight over Proposition 13 occurred in the late 1970s. In early February 1978, a group of businessmen met in Springfield, Missouri, to organize a tax protest of their own, a group they called "the Taxpayers Survival Association." Their leader was Springfield businessman Melton D. "Mel" Hancock, who was influenced by the National Tax Limitation Committee headquartered in Washington, D.C. The latter group was established in 1975 by Lew Uhler, whose aim was to create a grassroots national effort "to limit state and federal spending through legal restrictions and constitutional change." Uhler, a native of California, worked with and for Ronald Reagan when the latter was governor of California during the late 1960s and early 1970s and helped to shape and promote Reagan's anti-tax, downsizing of government positions as both California governor and U.S. president.

Hancock was born in the tiny Stone County community of Cape Fair in September 1929, just as the Great Depression was about to begin. He graduated from high school in Springfield in 1947 and Southwest Missouri State College (now Missouri State University) in 1951. After serving in the United States Air Force for two years, he worked in several different businesses before launching Federal Protection, Inc., a bank security leasing company in 1969.

From the beginning, Hancock and his supporters aimed to gather signatures to place on the ballot a proposed amendment to the Missouri constitution to limit taxation. By August 1978, Hancock's group had grown to five hundred members, and he and his followers had collected five thousand signatures in their effort to get an initiative petition on a statewide ballot. In 1979, Hancock temporarily abandoned his effort at a petition drive when asked by some lawmakers to give the legislature a chance to address the problem. When the legislature failed to satisfy Hancock's wishes, he again began collecting signatures, opining, "Our General Assembly has chosen to ignore the desire of the people to limit the growth of government by establishing tax and spending limitations." "Now," Hancock said, "we are going to ask the citizens to call for a substantial reduction in government spending."

Hancock and his followers succeeded in gathering enough signatures to place their issue on the November 4, 1980, ballot. The so-called "Hancock Amendment" required the state to refund money to taxpayers when revenues exceeded a specified ratio to personal income in the state. The goal was to prevent the Missouri state budget from growing faster than average family incomes. The amendment also required prior taxpayer approval of new local taxes and fees before they could take effect. After the amendment to the Missouri constitution was approved by fifty-five percent of those Missourians who voted in the election of 1980, the provision went into effect the next year. In 1994, Missouri voters approved "Hancock II," which further clarified and excluded exceptions to the original Hancock Amendment. The Hancock Amendment was one of the first, and among the most successful, efforts to limit taxation and government growth during this era of the taxpayer revolt. Supporters hailed its passage as a necessary tool needed to slow down government growth and excessive taxation. Critics, on the other hand, feared that the amendment would cripple future efforts to raise critically needed funds for education, infrastructure, and social services by state, county, and local governments. Over the ensuing decades, each side would find ample opportunity to tout their position as the better one for the people of Missouri.

Mel Hancock, meanwhile, rode the popularity of his namesake amendment to a new career as a politician. In 1982, he challenged popular incumbent U.S. Senator John C. Danforth for the U.S. Senate. Losing that race, he ran again for office two years later, this time for that of lieutenant governor, losing to Democrat Harriett Woods, who became the first woman in Missouri history to hold that position.

Hancock's third try for public office proved to be the charm; in 1988 he was elected to Congress from Missouri's 7th congressional district, succeeding Gene Taylor, the popular Springfield Republican. Hancock would go on to win three more congressional terms before retiring on January 3, 1997. He was succeeded in office by Roy D. Blunt.

Mel Hancock was also an early supporter of another anti-government movement of the era: the effort to impose limits on the number of terms that an individual could serve in the Missouri General Assembly, which began to gain momentum during the late 1980s. In 1990, a Republican lawyer from St. Louis, Greg Upchurch, founded an organization called "12-AND-OUT." The goal of this group was to pass a constitutional

Fig. 42: Missouri Senator Harriett Woods, the second woman to be elected to the Missouri Senate, appears in this photograph just to the right of Governor Joseph Teasdale at the 1979 signing of the Omnibus Nursing Home Act. Credit: State Historical Society of Missouri. Harriett F. Woods Papers, Collection No. S0051.

Fig. 43: Missouri State Representative Claire McCaskill working in her Capitol office, holding her son, late 1980s. Credit: State Historical Society of Missouri, Claire McCaskill Papers. Collection No. CA6530.

amendment in Missouri that would allow an individual to serve in the legislature no more than twelve years in a twenty-four-year period. In 1990, Upchurch told Scott Charton, an Associated Press reporter, that he got the idea after hearing about a similar term limit proposal in Oklahoma. Said Upchurch, "This is to let people who don't plan on making politics a career become involved in government." He went on to say, "We should prevent the chance for abuse of powers. I think we have had some terrible things occur that should never happen. . . ." He cited examples of two St. Louis-area legislators to prove his point. One was Dewey Crump, a Democrat from Maryland Heights, who was convicted of federal felony cocaine charges. The other, also a Democrat, was E. J. "Lucky" Cantrell, who was convicted of federal labor-corruption charges.

Not surprisingly, the term-limit proposal was unpopular among many sitting legislators, but it gained increasing acceptance in 1991 and 1992, as

Upchurch and his supporters lobbied relentlessly for the measure. In 1991, Upchurch teamed with former state representative Curtis Wilkerson to form a new group called "Missourians for Limited Terms." The new group set about gathering signatures aimed at placing a term-limits amendment to the state constitution on the ballot. Anticipating the populism of the "Make American Great Again" movement of the 2016 presidential campaign, supporters of the term-limits movement argued that establishing terms limits was a way "to get control of government and get rid of career politicians."

Ultimately, the group gained enough signatures to place the issue on the November 1992 ballot. As submitted, the proposed constitutional amendment would limit the service of any one person to eight years in the House and eight years in the Senate, or a total of sixteen years in the state legislature. Among its supporters was Missouri governor John D. Ashcroft. On election day, November 3, 1992, nearly three-fourths of Missouri voters who cast ballots endorsed the idea of term limits. Greg Upchurch was ecstatic: "This is great. I think it's one step toward reforming politics as usual." Tom Mericle, executive director of Common Cause-Missouri, disagreed. He argued that the measure would lead to "a bunch of neophyte legislators, having to rely on special-interest money, lobbyists and bureaucrats to help them get to know and understand how government works in Jefferson City."

Who was right? Eight years after the term-limits amendment passed, Missouri Senator P. Wayne Goode (D-St. Louis) was asked by a State Historical Society of Missouri historian for his opinion of term limits. Goode was, in many ways, the type of person targeted by Upchurch and Missourians for Limited Terms. First elected to the Missouri House in 1962, Goode served in that body from 1963 until 1984, much of that time as the chairman of the House Budget Committee. In 1984, Goode was elected to the Missouri Senate and served in that body until 2005, much of that period as chair of the powerful Senate Appropriations Committee. Goode's more than four decades as a state legislator were free of scandal; indeed, he was widely respected by members of both political parties. In the 2000 interview, he expressed great concern about term limits. "I am very concerned about what's going to happen with term limits," Goode told his interviewer. "I'm so concerned because there isn't going to be anyone who has that background or institutional knowledge. . . . [T]erm limits is just wrong. It is not going to work well for the public."

Term limits became fully implemented in Missouri in 2000, eight years after the term-limits amendment was passed. Critics of the measure continued to warn that term limits would lead to ineffective legislators, political gridlock, and undue influence of government bureaucrats and lobbyists. In 2011, David Valentine, senior research analyst for the University of Missouri Institute of Public Policy, and a former long-time director of the Missouri Senate's research division, issued a study on the results of term limits. His conclusion: because of term limits, "The legislature has become unable to do the job we need it to do." Twenty years after the passage of the term limits amendment, former Republican state senator, Tom Dempsey, fresh from serving his final term in the senate, noted that term limits left legislators with no incentive to compromise, "So sometimes you have decisions that end up being based on politics more than policy."

In 2018, twenty-six years after Missouri voters overwhelmingly passed the term-limits amendment, the *Kansas City Star* produced a piece on the impact of the measure for what it called its "Missouri Influencer Series." Its conclusion was contained in the headline above the story written by long-time political reporter, Jason Hancock: "Term limits have been 'a disaster' for Missouri, say many state leaders."

One of the most challenging developments of the 1980s in Missouri came with what came to be called the "farm crisis." Although this crisis hit its peak during mid-decade, its origins dated back more than a decade. The early years of the 1970s was actually a good time to be a farmer, both in Missouri and throughout the nation. For one thing, President Richard Nixon became concerned about the U.S. trade deficit, the first such deficit since World War II, and worked to devalue the American dollar in the hope that residents of foreign countries would find American goods, including agricultural products, more affordable.

The strategy worked, as it did indeed lead to an increase in foreign purchases of American agricultural products. So, too, did President Nixon's famous 1972 trip to China, the first such trip to that communist nation by a sitting American president. The Nixon trip opened Chinese markets to American agricultural products in a way never before experienced. Likewise, in 1973, the Soviet Union suffered huge crop failures, leading to the Soviet purchase of large amounts of American farm products, especially wheat.

American farmers, Missourians among them, responded to this greatly increased demand for their products by trying to ratchet up their rates of production, an effort that included bringing more farmland under cultivation. Farmers began investing in land and new and expensive equipment, often buying both on credit, in the hope that future sales would cover the costs of current investments and lead to profits. By 1978, the debt incurred on these kinds of purchases averaged an astonishing seventy-six percent of the purchase price. Farmers were also handicapped by the increased energy costs that plagued all Americans during the 1970s and 1980s.

As it always has, the overproduction of crops led to plummeting prices for farmers by the late 1970s, with farm income now woefully inadequate to service the debts that so many American farmers had incurred. But the farmers still had an ace in the hole: their land values had grown tremendously, and they were able to service their debts by regularly, sometimes yearly, borrowing against the equity in their land, albeit often doing so at inflated interest rates.

The anti-inflationary policies of the Federal Reserve, beginning in late 1979, and the "Reagan Revolution" of the early 1980s began to change things for farmers, and, indeed, for all Americans. Concerned about a mounting federal debt and a devalued dollar, Federal Reserve chairman Paul Volcker and President Reagan began to tighten the money supply, cut taxes, and downsize government, an approach known as "supply-side economics."

As the value of the dollar rose, farm exports became more expensive for foreign buyers and the prices for American crops declined precipitously. Tight money supplies made it more difficult for farmers to refinance their loans, so loan defaults became more common. And, as a series of mid-1980s droughts combined with all the other factors, the farmers of the state and the nation found themselves in a state of crisis. In 1981, there were 114 farm bankruptcies in Missouri; by 1985, that number had more than quadrupled to 535.

The crisis impacted farmers all over the state, and it spread to businesses that catered to and benefited from commerce with farmers. Journalist Joe Link described the impact in an article titled "The Struggle for Survival" that appeared in the September 28, 1985, issue of the *Missouri Ruralist*. Link's article focused on the small Chariton County community of Brunswick, population 1,272, but his description of what happened there was applicable across rural Missouri.

As the farm economy declined, the town's commerce proceeded to dry up along with it. Link quoted Brunswick Mayor Ray Stark: "Agriculture is the backbone of small towns like this. All of these small towns are going through the same thing. They all rely on agriculture." Bud Shull, a car dealer, told Link when he first opened a car dealership in Brunswick sixteen years earlier, the town had four other auto dealerships. In 1985, his was the only one left. "The boys just don't have the money anymore," Shull said of area farmers. During the previous year, the town also had lost a grocery store, a service station, a hardware store, and a clothing store. "It's sort of like everyone is down in the dumps," John Bartow, an appliance storeowner, told author Link.

The town suffered a huge blow when its only pharmacy closed. Residents then had to drive twenty-eight miles to Marshall, in adjacent Saline County, where they often did other shopping at higher-volume stores in which prices generally were lower. It was a vicious circle. As one storeowner put it, "This town depended on the little farmer. The little farmer traded with the little towns. You go out here you won't see the little farmer anymore. It's as simple as that."

One of the more unfortunate consequences of the farm crisis in Missouri during the 1980s was an increase in the number of suicides among farmers. In a 1985 news article about this tragic phenomenon, Rex Campbell, a sociologist at the University of Missouri in Columbia, noted that farmland prices peaked in Missouri in 1981 and started to decline in 1982. There were fifty-seven farmer suicides in 1982, sixty-nine in 1983 and seventy-one in 1984. Campbell also noted that 1982 was a drought year and that the number of farm auctions in 1984 was up almost one hundred percent over 1983. One of the saddest parts of the story Campbell relayed was that those farmers who were most likely to take their own lives were young persons: "The increase in suicides has been almost entirely among farmers less than 40 years of age." Campbell continued: "Our studies show younger farmers are more likely to be in financial trouble than are older operators. . . . [T]heir debts are the largest."

One of the great ironies of the 1980s farm crisis in Missouri was that many of the people whose job it was to produce food increasingly found themselves unable to afford groceries to feed their own families. In Harrison County, which had the largest number of farm bankruptcies in the state in 1985, there were 1,232 food stamp recipients in 1986, nearly double the 673 it had in January 1980. Unfortunately, however, many farmers could not qualify for food stamps because they owned too many assets in the form of either land or machinery or both. As a consequence, many farmers turned to food banks and organizations such as the Missouri Rural Crisis Center (MRCC). "They line up like [in] the Great Depression," said Roberta Arensberg, an MRCC staff member. "We have never had anything left."

The businesses were not alone in their abandonment of towns and cities in rural Missouri. There was also a large out migration of job seekers, especially young people, who saw no future for themselves in the communities in which they had been born and raised. Not surprisingly, the populations of many towns in largely rural, farming counties declined dramatically during the period from 1970 to 1990. Chillicothe, the county seat of northwest Missouri's Livingston County, is a case in point. In April 1970, the City of Chillicothe unveiled its "Comprehensive Plan" for the city. Planners saw nothing but progress and growth in the city's future. Among the reasons they saw Chillicothe as likely to keep growing was an anticipated "continued aggravated social unrest in metropolitan areas" that would prompt more and more city dwellers to relocate from urban areas such as Kansas City to smaller cities such as Chillicothe—in short, white flight. They predicted that Chillicothe's population of 9,519 in 1970 would more than double by 1990, bringing the total number of residents to a whopping 19,750. In 1970, city planners worried, "What will Chillicothe do with 20,000 people?" They need not have worried. By 1990, the town's population had failed to come anywhere close to doubling, and had instead declined to 9,046.

One welcome diversion for Missourians of all ages during the 1980s was the 1985 "I-70 Showdown Series," featuring Missouri's two Major League Baseball teams, the Kansas City Royals and the St. Louis Cardinals. Perhaps the series was an apt metaphor for the historic relationship between the state's two major cities. St. Louis began the decade leading Kansas City in population, but over the course of the decade, the unthinkable happened: Kansas City supplanted St. Louis as Missouri's most populous city. Similarly, in the 1985 MLB Championship Series, the Cardinals were heavily favored; they were, after all, the team with history on their side. Descendants of one of the oldest professional baseball clubs in America, the Cardinals were charter members of the National League when it formed in 1892. By 1985, they had won a league-leading ten World Series championships, and seemed destined to win their eleventh with a best-of-seven series of victories over the Royals. The Royals, by contrast, were a relatively new team, an

American League expansion franchise founded in 1969, less than twenty years earlier and nearly ninety years after the founding of the Cardinals. Although they had won one American League pennant in their relatively short life as a team (in 1980), the Royals had yet to win a World Series.

Fig. 44: Fans gather in front of Amtrak's "World Series Special" during the 1985 World Series between the St. Louis Cardinals and the Kansas City Royals. Credit: Missouri State Archives, RG 104, Missouri Division of Tourism Photograph Collection.

The Cardinals stepped out to any early lead, winning the first two games of the series in Kansas City, leading many "Cards" fans, this author among them, to believe that they would sweep the Royals in the next two games at home in Busch Memorial Stadium, thereby adding to their impressive list of series wins. But it was the Royals who won Game 3 on the riverfront in St. Louis on October 22, 1985, by a score of 6-1. The Cardinals came back to win the next game, 3-0, leaving the Royals on the verge of defeat. Incredibly, the "Boys in Blue" shocked and impressed baseball fans across the country, reeling off three straight wins to defeat the Cardinals four games to three. For this Cardinal fan, who grew up worshipping the "Greatest Cardinal of Them All," Stan Musial, the outcome bordered on the unbelievable.

Unfortunately, as the twentieth century entered its final decade, Missouri experienced one of the most dramatic and traumatic events in its recent history, the Great Flood of 1993. Occurring along the bottomlands of the Mississippi and Missouri rivers and all the many tributaries of the state's great rivers, the flood extended from the spring to fall of that year, making it among the most devastating floods in the history of the state and nation, made all the worse by the growing tendency toward intense development of flood plain areas and aggressive channeling of major rivers and tributaries.

Unusual weather patterns preceded the Great Flood by almost a year. Beginning in the summer of 1992, the Upper Midwest experienced above-average rainfall that saturated the soil and filled reservoirs, in some cases to overcapacity. Heavy winter snowfalls and a return of rains in the spring of 1993 added to the problem. Years later, Scott Watson, Senior Service Hydrologist with the National Weather Service, recalled, "There was a point in time from mid to late summer where we had around 49 days straight of rainfall."

Neither the Mississippi nor the Missouri river could handle the large volume of water. Levees were breached or broken as the heavily channeled rivers sought their natural boundaries. Tens of thousands of homes were destroyed or damaged, dozens of towns were inundated, and millions of acres of farmland remained under water for months. When the West Quincy levee gave way in Marion County on July 16, 1993, Mississippi River floodwater quickly engulfed 14,000 acres of farmland, blocked U.S. Highway 24, and closed the only bridge across the Mississippi River still operable between Burlington, Iowa, and St. Louis, a distance of 212 miles. People who normally used the bridge to get to work or shop or for any other reason had to find a new way to cross the river, boats being the only reasonable solution. Clarksville (Pike County), in far northeast Missouri, recorded a devastating 187 days of flooding; Winfield (Lincoln County)183 days; and Hannibal (Marion County) 174 days.

Hannibal, Missouri, witness to many floods throughout its more than a century and a half of existence, built a new $8 million floodwall that was completed on April 1, 1993, as it turned out, just in time to protect the city against the worst ravages of the Great Flood. Locals estimated the floodwall spared the city some $15 million worth of damage. Just to the south of the

Fig. 45: Aerial view of flooding in Jefferson City, including area around the State Capitol, 1993. Credit: State Historical Society of Missouri, Debbie Kilgore Photograph Collection, 1993-2002, Collection No. P0155.

downtown area, however, an entire Hannibal neighborhood was flooded, displacing approximately eleven hundred residents.

In St. Louis, the Mississippi River crested on August 1, 1993, at 49.58 feet, the highest level ever recorded there. That meant the river had reached an astonishing twenty feet above flood level. Water rose halfway up the grand riverfront staircase of the iconic Gateway Arch, the mighty river staying above flood stage at St. Louis for 147 days, or nearly five months.

During the disaster, life along the Missouri River was disrupted in many ways, some unforeseen, some dangerous. In the town of Hardin, in northwest Missouri's Ray County, a community cemetery was flooded, with 793 of the cemetery's 1,576 graves disturbed or ruined. On July 12, 1993, Missouri River floodwaters cascaded through the cemetery, dislodging caskets, vaults, and tombstones, destroying two-thirds of the cemetery and creating the eerie image of caskets floating freely in the floodwaters. Although 645 remains were eventually recovered, only 120 were identified, with 520 reinterred in an "Unknown" section of the cemetery. More than one hundred remains were never recovered.

In the Montgomery County town of Rhineland, located about forty-five miles east of Jefferson City, the entire town was overrun. With the Missouri River topping a levee protecting the town in multiple places, residents had about six hours to remove their belongings from their homes before the town was fully inundated. Ultimately, Rhineland residents decided to abandon their town location and move to a forty-acre site on a hill about a quarter of a mile north. Cedar City, a small Callaway County town just across the Missouri River from Missouri's capital city, was also destroyed by the 1993 flood and never recovered. The land that the abandoned town had encompassed was subsequently annexed into the City of Jefferson. The capital city itself was briefly cut off from northern Missouri when the river flooded and blocked U.S. Highways 63 and 54 just north of the city. According to the Missouri Department of Health, twenty-one deaths directly related to flooding occurred in the state between July 1, 1993, and August 31, 1993.

By the last decade of the twentieth century, it was apparent that Missouri was changing. Among the changes was an increase in the number of immigrants to the state. The 1990s, for example, witnessed a large influx of new residents because of the Bosnian War that took place in Bosnia and

Fig. 46: A Bosnian American woman in St. Louis joins the protest against President Donald Trump's January 2017 executive order on immigration. "War Refugee. Bosnian. Muslim. American. Proud." Photograph by Paul Sableman, February 4, 2017. https://www.flickr.com/photos/pasa/31911921344/.

Herzegovina between 1992 and 1995. That war, prompted by the fall of the Soviet Union and the breakup of Yugoslavia, witnessed unspeakable horrors, including efforts at ethnic cleansing, as Bosnians, Croats, and Serbs fought each other. Millions of refugees fled the area to escape the separatist warfare and genocide that characterized the grisly conflict. Tens of thousands of those refugees ended up in St. Louis, attracted by affordable housing and the availability of jobs that required minimal skills.

Likewise, the Hispanic population of Missouri almost doubled during the decade of the 1990s, increasing by ninety-two percent. Many of these immigrants ended up in the Missouri Ozarks, where they found work in poultry plants and factories. A case in point was the Tyson Poultry plant in the Barry County town of Monett. In 1990, Hispanics made up less than 1 percent of the county's population. By 2000 they comprised more than 5 percent of the county's population. By 2017, Hispanics accounted for nearly one-quarter of Monett's population and thirty-five percent of its students. Unfortunately, by century's end, there were more recent immigrants in the state than jobs available, the *St. Louis Post-Dispatch* reporting in late 1999 that by that date, immigrants in Missouri were three times more likely to live in poverty than American-born Missourians. An estimated thirty-four thousand Missouri immigrants lived in poverty in 1999. In addition, the Immigration and Naturalization Services (INS) reported that by late 1999, there were eighteen thousand undocumented immigrants living in Missouri, a sore spot for many Missourians, especially those living in rural, often more homogenous, parts of the state.

This reality was one of many concerns that troubled Missourians as they prepared for a new decade, a new century, and a new millennium. What, they wondered, would the twenty-first century hold?

SUGGESTED READINGS

Lawrence H. Larsen, *A History of Missouri, 1953–2003* (2004), published by the University of Missouri Press, is a good introduction to this period. Demographic changes in Missouri during the last three decades of the twentieth century are the subject of a number of works, including an essay titled "Losing Ground to Urban Sprawl," by Helene Miller, *Missouri Conservationist*, (September 2001); "Main Street Replaced by Superhighways," *St. Louis Post-Dispatch*, July 22, 1971; William H. Kester, "Economic Potential Not Being Realized," *St. Louis Post-Dispatch*, August 8, 1971; "Suburbs Lead Numbers Gain," *Springfield Leader and Press*, September 13, 1971; and "Population in City Continues Decline," *St. Louis Post-Dispatch*, June 28, 1975. Also helpful are Charles R. T. Crumpley, "Freeways Paved Way for Suburbs," *Kansas City Times*, December 13, 1979;

and Marjorie Mandel, "Kansas City Area Faces Population Drain," *St. Louis Post-Dispatch*, February 1, 1981.

Biographies and autobiographies of political figures from this era are helpful, among them is James N. Giglio, *Call Me Tom: The Life of Thomas F. Eagleton* (2011), published by the University of Missouri Press. Also, Harriett Woods, *Stepping Up to Power: The Political Journey of American Women* (2000), published by Westview Press, takes up the issue of the battle over the Equal Rights Amendment in Missouri. So, too, does Claire McCaskill's autobiography, *Plenty Ladylike: A Memoir* (2015), published by Simon & Schuster. Lana Stein, *St. Louis Politics: The Triumph of Tradition*, includes coverage of the last three decades of the twentieth century. It was published by the Missouri Historical Society Press. Also useful are the voluminous oral histories compiled by the State Historical Society of Missouri since it began its oral history program during the early 1990s. Transcripts of many of these oral histories, including those of former Missouri Senator Mary Gant and former Missouri State Representative and Senator P. Wayne Goode, may be accessed through this website: https://digital.shsmo.org/digital/collection/ohc.

College campus demonstrations in the wake of the Kent State killings in May 1970 were widely covered by Missouri newspapers. Especially helpful are articles in the *St. Louis Post-Dispatch*, *Kansas City Star*, *Columbia Missourian* and *Columbia Tribune*, and *Springfield News-Leader*.

The Hancock Amendment had a dramatic effect on Missouri public services; the debate over the amendment was covered widely by newspapers during the early 1980s and, indeed, ever since. Early articles about the amendment include Mike Sweeney, "Pros, foes expect challenges to amendment limiting taxes," *Springfield Leader and Press*, November 5, 1980; Marjorie Mandel and Robert Goodrich, "Tax Lid: Yes; Waste Plan: No," *St. Louis Post-Dispatch*, November 5, 1980; Brad Cain, "State, Local Officials Keep up Attack on Spending Lid," *Kansas City Times*, November 19, 1980.

The issue of term limits has been the subject of much commentary, including Phil Brooks, "Capitol Perspectives: Term Limits," November 1, 2018, available at www.mdn.org/mpanews. Also useful is "How it started: The campaign for term limits in Missouri developed out of frustration," *Springfield News-Leader*, October 3, 1992; and "Lawmakers are divided on

Merits of Term Limits," *St. Louis Post-Dispatch*, November 6, 1992. On John Danforth's transformative role in Missouri politics, see "Remembering 1968, when Jack Danforth upended GOP Politics," *Kansas City Star*, November 4, 2018.

Edward "Chip" Robertson Jr. explains the battle over the right to die that made its way to the Missouri Supreme Court during the 1980s. Robertson was one of the justices of the Missouri Supreme Court who heard the case. His essay, "In the Midst of All Such Excitement: The Nancy Cruzan Case," appears in Kenneth H. Winn, ed., *Missouri Law and the American Conscience: Historical Rights and Wrongs* (2016), published by the University of Missouri Press.

Chapter Ten

The Twenty-First Century
Challenges in the New Millennium

"We are witnessing the slow-motion collapse of the working class in America."

Missouri Senator Josh Hawley, October 11, 2019

MISSOURIANS, LIKE THEIR fellow citizens throughout the country, anticipated the twenty-first century with anxiety, even trepidation. Many wondered whether their computer-dependent culture would fail them at midnight on December 31, 1999, leaving them with cars, utilities, appliances, banks, businesses, and governments that would no longer function. In May of 1999 the Missouri Office of Information Technology reported that it had printed ten thousand brochures to help businesses prepare for what was widely referred to as "Y2K." They ran out of brochures within forty-eight hours. On New Year's Eve 1999, a SWAT team of government officials gathered at the Missouri State Emergency Management (SEMA) headquarters, not far from the State Capitol, ready to troubleshoot if anything went awry, when the clock struck midnight: when the digits "99" rolled over to "double zero," nothing happened, except of course the year had changed.

Even though all the doomsday scenarios had proved false, the anxiety before the change of the millennium was very real, across the nation and the world. Naturally, the anxiety over Y2K created a plethora of scamming opportunities, as anxiety always does. One such effort involved targeted phone calls to individuals, warning them that their bank was not "computer ready" for 2000, and urging them to transfer all of their money into a "safe" account, a transfer that the caller offered to facilitate, if only the recipient of the call would provide them with necessary personal information, including account numbers and passwords. An even more creative and aggressive effort to take advantage of Missourians' fears came from a real estate company in south central Missouri that tried to market rural real estate to survivalist types who were fearful that Y2K would lead to mass starvation and even civil war. The realtor promised fertile land where food could be grown and abundant water supplies so that Missourians with grit and survivalist skills could weather the Y2K storm, proving once again that Missourians, scammers among them, are an ever-resourceful people.

The lead-up to the new millennium and the false fears notwithstanding, the twenty-first century did not unfold the way many Missourians believed or hoped it would. When the 2000 federal census was taken, the Show-Me State's population total stood at 5,595,211. Although that figure represented an increase of nearly half a million persons over the 1990 total of 5,117,073, it officially registered Missouri's decline from the fifteenth most populous state in the country to the seventeenth, and a far cry from its ranking as the fifth most populous state in the nation a century earlier.

In the year 2000, demographers with the Missouri Economic Research and Information Center predicted that Missouri would shake off its anemic growth during the first three decades of the twenty-first century. They estimated that the state's population would grow at a rate of twenty-one percent by the year 2030. But two thirds of the way through that period, near the end of the second decade of the new millennium, the state's population growth was closer to two percent, or less than one-tenth of the rate projected. Clearly, the vision that many Missourians held for their state was not coming to pass. Increasingly, Missouri seemed to be a less desirable place to live than it had been for much of its earlier history.

Why was this? What had happened? What lay at the root of Missouri's relative decline? According to Matt Foulkes, Associate Professor of Geography at the University of Missouri, the Great Recession of 2007–2009 "curtailed our net migrations to the state." In a 2019 *Jefferson City News Tribune* article titled "Low job growth a factor in stagnant population," reporter Joe Gamm noted, "Census data show people of high and low tax bases both migrate for the same reasons—for jobs, families and, recently, for amenities," or what might be called the pleasantness of a place. A 445-page report titled "Equitable Economic Development Framework," produced for the St. Louis Development Corporation (SLDC) by Boston planning firm Mass Economics, noted that a key element missing in the St. Louis economy was "entry-level and middle wage jobs." As SLDC Director Otis Williams noted, "The big hole that we have in the city of St. Louis is we have lots of citizens who are not at the upper end of the educational spectrum." Another hint of an answer appeared in a *St. Louis Post-Dispatch* article by business editor David Nicklaus on July 3, 2020. He reported that Michael Neidorff, CEO of Centene, "the largest company headquartered in the area," had announced the previous day that his company was going to spend $1 billion to build a new Centene headquarters in Charlotte, North Carolina. This new venture meant creating six thousand new jobs.

But why had Neidorff and Centene chosen to build their new facility in North Carolina instead of in St. Louis, where they already employed a significant number of workers? Neidorff's response: "I always want to expand here. I love it here, but we're not able to recruit all the people [workers skilled enough for the jobs and willing to live in the St. Louis area] we want."

Neidorff's comments highlighted St. Louis's, and Missouri's, struggle to supply a well-educated and well-trained labor force, but he also emphasized other issues: a high murder rate in the city, inadequate airline connections, and persistent and unresolved racial divisions.

For nearly two centuries, Missouri's political leaders of both major parties had been operating under the assumption that low taxes and a reduction in government regulations would be enough to attract people and businesses to the state. It turns out, however, that low taxes may not have been incentive enough. The problem remains that people, including those who staff businesses large and small, want good schools for their children, good infrastructure and ease of travel, and good, even excellent, cultural resources, and social harmony. Critics argued that all those things were hard to find in Missouri. All, save perhaps for the social harmony, cost a good deal of money, money that the state of Missouri never raised—and still does not raise from tax revenue.

Professor Foulkes claimed that the state's failure to attract a large influx of migrants during the first two decades of the twenty-first century had a lot to do with jobs, and jobs have a lot to do with an educated work force. A major criticism of Missouri government in the twenty-first century has been its failure to support adequately public education. According to *U.S. News and World Report*, Missouri consistently ranked in the lower half of all states in the list of "Most and Least Educated States in America." Notwithstanding this reality, a 2019 analysis of per-pupil expenditures in the state by Michael Q. McShane of the Show-Me Institute did show an upward trend in per-student expenditures over the preceding five years.

One problem in Missouri's system of public education lay in the very high rate of teacher turnover, caused in part by low pay. According to a January 2019 *Kansas City Star* article, based on a Missouri Department of Elementary and Secondary Education report, "Only about a third of teachers hired these days stay on the job for at least five years." The report further indicated that the rate of teachers leaving their positions each year exceeded the national rate. "Missouri," the *Star* noted, "has the second-lowest average starting salary for teachers *in the nation.*" Only Montana was lower. Evidencing the relative decline of teachers' pay, the report indicated that, adjusted for inflation, teacher pay in Missouri had dropped 5.5 percent since the year 2000.

Public funding for higher education in Missouri was equally challenging. According to a 2020 study compiled by an Illinois State University organization known as "Grapevine," Missouri ranked forty-sixth in the nation for the amount of state funding it provides per student.

These educational funding challenges came at a particularly difficult time, as education was more critical in the twenty-first century than it had ever been. Many of the factory jobs in Missouri that had emerged after World War II, which required no formal training beyond high school, had disappeared or were rapidly disappearing in the early twenty-first century. Sadly, illustrations abounded. Lamar, Missouri, in the west-central county of Barton, was a factory town for more than half a century, from the 1950s well into the second half of the first decade of the twenty-first century. For many years, Lamar was home to O'Sullivan Industries, described as "the country's third-largest furniture manufacturer." At the peak of its production, O'Sullivan employed approximately eighteen hundred people in Lamar, roughly forty percent of the town's population. By 2007, O'Sullivan had closed its doors, laying off the last of its seven hundred employees still working there. There were no jobs for the people laid off. Examples such as Lamar abounded statewide.

The loss of jobs and the decline in population in rural and small-town Missouri had many tangential consequences. One of those was a dramatic decline in access to adequate health care. By 2019, thirty-seven percent of Missourians remained in rural Missouri, where their access to "adequate health care" was, according to Hospital Industry Data Institute statistics, "a nightmare." Rural Missourians increasingly had little or no access to physicians—only nine percent of licensed physicians in Missouri lived in rural areas of the state in 2014, a number that had declined by fifteen percent since 2011. Moreover, rural Missourians lived much farther away from hospitals than their urban counterparts. According to the study, six rural hospitals had been closed over the five years preceding 2019, including three just between 2018 and 2019. These included the one-hundred-bed Twin Rivers Regional Medical Center in the Bootheel town of Kennett and the fifteen-bed I-70 Community Hospital in Sweet Springs.

There was much concern about the general well-being of children in early twenty-first century Missouri. Toward the end of the second decade of the century, proponents of child health care in the state became alarmed at the number of Missouri children who were losing health insurance coverage. A June 2019 report indicated that the number of Missouri children enrolled in Medicaid and the Children's Health Insurance Program had declined nearly ten percent over the previous fourteen months. Critics pointed out that this was the second largest decline of any state in the union, after Idaho, and that the decline in Missouri was some five times the national average. They further claimed that these reductions were the result of the state's implementation of a new, more rigid and more restrictive eligibility system, one aimed at weeding out improperly enrolled state residents. State officials countered that the decline was due largely to an improved economy and the consequent enrollment of more children in private health insurance plans. On August 4, 2020, Missouri voters approved a state constitutional amendment aimed at expanding Medicaid eligibility in the state. Ironically, many rural voters who stood to gain from this expansion voted against it. It remains to be seen whether this proposed change in access to health care coverage in Missouri will result in improved health care for the state's most vulnerable citizens. During the 2021 legislative session, Missouri lawmakers refused to fund the expansion of Medicaid, despite voter approval of the constitutional amendment months earlier. Centene chairman and CEO, Michael F. Neidorff, called this action by Missouri officials an "embarrassment" and threatened to relocate his company out of the state because of it.

A related problem facing Missouri and Missourians in the twenty-first century is the presence and persistence of poverty in the state. According to the 2020 Missouri Poverty Report, presented by the Missouri Community

Action Network and Missourians to End Poverty, Missouri's poverty rate was 13.2 percent, meaning that 786,330 Missourians, including roughly one out of five children under the age of twelve, lived in poverty. The official poverty rate for the nation was only slightly lower, at 13.1 percent. Likewise, there was growing concern in the state over the increased number of individuals, including children, who faced "food insecurity." Indeed, in June 2019, the KIDS COUNT Data Book, released by the Annie E. Casey Foundation, ranked Missouri twenty-eighth among the fifty states in the category of "Child Well-being," a decline from twenty-sixth for the previous year.

Among the troubling trends in Missouri during the early twenty-first century was a sharp drop in life expectancy. A report from the Missouri Department of Health issued in late 2019 documented what journalist Charles Fain Lehman described as a decline, "not the result of a graying population, but rather a reflection of increases in death rates among younger persons for external causes such as drug overdoses, suicides and homicides." According to the study, a Missourian born in 2018 could expect to live nearly one year less than a Missourian born in 2012.

Young and middle-aged Missourians, those between the ages of twenty-five and fifty-five, were reported to be the most vulnerable to what was sometimes described as "deaths of despair." The Department of Health report documented an astonishing increase of 53.5 percent in Missouri suicides between 2008 and 2018. During that same period, accidental deaths in Missouri increased by 33.6 percent and homicides by 30.7 percent. Much of the increase in accidental deaths was the result of drug overdoses. Addressing this "crisis" in late 2019, Missouri's junior U.S. Senator, Josh Hawley, noted, "These numbers are tragic, but they are more than that. They are the signs of a crisis. We are witnessing the slow-motion collapse of the working class in America. All Americans suffer from deaths of despair, but we know from the evidence that it is working people and working families who are hit hardest."

The rate of homicides in Missouri's two major cities was especially troubling during the second decade of the twenty-first century. In 2018, St. Louis had more murders per 100,000 people, 66.1, than any other major city in the United States. Indeed, according to FBI statistics, St. Louis's reign as the American city with the highest murder rate dated back to 2014. According to an October 2019 report by *St. Louis Post-Dispatch* reporters

Erin Heffernan and Janelle O'Dea, "Children in [St. Louis] have been killed at 20 times the national rate for decades." According to their reporting, "584 kids [were] killed in St. Louis over [a period of] 30 years." In a five-month period in 2019, from early May to late September, 17 children under the age of 16 were killed by gun violence in St. Louis.

On the other side of the state in Kansas City, local officials also struggled with a high murder rate and high incidences of gun violence. In October 2019, the *Kansas City Star* reported that during the first ten months of the year, twenty-five persons between the ages of thirteen and nineteen died as a result of gun violence. Although the murder rate in Kansas City dropped from 30.93 per 100,000 population in 2017 to 27.78 in 2018, it still had the fifth highest murder rate in the nation for a major city.

Missouri's third and fourth largest cities, Springfield and Columbia, also experienced high incidences of gun violence. In October 2019, mayors of the four major cities met with Missouri Governor Mike Parson to search for a way forward out of the gun violence quagmire in the state. Among the ideas discussed were increasing community mental health and substance abuse funding for both victims and offenders, plus strategies for keeping firearms out of the hands of violent offenders, some version of what by that time had come to be called "red flag" laws. An obstacle to the latter was Missourians' strong "gun culture," and the perception of many residents of the state that any effort to restrict citizens' access to and use of firearms of any kind constituted a violation of citizens' Second Amendment right to bear arms.

In 2016, the Republican-controlled Missouri General Assembly passed Senate Bill 656, referred to by some as "the guns everywhere bill." SB 656 allowed the carrying of concealed weapons in Missouri without the need to obtain a permit, any kind of training, or background check. It also negated any local government ordinances aimed at restricting gun ownership or use. Moreover, it expanded the so-called "Castle Doctrine," giving Missourians greater license to defend themselves with lethal force if and when they felt threatened, either inside or outside of their homes.

Democratic Governor Jeremiah "Jay" Nixon, himself a well-publicized hunter, vetoed SB 656, explaining in his veto message, "I cannot support the extreme step of . . . eliminating sensible protections like background checks and training requirements, and taking away the ability of sheriffs to protect their communities." The governor's decision was praised by the

Missouri chapter of Moms Demand Action for Gun Sense in America, part of Everytown for Gun Safety. Speaking on behalf of the chapter, Becky Morgan praised Governor Nixon, while calling SB 656 legislation that "would make the every day in Missouri more dangerous." Morgan had seen the consequences of gun violence up close. In 1991, a mentally ill person who was under treatment bought a gun and used it to kill her father. Morgan was only nineteen at the time. Although that incident shook her to the core, it was the killing of twenty children and six adults at Sandy Hook Elementary School in Newtown, Connecticut, in December 2012 that prompted Morgan, by then a mother herself, to join the Moms movement.

The effect of the implementation of SB 656 was to transform Missouri from a state that had some of the strictest handgun laws in the nation to a state that had some of the least restrictive such laws by the second decade of the twenty-first century. According to a January 5, 2021, editorial in the *Kansas City Star*, 689 people were shot and killed in Missouri in 2020. This number represented "Missouri['s] . . . worst year ever for gun violence. . . ."

If Missouri's major urban areas were awash in gun violence, rural Missouri faced a different type of crisis, as it was in a serious state of population decline during the first two decades of the twenty-first century. Census data released in April 2019 indicated that fifty-two Missouri counties, mostly in rural parts of the state, had experienced population decline in 2018. Pemiscot County, deep in the Missouri Bootheel, saw the largest drop, at 3.2 percent. The counties with the next largest declines in population were also in the Bootheel: Dunklin (2 percent) and Mississippi (1.8 percent). Carter County, in the eastern Missouri Ozarks, matched Mississippi County with a 1.8 percent decline in population.

The total number of farms in the state was decreasing in the early twenty-first century, even as the size of Missouri farms increased, suggesting that farming was being taken over by large agribusiness concerns, entities overseen by corporate elites. Especially hard hit were family farms, once the backbone of Missouri economic and social life. The days of a family making a living from a quarter or even half section of land through the hard work of diversified farming of a combination of crops and livestock was rapidly disappearing. Between 2000 and 2014, the number of dairy farms in Missouri declined by a staggering fifty-four percent, from 1,796 to 895.

The rural counties in Missouri that were growing tended to be those that were quickly becoming "exurbs," communities that were farther away from metropolitan areas than suburbs, but still close enough to allow access to an urban area. The county with the largest percentage population increase in 2018 over 2017 was Lincoln County, at a rate of roughly 2.8 percent. The fact that Lincoln County is only sixty miles north of St. Louis points to another reality: urban sprawl. The availability of large tracts of affordable land made living in Lincoln County more attractive to St. Louis area workers than living in St. Louis or St. Charles counties, as had previously been the case, the daily commute of up to an hour or more each way seemingly no longer a deterrent. Ironically, of course, as increasing numbers of urban residents moved farther and farther from the urban core, they brought the problems of urban life with them: congestion, crime, and the need for more public services, which, in turn, brought an increased need for higher taxes, all of which they had sought to escape in the first place.

To a great extent, twenty-first century Missourians, especially those in rural parts of the state, suffered a malaise, a sense that things were not as they should be, and that the people and institutions they had long trusted, especially their governments, to make things right were no longer working. This negativity and suspicion carried over into and helped to define the 2016 presidential and gubernatorial elections in the state. Presidential candidate Donald J. Trump defied pundits' predictions by defeating the politically experienced Hillary Clinton. Trump bested Clinton in the Electoral College by a tally of 304 votes to 227, to take the White House, even though Clinton's popular vote total exceeded Trump's by nearly three million. In Missouri, however, Trump's victory was a resounding one, as he carried 111 of Missouri's 114 counties, losing to Clinton in only Boone, Jackson and St. Louis counties, as well as in the City of St. Louis. Trump garnered 56.4 percent of the Missouri vote, compared to Clinton's 37.9 percent. By any standard of measurement, this was a landslide victory for Trump, and solidified Missouri as a "red state," contrary to its "blue state" status throughout much of the previous century. Indeed, as journalist David Weigel had pointed out earlier, in a 2012 essay in *Slate Magazine*, the turning point in Missouri had been the 2008 election, when Missouri went for Republican presidential candidate John McCain over U.S. Senator Barack Obama. That election solidified the reality of the state's transition from "blue" to "red." As Weigel noted, "for 187 years [from 1821 until 2008] no Democrat won the presidency without carrying the state. When Democrats lost, they at least kept it close [in Missouri]. Even Michael Dukakis lost Missouri by only 4 points [in 1988]." Clearly, Trump's outsider mystique, his criticism of the status quo and of government bureaucrats who constituted "the swamp," played well in Missouri. Trump's drubbing of Clinton in Missouri was the worst showing in Missouri by a Democratic presidential candidate since George McGovern earned thirty-seven percent of the vote forty-four years earlier, in his 1972 challenge of President Richard M. Nixon.

Also claiming victory in the Election of 2016 was Navy Seal and Rhodes Scholar Eric Greitens, who defeated Missouri Attorney General Chris Koster in the race for Missouri governor. Both Trump and Greitens campaigned as anti-politician outsiders who wanted to end business-as-usual politics. Neither man had ever held an elective office.

In yet another 2016 statewide election that evidenced the appeal of outsiders over incumbents, thirty-seven-year-old Joshua Hawley, a University of Missouri law school professor with no prior political experience, defeated two-term Missouri state senator Kurt Schaefer, who chaired the powerful Senate Appropriations Committee. Hawley's margin of victory over his Republican primary opponent Schaefer was sixty-four percent to thirty-two percent. Tellingly, in a campaign appearance in Columbia, Hawley told a reporter, "The Missouri attorney general's office should become a platform for challenging federal laws and regulations." It was a sentiment that many Missourians, past and present, shared.

Despite Greitens's overwhelming defeat of Koster in the 2016 election, it was his "outsider" status and his tempestuous relationship with legislators of his own party that contributed to his downfall. There were contradictions aplenty during Greitens's short time in office. Though he claimed a commitment to transparency and open government, his opponents accused him of raising dark money and violating open-records laws by using software that caused opened messages to self-destruct. Although he claimed to be an advocate of collegiality and compromise, he was often at loggerheads with legislative leaders of his own party, the latter of whom often accused him of using strong-arm, even dictatorial, tactics. One of his biggest political setbacks came at the hands of the people who had elected him. On February 6, 2017, less than a month after taking office, Governor Greitens signed into law a bill making Missouri the twenty-eighth "right-to-work state" in the Union ("right-to-work" being a euphemism for union busting by anti-union political and business interests). This was a much-sought-after goal passed overwhelmingly by Republican supermajorities in the House and Senate during the previous legislative session. Opponents of this legislation mounted a referendum petition drive aimed at getting this issue on the ballot in August 2017. On August 5 opponents of right-to-work, who were also pro-union, won a decisive victory when Missouri voters chose to overturn the law by a more than two-thirds majority.

Greitens's reign as governor of Missouri began to unravel barely a year into his term. On January 10, 2018, in anticipation of an investigative report that was about to be released by a St. Louis television station, the governor admitted to an extramarital affair in 2015, before he began his campaign for governor. Subsequently, the husband of the woman with whom Greitens was involved produced what he alleged was evidence that the governor attempted to blackmail his partner. This action, allegedly, was aimed at preventing her from releasing information about their relationship. There followed an ever-growing cascade of allegations of wrongdoing from the governor's accusers and denials by Greitens and his ever-diminishing number of supporters. His record of combative interaction with and defiance of legislators, even within his own party, meant that there was no deep well of support from which Greitens could draw. Finally, in the face of impeachment proceedings in the Missouri House that began on May 18, 2018, Greitens resigned as governor, effective June 1, 2018.

Greitens was replaced on the day his resignation took effect by Lieutenant Governor Michael L. Parson, a man who was in virtually every respect the antithesis of the disgraced governor. Contrary to being an outsider like Greitens, Parson, nearly a generation older than the man he replaced, was a consummate insider, having served twelve years in the Missouri General Assembly before being elected to the state's second-highest office in 2016. Unlike the urbane and scholarly Greitens, who had grown up in St. Louis and earned a Ph.D. from Oxford University, Parson grew up on a farm in rural Hickory County, Missouri, joined the U.S. Army soon after high school graduation, and took night classes at the University of Maryland and the University of Hawaii while in the service. After six years in the Army, most of the time serving as a military policeman, Parson returned to Hickory County and served as a sheriff's deputy for two years before moving to neighboring Polk County to take a job as a criminal investigator and manage a service station. In 1992, Parson was elected Polk County

Fig. 47: Governor Mike Parson, U.S. Senator Roy D. Blunt, SHSMO Executive Director, Gary Kremer, and Lieutenant Governor Mike Kehoe, gather at the SHSMO Center for Missouri Studies on November 1, 2019. Credit: Notley Hawkins, State Historical Society of Missouri.

sheriff, a position he held for twelve years prior to being elected to the Missouri legislature in 2004.

Parson quickly became a popular governor who seemed to exude the transparency that Governor Greitens only talked about. The new governor met frequently with legislators and talked with them rather than at them. He travelled the state and delivered plain-spoken remarks to people from all walks of life who seemed to be more comfortable with his casual style than they had ever been with the elitist and somewhat distant Greitens. A conscience conservative in what had become a deeply red state, Parson seemed to many Missourians a shoo-in for the 2020 gubernatorial race, regardless of the current state of politics in the state and the nation.

President Trump retained his popularity in Missouri throughout his term in office, despite some of the actions he and his administration took. On May 31, 2018, the president announced he would be imposing steep tariffs on a variety of imports, including steel and aluminum from Canada, Mexico, and the European Union. According to a *St. Louis Post-Dispatch* report, "Within a few weeks of the start of the tariffs, sales [for

Mid-Continent Nail Maker of Poplar Bluff] had fallen by 50 per cent," and company officials had to lay off sixty workers because foreign steel was now cheaper than American-made steel. Mid-Continent warned that two hundred of its five hundred employees could be laid off by the end of July if the business did not receive an exemption from the tariff. Butler County, where Mid-Continent Nail Maker was located, had given Trump almost eighty percent of its votes in 2016.

Ten difficult months after the tariffs were imposed, Mid-Continent, the largest nail manufacturer in the United States, earned an exemption from the tariff by the federal government. Over the course of those ten months, however, Mid-Continent's sales fell by sixty percent, and the number of employees fell from more than five hundred to fewer than three hundred. Many employees left because of the uncertainty surrounding the business's future. Although Mid-Continent hoped it could recover in time, Chris Pratt, Mid-Continent's operations manager, noted, "We lost a huge volume of orders that were already on the books. . . . Some of those orders will never come back."

Likewise, Missouri farmers worried over the impact of President Trump's trade war with China. In March 2018, Missouri Farm Bureau President Blake Hurst, a farmer who raised corn and soybeans near Tarkio in northwest Missouri, noted, "Half of all soybeans (in Missouri, and nationally) are exported, and half of those go to China." Anxiety over adverse effects of agricultural tariffs was compounded by a summer drought in much of Missouri in the summer of 2018. One estimate indicated that as much as seventy percent of the state's soybean crop was affected by the drought; likewise, that year Missouri farmers produced the smallest corn harvest since 2012.

Among the social institutions that had long provided support to struggling Missourians was organized religion. But organized religion's sway over the lives of Missourians declined in the twenty-first century. In Missouri, as in the rest of the country, the number of people regularly attending or belonging to churches declined significantly, although Missourians remained somewhat more religious than most Americans.

Missouri Catholics, just like Catholics elsewhere in the country, felt the impact of the sex abuse scandal first reported by the *Boston Globe* early in 2002. In March 2002, Bishop Anthony O'Connell of the Palm Beach,

Florida, diocese resigned his position in the wake of allegations of sexual misconduct during his twenty-five-year-career at St. Thomas Aquinas Preparatory Seminary in Hannibal, Missouri. A native of Ireland who was ordained a priest for the Diocese of Jefferson City in 1963, "OC," as he was known, became Director of Students at the seminary following his ordination. He was named Spiritual Director in 1968 and Rector of the school in 1970. He also served as Director of Vocations for the Jefferson City diocese from 1969 to 1988.

Occupying positions of power in a Catholic culture that venerated priests and nuns, O'Connell abused his power and authority to prey on young Catholic boys for years. Although O'Connell admitted to molesting at least two seminary students in 2002, it was widely thought that the number of his victims was far higher. At least three graduates of the seminary's class of 1971, including one who subsequently became a priest, credibly claimed O'Connell had molested them.

The publicity surrounding O'Connell's crimes was the death knell for St. Thomas Aquinas Seminary, whose student enrollment had fallen from more than one hundred students during the early 1960s to only 27 in 2002. On April 17, 2002, Bishop John R. Gaydos of the Jefferson City Diocese, announced that the school would close at the end of that academic year. A few days later, my childhood friend, Tim Samson, and I drove to Hannibal for a final look at the seminary where the two of us had attended high school some four decades earlier, Tim for four years, me for two. Our pilgrimage included spending time in the gym and on the ballfield, walking through the dormitories where we slept, the dining room where we ate, the laundry room where we sorted clothing, the kitchen where we washed dishes, and the classrooms and study hall where we learned. We attended Mass with the faculty and students and visited with two elderly priests who had been our teachers forty years earlier. Both octogenarians, they were incredibly sad, disheartened, disappointed, and angry over the series of events that led to the school's closing. We shared their grief and their outrage.

The extent of O'Connell's crimes, the brazenness with which he carried them out, and the failure of the Catholic Church generally or the Jefferson City diocese specifically to protect young boys from him sent shock waves through the Catholic community. Ultimately, over the next decade and half, the Jefferson City diocese identified twenty-six priests who were "credibly accused" of sexual molestation while serving the diocese, along with three religious brothers who were members of the Presentation religious order. An additional four diocesan clerics were found to be "unsuitable for ministry out of concern for the safety of our youth."

In 2018, new Jefferson City Diocesan Bishop, Shawn McKnight, who assumed the leadership of the diocese in 2017, acknowledged that the diocese had spent $4.7 million dealing with the issue of sexual abuse between 2003 and 2015. This reality did not sit well with many Catholics, who were already dealing with a church whose declining membership placed a greater financial burden on those who remained faithful to the cause.

In truth, even apart from the sex scandal, the Catholic Church and other organized religious denominations, faced great challenges throughout the state and nation. According to a 2019 Gallup survey, church membership in the United States declined precipitously during the first two decades of the twenty-first century. During that same period, the percentage of American adults with no religious affiliation more than doubled. In 2020, approximately one out of five adult Missourians was unaffiliated with any religion. In June 2020, the Southern Baptist Convention reported its largest single-year decline in membership in more than a century. In St. Louis, over the decade from 2010 to 2019, baptisms for children in the Catholic Archdiocese of St. Louis fell by twenty percent, from 5,711 to 4,564 a year. Catholic school enrollment declined by twenty-five percent and the number of schools declined fourteen percent, from 152 to 131. Overall, most Catholics in the archdiocese failed to fulfill their Sunday obligation, with only about one-fourth of them attending church each week. The St. Louis Archdiocese, too, had its own sex scandal cases. According to a June 16, 2019, article in the *St. Louis Post-Dispatch*, "In 2015, a court filing in a sex abuse case revealed a matrix of 240 complaints against 115 priests and other church employees in the Archdiocese of St. Louis over a 20-year period ending in 2003."

Arguably, the oldest and the most persistent of Missouri's challenges, the issue of relationships between white and Black Missourians, remained in the forefront of concern in the twenty-first century, two centuries after race and slavery had been the touchstones of the state's entry into the Union. For all that had transpired between the races over that time span, Blacks and whites seemed as divided as ever. Indeed, they seemed to see the world differently and to live in separate spheres, reminding an observer of a line from the great Black novelist Richard Wright's 1940 classic, *Native Son*, whose protagonist, Bigger Thomas, exclaimed, "White folks and black folks is strangers. We don't know what each other is thinking."

Examples of conflict abounded. Concern in the state over allegations of racial bias in traffic enforcement led the Missouri General Assembly to create a law requiring the state's attorney general to compile a "Vehicle Stops Report" each year. This law went into effect on August 28, 2000. Nearly two decades later, these reports regularly indicated that African Americans were far more likely than whites to be pulled over by police—a phenomenon that came to be called "driving while Black." Indeed, the report issued by the state attorney general in 2019 indicated that Black drivers were ninety-one percent more likely than white drivers to be pulled over by police in that year. According to the *Kansas City Star*, "That is the largest racial disparity in vehicle stops in Missouri history."

Racial disparities existed on many other levels in twenty-first-century Missouri: in family income and accumulated wealth, rates of incarceration, level of education attained, unemployment rates, possession of health insurance, life expectancy, and more. By the twenty-first century, whites and Blacks in the state and nation had come to see themselves and each other very differently. Some argued whites saw a lack of Black initiative and individual responsibility, while African Americans saw systemic racial bias and discrimination.

The differing views surfaced in two major conflicts that focused the nation's attention on Missouri as never before in 2014 and 2015. The first of these events was the killing of eighteen-year-old Michael Brown, a Ferguson, Missouri, African American, by a white police officer on August 9, 2014. Multiple narratives emerged over what transpired prior to the shooting, but the one that took hold in the African American community was that Brown was shot while his hands were raised in surrender, imploring the officer not to shoot. Although a subsequent FBI investigation failed to find evidence that Brown was surrendering, the cry of "Hands Up, Don't Shoot," became a rallying call for protesters who claimed the officer had murdered Michael Brown.

Protests, both orderly and violent, followed Michael Brown's death for more than a week. Police efforts to suppress the protests, including establishing a curfew, were widely criticized. So, too, was Missouri Governor Jay Nixon's ceding authority to the Missouri State Highway Patrol to suppress the protests.

In the aftermath of Brown's death, the St. Louis County prosecutor convened a grand jury to determine whether to indict the white officer who shot Brown. On November 24, 2014, the prosecuting attorney announced the grand jury's decision not to do so. More protests and violence resulted in the wake of the decision, not only in Ferguson, but in more than one hundred seventy cities around the country. By this time the single word "Ferguson" had become synonymous with the conviction that Blacks in America for a very long time were and today still are the victims of systemic police brutality and violence, and that their citizenship rights were under assault, not only in St. Louis County but throughout the United States. Although the U.S. Justice Department subsequently reported that the officer who killed Brown had been justified in his actions, it also concluded that, in the words of Kevin McDermott of the *St. Louis Post-Dispatch*, "the city's municipal court system was essentially a money trap designed to milk poor black defendants through targeted traffic stops and self-perpetuating fines."

In Missouri the focus of racial unrest moved to the University of Missouri's flagship campus in Columbia. The university had a long history of racial discrimination and tension, the school refusing to admit African American students until forced to do so by court order in 1950. MU did not hire its first full-time Black professor until 1969. Throughout the decades that followed, racial tensions simmered just below the surface, periodically boiling over into physical and verbal confrontations.

In the fall of 2015, MU student government president Payton Head, a native of Chicago's South Side, posted a Facebook response to his experience of hearing racial slurs directed at him on campus. The post went viral, nurtured by the environment created by the Michael Brown killing. On September 24, 2015, a group of protesting students gathered at a campus event labelled "Racism Lives Here." The event called attention to the students' view that Payton Head's concerns had not been adequately addressed. A second "Racism Lives Here" event was held a week later. Subsequently, protesters formed a group they called "Concerned Student 1950," referencing the year African American students were first admitted to the university.

Tensions increased perceptibly on October 10, 2015, when student protesters blocked University President Timothy Wolfe's car during the Mizzou homecoming parade. Wolfe failed to engage the students, one of whom later claimed he was hit by Wolfe's car. That student, Jonathan Butler, subsequently went on a hunger strike, and protesters launched a student boycott in support.

The relationship between Concerned Student 1950 and university administrators continued to deteriorate, with students issuing a series of demands that included Wolfe's resignation or removal. On November 8, Missouri's Black football players announced they would not practice or play until Wolfe was gone. Additionally, Head Coach Gary Pinkel and the team's white players announced their support of Concerned Student 1950. One day later, after the Missouri Students Association joined the call for Wolfe's resignation, the president stepped down.

The fallout from the student protests and president's resignation was intense and widespread. Student protesters and their supporters were ecstatic over the extent of their power and influence. Critics, including some Missouri legislators, were enraged, with many Missourians, Mizzou alumni among them, disavowing their connection to and support of the school. Some pledged never again to support the university's athletic or academic programs or to send their children to the school. Indeed, the following fall (2016), the University of Missouri experienced a cripplingly sharp decline in student enrollment, while many of the state's other institutions of higher learning experienced increased enrollments. Among the victims of the Concerned Student 1950 movement, and the reaction to it, was any opportunity for increased racial healing in the state.

Not all was gloomy as the Show-Me State approached its two hundredth anniversary. While some regarded twenty-first-century Missouri as backward and slow to embrace new ideas, there were a number of areas in which Missourians seemed exceedingly forward looking and on the cutting edge of innovation. One was the prospect of the development of a futuristic high-speed transportation system that would reduce the travel time between St. Louis and Kansas City, by way of Columbia, from four hours to under thirty minutes.

The Missouri Hyperloop, as it came to be called, began to take shape in 2017, when a coalition formed between Virgin Hyperloop One, the University of Missouri, and the engineering firm of Black & Veatch. This group released a report in 2019, concluding that a hyperloop was feasible. Later that year, Missouri governor Mike Parson formed a blue-ribbon panel created to explore how a hyperloop might be constructed, how to fund it, and how to build a ten-to-fifteen-mile test track in the state. During the 2020 legislative session, a bill was introduced in the Missouri House aimed at building a hyperloop test track through public-private funding. The goal was to build ten to fifteen miles of such a track that would allow a train-like pod to travel through a tubular track at speeds up to 640 mph. In supporting the idea Missouri legislator Brad Fitzwater, the bill's sponsor, noted, "It would bring in investment dollars from around the world to make Missouri an innovative state." The estimated cost of building the hyperloop was $30 million to $40 million per mile, or approximately $7.3 billion to $10.4 billion total. Although Virgin Hyperloop ultimately chose West Virginia rather than Missouri for its "futuristic tube travel test track and certification center," a company spokesman noted in October 2020 that Missouri might still be a location for future hyperloop development.

In addition to the hyperloop, there was also the University of Missouri's NextGen Initiative, launched in 2019 on the University of Missouri campus in Columbia. The university broke ground in May 2019 on a $220.8 million facility that, its promoters, including University of Missouri System President Mun Choi, said, "would revolutionize the university's ability to understand and treat some of the world's most challenging diseases." Dr. Joseph Haslag, Director of the Economic and Policy Analysis Center at the university, projected that "NextGen will have a $5.6 billion impact on Missouri's economy" over the next five years. He further predicted "that by 2045, NextGen will have directly contributed to 7,000 new jobs."

St. Louis, meanwhile, seemed to be defying at least some of its critics and enjoying something of an economic renaissance near the end of the century's second decade. In October 2018, *St. Louis Post-Dispatch* business columnist David Nicklaus reported that Missouri companies had attracted $365 million of venture capital during the third quarter of 2018, "the largest three-month sum in records going back to 1995." Much of this money went to St. Louis area companies, including Essence Group Holdings Corporation, a St. Louis-based holding company that provides health insurance and software solutions through its subsidiaries.

The unemployment rate in the first decade of the twenty-first century in Missouri peaked at 9.8 percent in January 2010, the consequence of the Great Recession of 2007–2009. A decade later, by November 2019, unemployment in the state stood at 3.1 percent, 0.4 percent lower than the national rate.

A report presented by the Missouri Chamber Foundation in March 2019 foresaw impending success for the tech industry in the state. According to Bob Watson of the Jefferson City *News Tribune*, "Tech manufacturing in Missouri has grown by nearly 30 percent in the last five years, compared to a negative national growth rate of -0.7 percent." According to Watson's reporting, "Driving growth in Missouri is the manufacturing of electronic components, automatic environmental controls, bio-pharmaceuticals, battery storage and pesticides." The Chamber's fifty-six-page report predicted that Missouri would be among the top ten tech states in the nation within five years. The report also boasted that the average annual salary of Missouri tech workers was $101,470, nearly double the $57,000 average earnings for all jobs in the state.

No doubt the most exciting late-decade decision that would positively impact St. Louis and the state was the National Geospatial Intelligence Agency's (NGA) decision in 2016 to build its new NGA West facility in St. Louis. Described by the *St. Louis Post-Dispatch* as "the biggest federal project in St. Louis history," this venture called for a $1.7 billion effort to be launched north of downtown. Nearly one hundred acres was cleared near the intersection of Jefferson and Cass avenues to make way for the project. The new site was envisioned to replace an existing NGA facility on the south riverfront, where approximately thirty-five hundred people worked. In late 2019, a $712 million construction contract was awarded to two contractors: St. Louis-based McCarthy Building Companies, Inc., and HITT Contracting, Inc., headquartered in Fairfax County, Virginia. Groundbreaking for the project occurred on November 26, 2019, with U.S. Senator Roy Blunt, who helped lead the effort to keep NGA in Missouri, delivering the principal address. Construction began in 2020, with as many as thirteen hundred construction workers expected to be employed by the time the project peaked in 2022. The projected completion date was 2025. Robert Sharp, head of NGA, noted, "We're really in competition for our nation's best minds. And we are convinced that a lot of those great minds are right here in St. Louis. . . ." Even before construction began, NGA had negotiated an agreement with St. Louis University and was expressing hope for similar agreements with Washington University and the University of Missouri.

Likewise, in late June 2020, Accenture Federal Services CEO John Goodman announced that his company was building a new Advanced Technology Center adjacent to Maryville University, near Interstate 64 and Highway 41. CEO Goodman told a reporter that "We chose St. Louis because of your talent. You have a very strong workforce oriented toward tech, world class universities and where tech people want to live." And, Goodman added, "outstanding sports teams." This project promised to bring fourteen hundred new tech jobs to St. Louis County, two hundred within the first year.

Another hopeful sign for the future was the effort by Missouri Governor Mike Parson and his Kansas counterpart, Laura Kelly, to end the economic border war between the two states. For years, each state tried to lure employers to the Kansas City metro area to their side of the state line with all sorts of incentives that often proved to be disruptive and even harmful to local tax bases. In early June 2019, Governor Parson signed legislation aimed at ending the practice.

The onset of the COVID-19 pandemic early in 2020 threatened to change everything. Missouri officially took notice of the novel coronavirus (COVID-19) on January 17, 2020, when the Missouri Division of Health and Senior Services distributed a health update to the state's health care providers and public health care practitioners regarding the outbreak of the virus in December 2019 in Wuhan City, Hubei Province, China. Five days later, DHSS updated the original report, noting that the virus had spread to the United States.

One month later, DHHS reported that its director, Dr. Randall Williams, attended a meeting at the White House to discuss federal, state, and local health officials' strategy for dealing with the virus, should they have to. Additionally, DHHS announced that the Missouri State Public Health Laboratory had been approved by the Centers for Disease Control (CDC) to begin testing for the virus.

The first reported case of the coronavirus in Missouri came from St. Louis County on March 10, 2020. The victim was a twenty-year-old woman who had recently returned home after studying in Italy. Within days came the news of a second case in Springfield, also travel-related, this time a person in his or her twenties who had recently been to Austria. The third case was another St. Louis County case. On March 18, Missouri reported its first coronavirus death, a Boone County man in his sixties who had also recently traveled outside the United States.

By March 23, the number of coronavirus cases in Missouri had grown exponentially, to 183. To that date, there had been three coronavirus deaths in the state, one each in Boone, St. Louis, and Jackson counties.

Governor Michael Parson issued an executive order on March 13, declaring a state of emergency in Missouri. The mayors of Missouri's major population centers took even more forceful action. On Saturday, March 21, St. Louis Mayor Lyda Krewson announced that she and St. Louis County Executive Sam Page were enacting a thirty-day stay-at-home order for city and county residents, effective Monday, March 23, 2020. Similarly, Kansas City Mayor Quinton Lucas issued a stay-at-home order for residents of Kansas City and surrounding counties, effective Tuesday, March 24, 2020.

St. Louis area public and private schools closed on March 18. Schools in Kansas City had closed the day before, on March 17. University of Missouri President Mun Choi announced that all in-person classes were suspended on March 16. Subsequently, he closed the University until further notice, with all classes moving to virtual platforms.

Life as Missourians had long known it all but came to a standstill by mid-March 2020. The NCAA tournament was cancelled, so there was no March Madness. The Major League Baseball season opening was delayed, and spring training was cancelled. The NBA playoffs were cancelled. A sports-centered people were forced to get along without their favorite spectator sports.

One consequence of the coronavirus pandemic during the late winter and early spring of 2020 was a dramatic increase in gun and ammunition sales in the state, evidencing a widespread fear among Missourians that the spread of the virus could lead to lawlessness and a kind of jungle survival ethos. According to the *St. Louis Post-Dispatch*, "On March 10, the day the U.S. reached 1,000 cases of coronavirus, the gun industry saw an unprecedented 276% sales surge in ammunition nationwide." Likewise, federal background checks for firearms sales were up three hundred percent. Gun and ammunition stores in the St. Louis area were doing a brisk business, with one shop owner, a proprietor of St. Louis County's Mid-America Arms, telling a reporter that the shop had done three weeks' worth of business in one week." He attributed the surge to panic. "People are panic-buying," he said.

Similarly, across the state in Kansas City, gun and ammunition sales surged. In Lee's Summit, a Kansas City suburb, Bren Brown, owner and CEO of a firearms store called Frontier Justice, reported brisk sales, noting, "Desperate times bring desperate measures and people want to be able to protect themselves and their loved ones which, of course, is their second amendment right." According to the *Kansas City Star*, "In June, over 77,000 guns were sold [in Missouri], the most in one month since 2000."

Governor Mike Parson initially ordered people to keep "social distance" between themselves, but his critics argued that he was too slow in issuing what they thought was a necessary statewide stay-at-home order. That order finally came on April 3, 2020, effective from April 6 through April 24. On April 16, he extended the order through May 3. By then (April 16), however, Missouri reported 5,111 cases of COVID-19, with 152 deaths, the number of confirmed cases and virus-related deaths statewide continuing to climb throughout the summer months and into the fall. On September 12, 2020, the Missouri Department of Health and Senior services reported that the number of COVID-19 cases in Missouri had exceeded one hundred thousand.

In the spring of 2020, as Missourians moved toward their bicentennial commemoration of statehood, no one knew where, when, or how the social and financial crises caused by the global pandemic would end. Some thought the response to the disease might be worse than the disease itself. Among the critics of the mass closings and stay-at-home directives was Cindy O'Laughlin, state senator from northeast Missouri, who represented the state's 18th senatorial district. In a Facebook post, O'Laughlin questioned what she called the "shut everyone down" mode, suggesting it might even be unconstitutional to require "perfectly healthy people" to be "confined to their homes or only able to do essential things as in Kansas City or St. Louis. Frankly I consider this unconstitutional and it needs [to be] challenged."

And challenged it was. On April 21 more than seven hundred protesters gathered at the Missouri State Capitol to protest Governor Parson's stay-at-home order. Self-identified as the "Reopen Missouri Rally," the group marched with signs and flags from the Capitol to the Governor's Mansion, demanding that they be allowed to go back to work. St. Charles resident Lonett Nordquist told a television reporter, "We are beyond what is constitutionally acceptable. We deserve to be able to go back to work and support our families. And the fear that the media is pushing isn't true." The protest occurred on a day when Missouri recorded sixteen new COVID-19 deaths and 156 new cases, bringing the state's total number of deaths to 215 and number of cases to 5,963.

Although most Missourians seemed to side with the governor, the number of people who sided with the re-open sentiment increased with each passing day. By the start of May, a kind of fault-line began to emerge between those who took the pandemic seriously and those who believed it was "fake news," driven by mainstream media types who wanted to bring down President Trump.

In Kansas City a large group of people gathered at the Plaza to protest Mayor Quinton Lucas's decision to extend the city's stay-at-home order through May 15. Similarly, protesters emerged in Clayton near the seat of St. Louis County government. Protester Janet Ayers registered her complaint against the stay-at-home order, stating, "Well I would rather die than to be a slave, and telling me that I cannot go to a store and purchase what I think is necessary for my life is not living in a free country."

The decision to wear or not wear a mask divided Missourians and became something of a political symbol of the division over staying at home versus opening up the state. On May 10, the *Kansas City Star* reported on the discord in the Kansas City metro area. Ken Hall, a Liberty business owner, when asked why he did not wear a mask, responded, "Because I don't give a [expletive]. It is what it is. You're either going to get it or you're not. I'm not afraid of it. We all live, we all die. When that happens is not your choice." Like so many who shared his position, Hall blamed the media for engendering fear of the virus.

During the summer of 2020, there were multiple instances of violence recorded on the part of would-be customers who were denied service in Missouri businesses because they refused to wear masks after being asked to do so by business owners. On September 2, the *St. Louis Post-Dispatch* reported that a twenty-nine-year-old St. Louis man opened fire outside a Family Dollar store in the Gravois Park neighborhood after being denied service for failure to wear a face mask. The man exchanged gunfire with another man outside the store and was struck in the hip by a bullet. The assailant was charged with first-degree assault, armed criminal action, and unlawful possession of a firearm.

Fig. 48: Masks and mask requirements became common in 2020 during the COVID-19 pandemic. This image was taken in a Columbia store. Credit: Beth Pike, State Historical Society of Missouri.

Frustration turned to rebellion and open defiance over the Memorial Day weekend in 2020. As Missouri's number of total positive cases of COVID-19 surpassed twelve thousand on Memorial Day, news outlets reported that large crowds from all over Missouri and neighboring states gathered at popular venues at the Lake of the Ozarks. During and in the days after the Memorial Day weekend, viewers around the nation and the world watched videos on news broadcasts and social media posts that showed crowds of swimsuit-clad revelers, almost none of whom were wearing face coverings, crowded together at the resort area's bars, restaurants, and pools. Alan Hull, front-desk manager at Days Inn in Osage Beach, told a *Post-Dispatch* reporter, "We are a lot busier this year [than in past years]. All the hotels here around the lake are busy."

While many Missourians expressed outrage at the sign of videos of crowded bars, such as at Coconuts Caribbean Bar & Grill in Gravois Mill, Backwater Jack's Bar & Grill in Osage Beach, and Lazy Gators in Lake Ozark, Camden County Sheriff Tony Helms issued a statement indicating that because a failure to social distance was not a crime, "the sheriff's office has no authority to enforce actions in that regard." He added, "We expect residents and visitors alike to exhibit personal responsibility when at the lake." The problem was that many Missourians failed to act with personal responsibility, focusing instead on their "right" to act as they pleased. Upon seeing the images of Memorial Day revelers partying shoulder-to-shoulder, Missouri director of the Department of Health and Senior Services, Dr. Randall Williams, warned that, "COVID-19 is still here, and social distancing needs to continue to prevent further spread of infection." St. Louis mayor, Lyda Krewson, expressed frustration at such risky behavior: "Now, these folks will be coming home to St. Louis and counties all over Missouri and the Midwest, raising concerns about the potential of more positive cases, hospitalization, and tragically, deaths." Krewson added, "it's just deeply disturbing."

On June 11, 2020, Governor Parson announced that Missouri would fully reopen and enter Phase II of its "Show Me Strong Recovery Plan" on June 16, 2020. Meanwhile, challenges facing Missourians only got worse. Over the course of the same weekend during which the Lake of Ozark videos went viral, on May 25, 2020, Memorial Day, George Floyd, an African American, was killed in Minneapolis, Minnesota, the incident captured on cellphone video of bystanders who watched in horror as a white police officer pinned a clearly distressed Floyd to the sidewalk by kneeling firmly on the prone and handcuffed man's neck for more than nine minutes. Within days after the brutal incident, Floyd's death launched protests over police brutality against African Americans in all fifty states, including Missouri.

For weeks following Floyd's death, Missourians marched for racial justice. In Kansas City, protesters advanced on the city's police headquarters and through the streets of the iconic Country Club Plaza. They marched day after day, week after week, calling for an end to systemic violence and injustice against people of color, and demanding removal of statues and symbols that recalled or paid tribute to vestiges of racism.

Protests also occurred across the state: including in St. Louis, Columbia, Springfield, Jefferson City, Cape Girardeau, Sedalia, Independence, Joplin, O'Fallon, and Rolla. The protesters were a diverse group, more often than not composed of a majority of whites. The protests were usually peaceful, although there were instances of violence, especially in Kansas City and St. Louis.

Fig. 49: Black Lives Matter protesters march in Columbia in the wake of George Floyd's death in Minnesota. June 6, 2020. Credit: Beth Pike, State Historical Society of Missouri.

The death of Floyd, and subsequently of Rayshard Brooks in Atlanta, raised awareness of the "Black Lives Matter" movement, and prompted calls for racial justice from a growing number of whites and Blacks, although Missourians remained divided over whether African Americans were, in fact, the victims of racial injustice in daily life. In St. Louis, a white couple, Mark and Patricia McCloskey, gained national attention on June 28, 2020, when they confronted a crowd of approximately five hundred Black Lives Matter protesters with guns drawn as the protesters marched near their home in a private, gated neighborhood in St. Louis. The McCloskeys claimed they were simply defending themselves and their property, but the protesters argued that the gun-wielding couple clearly meant to intimidate them and restrict their right to protest peacefully. Ultimately, the McCloskey case became a wedge political issue, with prominent Republican political figures, including President Trump, siding with them while many Democrats sided with the Black Lives Matter protesters.

Meanwhile, the coronavirus pandemic only continued to spread, striking Missouri's African American population especially hard. In June, the *St. Louis Post-Dispatch* pointed out that "Black residents make up 12% of the state's population, but well more than one-third of coronavirus deaths. In St. Louis and St. Louis County, [Blacks] are dying at nearly double the rate of whites." By the July 4th holiday weekend, Missouri had more than twenty-four thousand confirmed cases of COVID-19, and 1,063 Missourians had died from the virus. On July 4, the Kansas City metropolitan area, which included Kansas border counties, reported three hundred new coronavirus cases and a total of more than nine thousand since the pandemic began. The St. Louis metropolitan area, including Illinois border counties, reached the one thousand death mark on June 19, 2020. By early July, COVID-19 cases could be found in every one of Missouri's 114 counties and the city of St. Louis, save for Hickory County in southwest Missouri. Even that county would soon find the virus among its residents.

The coronavirus took a devastating toll on Missourians, beyond the pain and suffering of the disease itself. In mid-June 2020, the Missouri Department of Economic Development reported that the state had shed two hundred sixty thousand jobs over the previous year, some sixty thousand in the leisure and hospitality sectors alone. Unemployment stood at 10.1 percent in May 2020, compared to 3.1 percent the previous May. On June 30, 2020, Governor Mike Parson announced that he was slashing the fiscal year 2021 budget by nearly $450 million because of declining state revenues, driven by the coronavirus pandemic. Missourians, like their fellow citizens throughout the country, wondered when, and even if, their lives would ever return to normal. In a December 2020 report for the *Missouri Independent*, reporter Rudi Keller noted that "The October [2020 jobs] report showed the state work force shrank by 160,000 in six months, to 1.98 million, the smallest since October 2000." To put it bluntly, the "COVID recession erace[d] 20 years of Missouri's workforce growth."

As the 2020 state and national elections approached, Missourians pondered the effect the pandemic would have on political contests. Although the pandemic and the associated economic downturn undoubtedly played a role in President Donald J. Trump's failure to win a second term in the White House, Trump and Missouri Governor Mike Parson both performed well in the Show-Me State. Trump lost by more than seven million votes nationwide, but in Missouri he defeated Democrat Joseph Biden 1,718,736 votes to 1,253,014, garnering more than fifty-six percent of the votes cast in the state. Only Jackson, Boone, and St. Louis counties went for Biden, plus the City of St. Louis. The race reflected Missouri's racial divide, with sixty-two percent of whites voting for Trump, and eighty-eight percent of Blacks opting for Biden. The contest also mirrored the historical urban-rural split in the state. President Trump won overwhelmingly in rural counties of the state. According to the *St. Louis Post-Dispatch*, "In one bloc of 13 [rural] counties centered around [southwest Missouri's] Shannon County, [Trump] secured 80% of the vote in each. His best showing in the state came in far northern Mercer County, where he won 86.6% to 12.5%." Statewide, Trump carried eighty-six percent of white Evangelical Christians in the state.

Governor Mike Parson outperformed President Trump in the state, defeating Democratic State Auditor Nicole Galloway by sixteen points, the best showing by a Missouri gubernatorial candidate since John Ashcroft defeated Democrat Betty Cooper Hearnes in 1988.

Trump's failure to win the 2020 presidential election, and his unwillingness to accept defeat, reverberated throughout the state and nation. In early December 2020, at least sixty-six Missouri Republican lawmakers signed a letter asking Congress to reject electoral votes from swing states that went for President-elect Joseph Biden. No Missouri politician advocated this position more visibly than the state's junior U.S. senator, Josh Hawley. Hawley's stand divided Missourians, especially in the wake of his pronounced "fist pump" on the morning of January 6, 2021, acknowledging protesters on the grounds of the U.S. Capitol in Washington, D.C.

The subsequent assault on the U.S. Capitol on January 6 by protesters who sought to preserve Donald Trump's presidency divided Missourians and their fellow Americans in a way hardly seen since the American Civil War. Missouri Republican Party patriarch, former U.S. Senator John C. Danforth, bemoaned the Capitol assault, and sharply criticized his former protégé, Hawley, blaming the latter for contributing to the chaos and violence and calling his prior support of Hawley, "the worst mistake I ever made in my life." Others praised Hawley as a hero and the actions of the attackers as patriotic.

In the wake of the chaos accompanying the 2020 presidential election, the January 6 attack on the Capitol, and the horrific consequences of the COVID-19 pandemic, which claimed the lives of more than eighty-four hundred Missourians as the one-year anniversary of the state's first

COVID-19 death approached, residents of the state pondered a way forward. What would the two hundredth anniversary of statehood mean for
Missourians?

SUGGESTED READINGS

Lawrence H. Larsen, *A History of Missouri, 1953–2003* (2004) offers a good
starting point for understanding twenty-first century Missouri, although
the history of this period remains to be written. The impact of the Great
Recession on migration to Missouri and the dearth of job development in
the new century is discussed in Joe Gamm, "Low job growth a factor in
stagnant population," *Jefferson City News Tribune*, August 4, 2019. Much of
Gamm's argument is drawn from studies done by the Missouri Economic
Research and Information Center, whose reports can be accessed at meric.
mo.gov. The St. Louis Development Corporation's "Equitable Economic
Development Framework" study can be accessed at https://www.stlouis-
mo.gov/sldc/framework/index.cfm. *St. Louis Post-Dispatch* business columnist David Nicklaus has written a considerable amount about the economic
development of Missouri generally and St. Louis specifically during the
current century. His columns can be accessed at stltoday.com/business/
columns/david-nicklaus. Teacher pay in Missouri is addressed in a January
11, 2019, *Kansas City Star* editorial titled "How bad are starting salaries for
Missouri teachers? Even Mississippi pays more."

Newspapers also covered demographic changes in Missouri during the
first two decades of the twenty-first century, including Jim Salter, "Census:
52 Missouri counties lost population in 2018," *Columbia Missourian*, April
20, 2019.

The economic fallout from President Trump's 2018 tariffs was the sub-
ject of many newspapers articles at the time, including Chuck Raasch,
"Missouri exporters worry about effects of Trump-induced trade war," *St.
Louis Post-Dispatch*, March 6, 2018; and Bryce Gray, "'Hit from every direction: Tariffs and drought weigh heavily on farmers," *St. Louis Post-Dispatch*,
October 19, 2018. Newspapers and other periodicals covered politics of the
period. Among useful articles is David Weigel, "Swung State: For the First
Time, Democrats Aren't Trying to Win Missouri's Electoral Votes. Why?"
in the October 3, 2012, issue of *Slate*.

A few books that address issues of this period will surely be studied in
further detail by future historians. Jonathan M. Metzl, *Dying of Whiteness:*

How the Politics of Racial Resentment is Killing America's Heartland (2019), published by Basic Books, documents the adverse consequences of Missouri's gun culture in the twenty-first century.

The high murder rates in Missouri's cities during the twenty-first century were covered by daily and weekly newspapers in the state, with articles such as "584 kids killed in St. Louis Over 30 years; 'It wrecked us,'" by Erin Heffernan and Janelle O'Dea, *St. Louis Post Dispatch*, October 20, 2019.

The sexual abuse scandals associated with the Catholic Church in Missouri were the subjects of many newspaper articles over the past two decades and more. Joe Gamm's "State releases clergy abuse report," *Jefferson City News Tribune*, September 14, 2019, is very helpful in understanding the depth and breadth of the problem.

The killing of Michael Brown in Ferguson in August 2014 resulted in the publication of a number of works that provide insight into race relations in twenty-first-century St. Louis and Missouri. Two reports published by the U.S. Department of Justice in 2015 are useful. The first is *The Ferguson Report: The Department of Justice Investigation of the Ferguson, Missouri Police Department* and *The Department of Justice Report Regarding the Criminal Investigation into the Shooting of Michael Brown by Ferguson, Missouri Police Officer Darren Wilson*. Scholarly attempts at understanding and explaining Michael Brown's death include the following: Jeff Smith, *Ferguson in Black and White* (2014), a self-published e-book, available through Amazon; Wesley Lowery, *They Can't Kill Us All: Ferguson, Baltimore and a New Era in America's Racial Justice Movement* (2016), published by Little, Brown and Co.; and Colin Gordon, *Citizen Brown: Race, Democracy, and Inequality in the St. Louis Suburbs* (2020), published by the University of Chicago Press.

Daily and weekly Missouri newspapers documented the rise of COVID-19 and the efforts by state and local officials to deal with both the disease and the economic fallout from it. Essays such as Jacob Barker, "Staggering number of people seeking help," in the *St. Louis Post-Dispatch*, March 27, 2020, are helpful. The dramatic increase in firearms sales is the subject of Danielle Duclos, "Firearm sales spike in Missouri, as in much of U.S.," *Columbia Missourian*, April 19, 2020. The controversy over wearing face masks during the COVID-19 pandemic is covered in a number of local contemporary newspapers, including Rachel Rice, "Pepper spray, knives, guns: Mask disputes flaring as workers try to enforce rules," *St. Louis Post-Dispatch*, August 4, 2020.

Epilogue

Missouri: Land of Promise

"**Missouri, possessing such great advantages of soil, climate and navigation, cannot fail to reach exalted destinies. . . .**"

Missourian [St. Charles], September 5, 1821

THE MISSOURI TERRITORY was widely regarded as one of the most desirable locations in the country in which to seek a new life during the years immediately following the ending of the War of 1812. Encouraged by boosters who described the region as a veritable paradise on earth, immigrants flocked to the region, especially to the area of the so-called Boonslick, a place characterized by rich, fertile land paralleling the Missouri River westward from St. Charles into the interior, to Howard County and beyond. So enticing was this region that historian Robert Lee has recently described it as "the most intensely growing settlement in the United States after the War of 1812."

This rapid population growth led to an effort to achieve statehood status, which in turn led to a conflict in the U.S. Congress over whether Missourians should, if they gained admission to the Union, be allowed to own slaves in the new state. The conflict was settled through a compromise that permitted current and future Missourians to own slaves, the beginning of a circumstance that made the issue of race central to the Missouri experience, both at its founding and over the course of the next two centuries.

Once members of the Union, Missourians went about settling and "civilizing" their state and connecting it to the larger nation. In the process, they struggled with the issues of the role of government in the lives of individuals, and the level to which government, whether state or federal, should be funded by its citizenry. Frequently, they opted in favor of frugality, some would say even penury, thereby handicapping efforts at building the state's infrastructure and providing services to its residents.

Although most Missourians did not own slaves, slaveholders in the state exercised a disproportionate level of control over governance, causing an ongoing conflict between those who advocated the use of slave labor and those, especially the German immigrants, who thought slavery stifled and inhibited free enterprise capitalism. The dispute came to a head during the American Civil War, a conflict that deeply divided Missourians and caused neighbors and relatives to fight each other over the state's and the nation's destiny. Ultimately, most Missourians sided with the Union cause, even many of the slaveholders whose commitment to the federal government was stronger than their commitment to the peculiar institution of slavery. Missouri became the first of the slaveholding states to abolish slavery, nearly a full year before the federal government accomplished that task with the ratification of the Thirteenth Amendment to the U.S. Constitution in December 1865.

The war slowed Missouri's economic growth and even caused many of its citizens to flee the violence that had become endemic to the state during the fighting. But war's end witnessed another sharp increase in the state's population and a renewed effort to attract immigrants to Missouri through railroad and town building and the spread of scientific agriculture. In 1880, in a report titled "Missouri, The Imperial State, Its Wealth and Resources," the state's Board of Immigration proclaimed, "Nowhere upon the continent can the people of any single State or Territory enjoy all the luxuries and blessings of an advanced civilization, depending entirely upon their own productions and resources so completely as in Missouri." Civil War animosities were gradually overcome, in large part because of the increased understanding that economic growth required cooperation on the part of all citizens. For at least a brief period, state support of the expansion of railroads finally succeeded in tying the state to national and even international markets.

The great promise of Missouri, first evidenced during the antebellum period, bore fruit during the last decades of the century. Between 1880 and 1900, Missouri's population increased by almost a million residents, from 2,168,000 to 3,106,665, a growth rate of forty-three percent. By 1900, Missouri became the fifth largest state in the Union, and its biggest city, St. Louis, the fourth largest city nationally. Missouri was proud of its big city and showed off St. Louis and itself to the world at the 1904 Louisiana Purchase Exposition, better known as the 1904 World's Fair. With this well-attended gala, the "Show-Me State" entered the twentieth century as a prosperous and promising place to live.

But Missouri could not sustain its national ascent and growing stature as the twentieth century dawned, and it soon began to decline, at least in relative terms. Put simply, immigrants and migrants from other countries and other states increasingly found Missouri a less desirable place to live than many other parts of the country. Beginning in 1910 and proceeding down to the present day, Missouri began to decline in its ranking among the most populous states in the nation. In 1910, it dropped to the seventh most populous state; by 1940, it was tenth. In 1970, it dropped to thirteenth, and by the year 2020, it was the eighteenth most populous state in the Union. St. Louis fell even more precipitously. By 1940, it was the eighth most populous city in the country; by 1970, it had fallen to eighteenth, and during the decade of the 1980s, it ceased to be even the most populous city in Missouri, having been overtaken by Kansas City. By 2020, St. Louis was America's sixty-ninth most populous city.

Determining why this relative decline occurred and a good remedy for its reversal remains one of the great mysteries of the past two centuries of Missouri statehood, and the answer is, admittedly, beyond the scope of this brief history. But the commemoration of two hundred years of statehood is a good time for all Missourians to ponder and reflect upon the policies and points in our past that have served us well, as well as those that have left us wanting.

We seemed to have fared much better as an agricultural, rural people than as a collectivity of urban residents. During the nineteenth century, most Missourians made their living on farms, and we attracted immigrants to the state, both domestic and foreign, through the availability of affordable land and accessible markets. We did not make the transition to being an urban people ("urban" being defined as towns or cities with 2,500 or more residents) until the 1920s. For much of the rest of the twentieth century, and especially over the past fifty years, we have, for reasons predictable and otherwise, struggled to present our state as a land of promise and have lost population, relative to our previous standing.

As we prepare for our third century of statehood, it may be a good time to examine some of our fundamental assumptions about what makes for a good life in Missouri, and what might attract outsiders to our state. Perhaps we need to rethink our views of the relationship between the level of taxation we are willing to support and the kind of government services we expect to receive. For most of our history, our state governmental leaders, Democrats and Republicans, have told us that we will prosper as a state and as a people to the degree that we keep taxes low. No one expressed this notion more clearly than Democratic Governor John S. Phelps, a Springfield lawyer. Elected as Missouri's governor in 1876, Phelps said in his inaugural address: "We must economize, we must reduce the expenditures of Government. It may be difficult to do so, but it must be done." He elaborated: "We should endeavor to place taxation at its lowest limit. . . . We invite population. And if to all our sources of wealth and prosperity we can, with truth, say the taxes of the municipal and State governments are low, we offer strong inducements for the enterprising, industrious and intelligent people to make their abode with us." In short, the contention was that low taxation would bring increased population and that increase would, in turn, bring wealth to our state. Nearly one hundred fifty years later, and during the intervening years, our political leaders have continued to promote this same message, even as we watch the relative decline of our population and well-being. Although there are notable exceptions, in the twenty-first century we Missourians find ourselves at or near the bottom of the lists of things that matter most to all Americans: quality of education, access to health care, life expectancy, standard of living attained, and more.

Moreover, our historical rural-urban divide continues to hurt us. In a March 10, 2021, op-ed written on behalf of Lindenwood University's Hammond Institute for Free Enterprise, Rik W. Hafer, Professor of Economics and Director of the Institute's Center for Economics and the Environment, called attention to a recent Brookings Institution study comparing 192 major metropolitan areas across the country as "engines of economic growth." According to this study, "In terms of overall economic progress, the St. Louis metropolitan area . . . ranked 44th out of the 53 large metro areas. . . . The Kansas City metro area . . . ranked 36th. Better, but solidly in the lower half." Moreover, according to Professor Hafer, the poor showing by Missouri's two major metro areas affects more than the residents of those two areas: "When these engines of economic growth sputter . . . they keep the [entire] state from realizing its potential." The state's rural-urban divide, indeed, all its divisions, are thwarting the state's growth. "Missouri's policymakers must recognize," Hafer summarized, "that urban and rural interests are closely linked. Until that happens, Missouri will continue to lag other states, its citizens enjoying little improvement in their prosperity."

Perhaps we need to reinvigorate representative government, learn again to trust our government more, and demand that our government show more trust in us. It is striking to me how negatively we regard our government and governmental officials. As Congressman William Hungate said upon the occasion of his retirement from the Congress in 1975: "Politics has gone from the age of 'Camelot,' when all things were possible, to the age of 'Watergate,' when all things are suspect." We Missourians reached a point during the 1980s and 1990s when we distrusted our political leaders so much that we tried to restrict their ability to raise revenue (through the Hancock Amendment) and to limit their time in office (through term limits) because we thought doing so would reduce the amount of damage politicians could do. The Hancock Amendment and term limits were not initiatives intended to empower our elected officials. Rather, they were born out of mistrust of those very officials, and a desire to limit their power. But distrust runs both ways: more than once in the recent past, our elected officials have defied and then attempted to thwart the will of the people who elected them by trying to overturn decisions the people made. Among the notable recent examples of this is the defiance of the public will exhibited by legislators who tried to replace the people's "Clean" initiative of 2018 (which passed by a 62 to 38 percent margin) with one of their own, known colloquially as "Cleaner." Ultimately, they succeeded in November 2020 in a close referendum on the issue; the "Cleaner" amendment passed by a popular vote of 51 to 49 percent. On another issue, in many rural communities in Missouri, most recently in Livingston and Cedar counties, local citizens and governments have found it difficult to control the presence of CAFO's (Concentrated Animal Feeding Operations) in their communities because of a law passed by state officials in 2019 that effectively nullified many local health ordinances. Other examples of a disconnect between state officials and the general public remain readily available. Perhaps none is more graphic than the conflict that emerged in early 2021, when state governmental officials insisted that 46,000 Missourians who were mistakenly overpaid unemployment benefits must repay these monies, even though the fault was not theirs and the federal COVID-19 federal relief guidelines allowed states the authority to forgive overpaid federal unemployment benefits. Finally, during the 2021 legislative session, Missouri lawmakers moved to give themselves the authority to limit the power of local officials to impose health orders. The outcome of that effort is yet to be determined.

The tribalism that governs our lives today and causes us to identify all of those who disagree with us as venal, evil people who must be despised, conquered, and even punished, is, quite simply, destroying the atmosphere of neighborliness and collegiality that we also claim to value. Might it be possible for all of us, elected officials and the general citizenry, to return to (or create) a time when goodwill is assumed, and the welfare of the people is the primary consideration? During the late 1990s, a State Historical Society of Missouri historian interviewed former Missouri Senator Warren D. Welliver, a Boone County Democrat who served in the Missouri Senate during the 1970s. Senator Welliver's kindest words in the interview were reserved for one of his fellow senators, a Republican from Barry County named Emory Melton. Welliver recounted this about the two men's relationship: "We were the closest of friends. I always got my seat right next to Emory, because he read the bills. And if I got caught on one I hadn't read . . . I could turn around and say, 'Emory? What about this bill?' He'd say, 'Well, Warren, I've got to do this. But you ought to vote the other way.' And you could just depend on him." Imagine that level of collegiality and trust in politics, or at any stratum of society, today!

Arguably, we Missourians have been at our best when we faced common crises, whether it was a war, an economic depression, or a natural disaster. In light of that historic reality, the intense and divided response we have exhibited in the face of the COVID-19 pandemic is especially troubling. Instead of bringing us together to face a common enemy, COVID-19 seems to have revealed and exacerbated already existing tensions between us. How can the wearing of a mask or social distancing in the face of such a real and present danger be sources of such division and hostility?

The ultimate expression of hostility between groups or individuals is violence against each other, and twenty-first-century Missouri is, unfortunately, home to an abundance of violence. As the state commemorates its two hundredth anniversary, violence rages in our largest cities. Kansas City, St. Louis, Springfield, and Columbia are at or near record numbers of annual homicides. Increasingly, Missourians do not feel safe in our cities; yet, our cities are the places where the greatest economic opportunity resides.

Domestic violence is a particular concern in Missouri, in both rural and urban areas. A 2018 study by the Violence Policy Center in Washington,

D.C., ranked Missouri second in the nation in the number of women murdered by men. More than nine out of ten of the female murder victims knew their assailants. Additionally, Missouri ranks number twenty in the nation in the number of suicides and twenty-second in opioid overdose death rates. U.S. Senator Josh Hawley was right when he designated these as "deaths of despair." They happen far too often in Missouri.

And then there is the issue of race. The consequences of slavery and racial segregation and discrimination have plagued Missouri and Missourians for our entire existence as a territory and a state. As demonstrations and protests during the summer of 2020 made clear, white and Black Missourians (and Americans) neither fully understand nor accept each other. The result is tension, hostility, and a reluctance to interact in meaningful ways. This reality, too, retards our individual and collective progress and deters would-be newcomers to our state.

The good news is that these are all remediable problems, especially for a people as resourceful as Missourians. Our nickname is "the Show-Me State," a sobriquet whose origin is debated by scholars. What is not debated is the meaning of the phrase; we see ourselves as demonstrably skeptical but relentlessly willing to follow the best proven path forward. The path forward for us now, as we face our third century as a state, is that of cooperation, compromise, and understanding. We are an incredibly diverse people, as different as Swampeast is from the Ozarks, and St. Louis is from Kansas City. Facing the challenges of the Civil War early in 1861, in the wake of secession, but before the firing on Fort Sumter, Missouri Provisional Governor Hamilton R. Gamble pondered the role his state could play in the greatest of all conflicts that Americans have faced. He had this to say: "If it be the glorious mission of Missouri to aid in arresting the progress of revolution and in restoring peace and prosperity to the country . . . she will but occupy the position for which nature designed her by giving her a central position. . . . And why should she not?—she was brought forth in a storm and cradled in a compromise."

Perhaps it is once again time for Missourians to face that which divides us and come together, to improve our lives, protect our beautiful natural environment, and show all Americans the way forward. This place of promise, our Missouri, the heart of the heart of the nation, can still be a beacon of light for the rest of the country—perhaps that is our real "exalted destiny," one for which both time and history have prepared us.

Index

About the Author

Photo credit: Aubrey Rowden

Gary R. Kremer is a fifth-generation Missourian, born and raised in a small, homogeneous German Catholic community in Osage County. Since 2004, he has served as the Executive Director of the State Historical Society of Missouri and a Senior Fellow in the Society's Center for Missouri Studies. Among his many publications are *James Milton Turner and the Promise of America: The Public Life of a Post–Civil War Black Leader*; *George Washington Carver: In His Own Words*; *Women in Missouri History: In Search of Power and Influence*; *George Washington Carver: A Biography*; and *Race and Meaning: The African American Experience in Missouri*. He is also the Editor-in-Chief of the *Missouri Historical Review*.